CHINESE FOREIGN POLICY DURING THE CULTURAL REVOLUTION

A PUBLICATION OF THE GRADUATE INSTITUTE
OF INTERNATIONAL STUDIES,
GENEVA

Also published in this series:

The United States and the Politicization of the World Bank
Bartram S. Brown

Trade Negotiations in the OECD
David J. Blair

World Financial Markets after 1992
Hans Genberg and Alexander K. Swoboda

Succession Between International Organisations
Patrick R. Myers

Ten Years of Turbulence: The Chinese Cultural Revolution
Barbara Barnouin and Yu Changgen

The Islamic Movement in Egypt: Perceptions of International
Relations 1967–81
Walid M. Abdelnasser

Namibia and Southern Africa: Regional Dynamics of Decolonization
1945–90
Ronald Dreyer

The International Organization of Hunger
Peter Uvin

Citizenship East and West
Edited by André Liebich and Daniel Warner
with Jasna Dragović

Introduction to the Law of Treaties
Paul Reuter

The Imperiled Red Cross and the Palestine-Eretz-Yisrael
Conflict 1945–1952
Dominique-D. Junod

Ideology and Economic Reform under
Deng Xiaoping 1978–1993
Wei-Wei Zhang

CHINESE FOREIGN POLICY DURING THE CULTURAL REVOLUTION

Barbara Barnouin
Yu Changgen

KEGAN PAUL INTERNATIONAL
London and New York

1998

First published in 1998 by
Kegan Paul International
UK: P.O. Box 256, London WC1B 3SW, England
Tel: (0171) 580 5511 Fax: (0171) 436 0899
E-mail: books@keganpau.demon.co.uk
Internet: http://www.demon.co.uk/keganpaul/

USA: 562 West 113th Street, New York, NY 10025, USA
Tel: (212) 666 1000 Fax: (212) 316 3100

Distributed by
John Wiley & Sons Ltd
Southern Cross Trading Estate
1 Oldlands Way, Bognor Regis
West Sussex, PO22 9SW, England
Tel: (01234) 779 777 Fax: (01234) 820 250

Columbia University Press
562 West 113th Street, New York, NY 10025, USA
Tel: (212) 666 1000 Fax: (212) 316 3100

Copyright © The Graduate Institute of International Studies, Geneva, 1998

Phototypeset in Palatino by Intype London Ltd
Printed in Great Britain by TJ Press, Padstow, Cornwall

British Library Cataloguing in Publication Data
Barnouin, Barbara
    Chinese foreign policy during the cultural revolution
    1. China – Foreign relations – 1949–1976
    I. Title II. Yu, Changgen
    327.5'1'009046

    ISBN 071030580X

Library of Congress Cataloging-in-Publication Data

Barnouin, Barbara.
    Chinese foreign policy during the Cultural Revolution/
    Barbara Barnouin and Yu Changgen.
        p. cm.
    Includes bibliographical references.
    ISBN 0–7103–0580–X
    1. China—Foreign relations–1949–1976. 2. China—History—
Cultural Revolution, 1966–1969. I. Yu Changgen, 1930– .
II. Title.
DS777.8
327.51–dc21   97–25796
                                                                    CIP

CONTENTS

INTRODUCTION

A nation's foreign policy is determined – to a large extent – by domestic and external environments. Though there are certainly other factors to be reckoned with, such as history, ideology, personality and leadership, the domestic and external environments have generally been singled out as the crucial factors in the determination of foreign policy of any nation. But what exactly is the weight of the two factors in this process, how do they relate to each other, which of them, at a given time, has the stronger impact – all this can be evaluated only through a process of careful investigation of the policy behaviour of the nation in question.

In the case of China during the Cultural Revolution, domestic criteria clearly played an important role during the initial phase, a phase characterized by the radicalization of Chinese political thinking and a phase that was replete with unusually sharp rhetoric. In fact, the turmoil within the country at that time was of such dimensions, factionalism so rampant, ideological discourse so incendiary, that all this had a strong impact on foreign affairs – on the Ministry of Foreign Affairs, on Chinese perceptions of the outside world and on the decision-making process pertaining to this sector. Inevitably, this brought about a change in Chinese foreign policy, rendering it more ideological and more revolutionary and defining, as its main objective, the spread of the Chinese revolutionary movement and of Mao Zedong Thought throughout the world. This process – albeit utopian – damaged China's diplomacy and led to its increased isolation from the international scene.

The linkage between domestic and foreign policy thus was evident during the first phase of the Cultural Revolution, but it was not so clear during the second phase. In fact, it had become opaque. While domestic preoccupations continued to dominate the leadership's concerns and while its incendiary rhetoric regarding the external world continued to be strongly influenced by internal revolutionary concepts, a slow dissociation began to emerge between the revolutionary agitation occurring inside China and the designing of its foreign policy at the upper spheres of the national leadership. While China was in turmoil, its foreign policy was becoming more sober, more governed by national interest, more concerned with national security and more preoccupied by its increasing isolation. China was becoming more susceptible to an adverse external environment.

The inauguration of this new process of normalization – eventually the major catalyst of fundamental changes in Chinese foreign policy – occurred in the middle of domestic pandemonium and factional fighting. Zhou Enlai, who appeared to the world as the architect of the normalization process on the Chinese side was, at that time, the victim of fierce factional strife which threatened his political future.

In this study the Cultural Revolution as such will not be analysed, for this has been done elsewhere.[1] What is proposed here is first of all to examine the effect it had on the very functioning of the Chinese Ministry of Foreign Affairs, and how the turmoil of the Cultural Revolution, of which the country had become a victim, spilled over to this highly elitist and prestigious Ministry. In sum, we will focus on the chaos that engulfed the institution.

In the Western world it might be difficult to imagine that the staff of a Foreign Ministry, instead of implementing foreign policy, became bogged down in a domestically determined political movement. In fact, so profound was the involvement that only a small segment of the staff continued to handle foreign affairs while the majority of the functionaries in the Ministry, and in the embassies abroad, were busy keeping abreast of domestic events and of the changing political fortunes which depended on internal factional strife. This situation began to change slowly only after *détente* with the United States, after China's entry into the United Nations and the ensuing spread of its diplomatic relations with an increasing number of Western countries.

The second point on which this study proposes to focus· is

the decision-making process in foreign policy. Who took the major decisions? How were they taken, and what were the different inputs that went into the designing of foreign policy?

The personality factor is increasingly recognized as a crucial one in the designing of foreign policy, perhaps even more important than some of the established institutions. Already in the 1960s, Joseph Frankel had considered it 'as a legitimate and important topic of historical analysis' in all investigations of external state behaviour.[2] More recent studies have gone further; they have evoked a panoply of psychological theories to understand the decision-makers' 'cognitive system', how it is established and how it operates 'so as to structure perceptions and hence determine behaviour.'[3]

If Western academic analysis is increasingly veering around to the theory that the personality factor is equally important where institutions are 'the most permanent element of politics in Western societies',[4] the role of the individual is more important in a country like China where institutions are not well established.

There does not appear to be any doubt – at least in the minds of these authors – that Mao Zedong was the principal if not the sole authority that determined the broad framework of the country's foreign policy. According to the judgement of Chinese specialists on foreign affairs, Mao had reached such a position of power that he was able to define unilaterally the course of his country's foreign relations. This was even more the case during the Cultural Revolution, since institutional input was no longer possible, with all the turmoil China was facing, and since the Foreign Ministry was no longer really operating. In sum, to understand China's foreign policy, it is vital to understand Mao, his ideas, his thinking. It is for this reason that the second chapter examines Mao's ideological approach to foreign policy, and his perception of the outside world, both of which are intimately linked.

The third aspect of this study concerns the substance of foreign policy during the Cultural Revolution. The spill-over of revolutionary concepts on to Chinese diplomacy generated a major conflict – within the second-rank leadership – between the traditionalists and the defenders of revolutionary concepts. As all of this had major ramifications for the actual implementation of foreign policy, Chapter 3 focuses on the discordant voices raised by the two groups.

While dealing with the substantive aspects of Chinese external relations, the authors have avoided going into all the encyclopaedic factual details of Chinese policies in Asia, Africa, Latin America or in Europe. Since they were all minor variations of the same themes, it would have led us to indulge in considerable repetition. We have therefore focused our attention on China's policies towards three major actors in the international system – the United States, the Soviet Union and Japan – for it was they who contributed to the introduction of tactical innovations in China's foreign policy behaviour. Finally, Chapter 4 deals with the new approach to foreign policy engendered by the Soviet threat to China's national security.

During the entire period of the Cultural Revolution China's declarations on foreign policy were full of rhetoric and revolutionary belligerence. While in the first phase foreign policy mirrored the turbulent domestic situation, from the late 1960s onwards the linkage was broken. Foreign policy was extricated from the vicious circle of domestic developments. Chinese foreign policy behaviour became less revolutionary, more sober and increasingly determined by concerns of national security. But all this was tactical. For soon after China had started to leave its state of isolation from the Western world and a certain balance of forces had been achieved in the triangular relationship between China, the Soviet Union and the United States, the process of normalization began to stagnate. It gathered momentum only in the late 1970s when Deng Xiaoping's leadership was firmly established

Besides using Chinese and Western sources, large parts of this study rely on oral history. This is particularly relevant for the first chapter in which 'Personal Notes' are frequently mentioned as a source. These notes refer to discussions and interviews held between 1988 and 1995 with a large number of persons who were involved in, or who were victims of, the Cultural Revolution in the Chinese Foreign Ministry. Given the sensitivity of the subject and the official Chinese reluctance to permit Chinese scholars to delve too deeply into the Cultural Revolution, a great majority of the persons interviewed did not wish to be quoted. In complying with their request, the authors have consolidated all the information under 'Personal Notes'.

The Appendix of the short study contains a diagram of the 'Foreign Affairs System', a chronology of events, and the full texts of or excerpts from relevant documents pertaining to China's foreign policy during the period under examination. The first series of texts (Documents 1–6) are first translations (by the authors) of texts published in China within the last few years by the Central Documentation Press and by *Liaowang*, a magazine issued under the auspices of Xinhua News Agency. Although they are heavily edited and therefore somewhat biased they contribute to the understanding of the fluctuations in foreign policy of the period. The reports of the group under Chen Yi, edited by Xiong Xianghui[5], in particular, reflect the causes behind Chinese interest in a Sino-American *rapprochement*. Wang Li's speech to the Foreign Ministry, discovered in a red guard tabloid of August 1967 and authenticated by witnesses, represents one of the major events in the Foreign Ministry at that time. The last four documents – though already published – are included since they reveal the overall approach of the Chinese authorities to foreign affairs during the Cultural Revolution.

1

THE MINISTRY OF FOREIGN AFFAIRS

The Cultural Revolution, a political movement of unprecedented intensity, penetrated the administration and the Party from the political centre in Beijing down to the level of townships throughout the vast territory of China. All of the most important economic sectors, industries and communications were affected by the Revolution, and even the rural areas close to the cities did not escape the movement. Since, at central government level, the Revolution was particularly pronounced the Chinese Foreign Ministry, one of the most prestigious and elitist ministries in the country, was also deeply involved in these developments.[1]

The Cultural Revolution in the Foreign Ministry mirrored the events as they unfolded on the national scale. It can be divided into several stages. The first stage – from June to the end of 1966 – was directed by the Ministry's Party committee under the leadership of Ji Pengfei and Chen Yi. It began with the campaign 'to sweep away all demons and devils and eradicate poisonous weeds'. According to the then-prevailing political line – introduced in Mao's absence from the capital by Liu Shaoqi – work teams were used to carry out the campaign. But these work teams did not last long, for they were withdrawn on the orders of Mao, who claimed that they had suppressed the masses and thus had carried out revisionist policies. The major issue at that stage was not so much the utilization of work teams; they had been employed in most previous campaigns and their activities had become common practice. Rather it was the definition of the targets of the campaign which had become the fundamental problem. While Party committees in general – and the Party committee of the Foreign Ministry as well – focused their criticism on a large number of average

1

cadres – thus following what was later termed the Liu-Deng line – the Maoist line was to emphasize criticism of high-level cadres. In January 1967 Chen Yi, the Foreign Minister who had failed to implement Mao's line earlier, was forced to make self-criticism.

Following the example staged by the Shanghai rebels, the second stage was inaugurated by the 'seizure of power' by the Ministry's rebel organization in January 1967. This power seizure consisted essentially in taking over, from the Party committee, the right to lead the Cultural Revolution in the Ministry. Since a number of factions developed at ministerial level, the question of who represented the truly revolutionary faction soon became a matter of contention. This was also the period of Chen Yi's second self-criticism which the revolutionary Left requested after Chen's involvement in the February Adverse Current. This stage lasted until October 1967 when Zhou Enlai declared that the rebels in the Foreign Ministry had connections with an ultra-leftist and criminal association called the May 16th group.

From October 1967 till 1971 (the third stage), the Cultural Revolution in the Ministry was led by the 'Committee of great unity' which at first grouped the three rebel factions (two of them conservative) at the Ministry. The Committee was soon dominated by the conservative factions which, with the assistance of the People's Liberation Army (PLA), carried out the campaign 'to purify class ranks' from 1968 onward.

In the fourth stage, beginning in 1971, the Party committee resumed its functions. It continued the campaign to purify class ranks with its different facets and also directed the campaign to criticize Lin Biao, Confucius and Zhou Gong (Zhou Enlai).

The First Stage

In late 1965 and early 1966, the Cultural Revolution was in its preliminary stage. It was directed primarily against the Beijing literary establishment headed by Peng Zhen, a powerful Politburo member and the Mayor of Beijing, who had promoted a relatively liberal atmosphere in the fields of literature and art. Mao disliked these developments, viewing them as a manifestation of bourgeois ideology. He instigated the official criticism of a number of literary works which, in his view, were representative of bourgeois degeneration. Debates about literary works and their political significance were taking place in many intellectual circles. The writings of Wu Han, Liao Mosha and Deng Tuo – all three members of the Beijing municipal party committee – which the official propaganda considered as works incompatible with socialist ideology, were widely criticized; and a number of popular films such as *Early Spring*, *Sisters of the Stage*, *Shop of the Lin Family* and *Besieging the City* were subjected to increasingly defamatory attacks.[2]

The discussions about literature and films were, however, not confined to literary circles. They were also taking place in government and other institutions, including the Foreign Ministry, where the entire personnel became involved in deliberations about the socialist nature of certain works of art. This was not unusual, but was part of the Chinese political culture where ideological campaigns tended to affect most work units. In the Foreign Ministry, literary works became required readings for everybody, and films shown in the Ministry's auditorium had to be viewed by the entire staff. In follow-up meetings the works were critically examined as to their socialist value. In their early stages these discussions remained relatively 'academic' without immediate political repercussions.[3]

Work team policies or Fifty days of White Terror

In May 1966, a significant change of style occurred in the Ministry's debates. It was directly linked to the adoption of the 'May 16th circular' by the Central Committee, a document criticizing the relative moderation of the campaigns hitherto conducted in the name of the Cultural Revolution. A Central Cultural Revolution Group (CCRG), headed by Chen Boda, was established with instructions to give the movement an ideological and political turn geared towards the elimination of all 'anti-socialist and bourgeois' tendencies among academics and in the literary world.[4] Moreover, the Cultural Revolution should not be confined to these areas but apply to other parts of society where, as Mao expressed it, a large number of representatives of the bourgeoisie and of counter-revolutionary revisionists had 'sneaked into Party, government, army and various cultural domains'.[5] In the Foreign Ministry, the campaign began to take a different form. According to the newly introduced policy, it moved from literary criticism to the stage of 'linkage with the realities of the Ministry'. At first it was not clear, to the majority of the Ministry's personnel, what this linkage might consist of and, in view of this uncertainty, most of the staff preferred to adopt a cautious attitude.[6]

Before long the new, more radical, orientation of the revolution became clear. On 25 May, a big character poster appeared on the campus of Beijing University, fiercely attacking the university's president Lu Ping and the Beijing municipal Party committee for 'sabotaging the Cultural Revolution'. The poster which was openly praised by Mao as the 'first Marxist-Leninist big character poster' was broadcast over the radio and published, on 1 June 1966, as a *People's Daily* editorial with the allegorical title: 'Sweep away all oxen, ghosts, snakes and spirits'. An attack on such an important Party committee was extremely unusual, but, due to Mao's support, it became a nation-wide event paving the way for more ample criticism of the Party establishment in general. However, Party leaders at all levels failed to grasp the significance of the message which was, in fact, directed against them. Their first reaction was to search for 'representatives of the bourgeoisie' within the Party, but not necessarily at leadership level. This was also the case in the Foreign Ministry. On 6 June, all Ministry staff was invited to participate in a mobilization meeting where Ji Pengfei made the major speech emphasizing the practical implications of the slogan heading the *People's Daily* editorial and especially the necessity to uncover 'representatives of the bourgeoisie' among the Ministry's personnel.

The rank and file among the Foreign Ministry staff had a different interpretation of the new policy trend. Encouraged by the poster at Beijing University a number of young staff members began to criticize certain leading members of the Ministry's staff, denouncing what they perceived as their bureaucratic style of work and their bourgeois way of life. A big character poster signed by 44 young people from the translation team under the general office of the Ministry created a sensation by enumerating a large number of 'facts' which revealed the 'decadent' style of life of some of the leading officials, including some ambassadors. Moreover, it accused them of acting as arrogant overlords in their relations with subordinates. Echoing the 'May 16th circular', the poster concluded that a 'privileged stratum had been established within the Ministry'.[7]

Dismayed by this attack on the Party leadership, Ji Pengfei and the Party committee responded with outrage. After their reaction had filtered through to the Ministry personnel numerous posters appeared in support of the leadership, denouncing the previous poster as 'poisonous weed'. A work team composed of members of different departments was sent to the translation department to 'examine' the 44 authors. They thus became the first targets of the Cultural Revolution within the Ministry.[8]

At the same time, the Cultural Revolution in the Ministry – still under the direction of the Party committee – began to seek out a small number of persons in leadership positions as targets of criticism. Of the three persons who were thus singled out two were vice ministers: Wang Bingnan – former ambassador in Warsaw who had conducted the Sino-American talks – and vice minister Chen Jiakang – former ambassador to Cairo. Both were accused of having neglected ideology in their work and of having adopted a bourgeois style of life. The third was the director of the Institute of International Relations, Meng Yongquan who, according to his critics, had promoted revisionist concepts in international studies. The two vice ministers escaped the fate of being labelled as 'capitalist roaders'. Instead, they were considered to have committed serious mistakes, which was a much lesser offence. Meng Yongquan, however, was judged more severely. In the heady atmosphere of revolutionary radicalism prevailing at the Institute of International Relations he was labelled a revisionist.

On the whole, the campaign against high officials in the Ministry remained relatively low key. But for the majority of the Ministry staff the situation evolved differently. As the campaign to 'sweep away all monsters and to eradicate all poisonous weeds' began to gather momentum, it became a campaign of mutual attack. In order to avoid being chosen as targets themselves, people felt compelled to prove their loyalty to the Party and their willingness to participate actively in the movement. Thus they began to compete with each other in the task of discovering other people's political mistakes. Everybody's attitude towards the socialist system and towards socialist policies over the years became subject to scrutiny.

5

Big character posters proliferated all over the Ministry's premises, carrying detailed reports on what their authors had been able to discover. As a result people became exposed in many different ways. Some were accused of having criticized the 'Great Leap Forward' in the early 1960s. Others were found to have opposed such basic ideological principles as 'putting politics in command', or of 'being both red and expert'. Even the private sphere did not escape the scrutiny of others. In this connection, a few illicit liaisons and other instances of sexual misconduct were discovered. Only a short time elapsed before each department had uncovered political offenders who were examined and criticized until a decision could be taken as to whether they still 'belonged to the people's ranks' or had become 'enemies of the people'. It is important to note that during this campaign, although it was relatively short-lived, the foundation was laid for future conflicts. The atmosphere of mutual suspicion created among colleagues and the fear of harassment by random accusations, all this encouraged by the Ministry's Party committee, undoubtedly contributed to the enthusiasm which was later aroused by Mao's demands to attack the Party apparatus itself.

Criticism of the Liu–Deng Line

Mao, after his return to Beijing on 18 July 1966, criticized the manner in which the Cultural Revolution had hitherto been carried out. He was particularly opposed to the work teams that had been dispatched to numerous departments and work units and to their way of operating. In his view, the work teams had become the instrument of bourgeois reactionaries who had followed a revisionist line by suppressing the masses rather than mobilizing them. Many people who had aired their views against the Party leadership had been treated in the same manner as during the anti-rightist campaign of 1957 and had been unjustifiably labelled 'sham leftists and real rightists'. In Mao's view, the masses should not be repressed; they should be encouraged 'to educate and to liberate themselves'.

As a result of Mao's formal condemnation of work team policies as a manifestation of the bourgeois reactionary line, all work teams were hastily withdrawn in early August 1966.[9] At the same time, the Cultural Revolution became increasingly radical. The new trend was confirmed during the 11th Plenum of the Party Central Committee convened in the first half of August 1966 to adopt the Decision of the Central Committee of the CCP Concerning the Great Proletarian Cultural Revolution, a decision which was later known as the '16 points'.

Until the end of 1966, criticism and repudiation of the line represented by Liu Shaoqi and Deng Xiaoping which, according to Mao, had suppressed the masses became the order of the day. As a result, those who had been persecuted by the work teams became again the first and most important group to stage a rebellion against their superiors. Soon they were joined by others who wanted to respond to Mao's claim that 'rebellion is justified'.[10]

The 11th Plenum had serious repercussions on government institutions. During the Plenum, Mao had brought forward his big character poster, 'Bombard the Headquarters', accusing Liu Shaoqi and Deng Xiaoping of having established a 'bourgeois headquarters' within the Party. With the demotion and later the fall of Liu and Deng, and the upgrading of Lin Biao and the Central Cultural Revolution Group (CCRG), the hierarchical order of the leadership, the process of decision-making and the role of government institutions changed considerably.

The first victim of the Cultural Revolution was the Central Committee propaganda department. Mao had condemned it as the 'palace of the King of Hell'.[11] Soon it was paralysed and its external propaganda operations were taken over by the CCRG, with the Xinhua News Agency and the *People's Daily* as the main instruments for the promotion of their policies. The second organization paralysed due to Deng Xiaoping's fall was the Central Secretariat. Its functions were taken over by the CCRG in February 1967.[12]

In the Foreign Affairs System[13] under the State Council, the situation was even more serious. Under Liu Shaoqi's work teams policy, which was at its height in June 1966, the State Council Office of Foreign Affairs and its political department had dispatched eight work teams to several institutions and schools of the foreign affairs system. The Ministry of Foreign Affairs sent seven of these teams to its schools and subordinate institutions. Some of them had applied a rather vigorous treatment to those who had tried to 'make revolution' by attacking the leading cadres in their institutions. This was especially the case of the work team led by the deputy head of the State Council office of foreign affairs, Zhang Yan, who operated within the Commission of Cultural Relations with Foreign Countries and of another, headed by the vice minister of the Ministry of Foreign Affairs, Liu Xinquan, who handled the case of the Beijing Institute of Foreign Languages. Both work teams condemned a number of people for having attacked leading cadres of the commission and of the institute labelling many of them as 'counter-revolutionaries' and subjecting them to 'struggle sessions'. Some of them were even sent into custody.[14]

After the abolition of the work teams the Commission for Cultural Relations with Foreign Countries and the Commission for Overseas Chinese came under attack by their former victims. Soon they were unable to function. The Ministries of Foreign Affairs and Foreign Trade – since they had sent work teams to the institutes of foreign languages – became, in turn, targets of attack by radical red guards from these institutes.

According to the practice of the Party, those who were attacked had to make self-criticism acceptable to the 'masses' of their respective systems. They had to convince them that their confessions were sincere, so that they could be 'liberated'. Pending such 'liberation' normal work procedures of the ministries were disrupted.

Since similar problems existed in other systems under the State Council Zhou Enlai, in his role as the premier, was in a particularly difficult position. First, he himself had given his agreement to the work team policies decided at a meeting of the Politburo in early June 1966. Nevertheless, since he was on a state visit to Albania, Romania and Pakistan during the second half of June, when the policy was implemented, Mao did not consider him responsible in this case. Second, he was deprived of the assistance of many of his deputies on the State Council who were criticized within the framework of the campaign against the Liu–Deng line and thus unable to proceed with their work. Zhou's concern was to see the State Council return to its normal functions, but since a large number of the Foreign Minister's deputies had come under pressure, they had to be 'liberated' in order to revive the system and, in order to be liberated, they had to make self-criticism in front of the 'masses'. This was proving difficult for Chen Yi, who had great reservations about the Cultural Revolution and who had openly complained about its excesses. But Zhou finally succeeded in persuading him to 'confess his mistakes' which was the precondition to enable him to resume his responsibilities.[15]

Liu Shaoqi, Deng Xiaoping and the Party establishment were in serious trouble. A central working conference (9–28 October 1966) stressed the importance of a new offensive against the 'bourgeois reactionary Liu–Deng line' on a nation-wide scale. The ramifications of this new campaign on the Foreign Ministry were unavoidable, for the Ministry's personnel had to debate the question whether the bourgeois reactionary line had in effect been implemented by the Party committee during the earlier stage of the Cultural Revolution. While Ji Pengfei – supported by the majority of the Ministry's personnel – insisted that the Party committee had faithfully adhered to Mao's proletarian line, a minority – mostly young people who had become targets of the 'white terror' – expressed disagreement with this opinion. In numerous debates about what a 'reactionary line' was, a simple criterion had been established to distinguish it from the 'revolutionary line'. If the movement had been directed against rank-and-file staff members, then it was considered 'reactionary' (*maotou xiangshang*). If, however, leading cadres had become its targets, then it was 'revolutionary' (*maotou xiangxia*). Although the Party committee, during the '50 days', had criticized three leading members of the Ministry, the bulk of its persecution had been directed against rank-and-file staff members. It was thus concluded that it had pursued a reactionary line.

With the mounting intensification of the campaign against the Liu–Deng line the Party committee's position became increasingly indefensible. In fact, political radicalization had become so strong that, when the committee turned to Chen Yi to endorse their argumentation, the Foreign Minister himself admitted that he had followed a bourgeois reactionary line by implementing work team policies. The same applied to Li Xiannian, vice premier in charge of the Finance and Trade System of which the Ministry of Foreign Trade was a part who also conceded, clearly under heavy pressure, that he had followed the wrong line.

The Second Stage

Encouraged by the failure of the Party committee to justify its policies during the '50 days' and to prove that they had concurred with Mao's revolutionary line, a number of young activists in the Ministry planned a meeting to openly criticize the bourgeois reactionary line which, in their view, had been pursued by the committee. Of about 2,000 ministerial staff less than 100 appeared at the meeting and many of them came only out of curiosity. Yet the meeting, which took place on 20 December, proved to be a success. It was followed by a series of similar meetings which attracted an increasing number of participants. In view of these developments, the initiators decided to set up a liaison station (*lianluo zhan*) within the Ministry[16]. Similar organizations were established in other government institutions.

The seizure of power

A sudden change in official policies occurred when the 'January storm' began to spread throughout the country. On 6 January 1967, Shanghai rebels seized power in the city's municipal Party committee and its government. Mao approved of their activities and proposed it as an example to be emulated. As a result, power seizure became official policy which incited red guards and rebels to 'seize power' in their respective schools and work units.

These developments stimulated the Foreign Ministry liaison station to seize power as well. To this end it convened a meeting on 18 January 1967 where it declared that it was from now on operating under the name of 'revolutionary rebels liaison station' and that it was seizing power at ministerial level. This action was followed up by a small number of rebels who expressed their decision to seize power in the Ministry's departments. A small 'nucleus group' to represent the liaison station was established. It was composed mainly of relatively young activists who had joined the Foreign Ministry fairly recently and who were generally known for their radical opinions.

In the evening of 18 January, Chen Yi, on Zhou's behalf, received representatives of the liaison station to express his support for their activities. He made it clear, however, that foreign affairs as such would remain the domain of the central-policy makers and that he would not permit any interference in the implementation of foreign policies. In his view, the seizure of power could only imply the right to lead the Cultural Revolution within the Ministry.[17]

Zhou Enlai had sound reasons for extending his support to the Foreign Ministry rebels. First, with Mao's formal backing power seizure had become an official policy and thus could not be evaded. Second, under the circumstances, Zhou preferred this policy to be implemented by the Ministry's own personnel rather than by outsiders. He especially wanted to avoid all pretexts for eventual interventions by red guards from the foreign languages institutes who demonstrated great eagerness to seize power in the Foreign Ministry. At the same time he advised Chen Yi to urge the staff of the Office of Foreign Affairs at the State Council, who had not yet established rebel organizations, to do so and to declare the seizure of power at that Office.[18]

The immediate consequence of Zhou's recognition of the seizure of power in the Foreign Ministry was an increase of the ranks of revolutionary rebels and a number of structural changes in the Ministry.

The leading political and administrative organ of the Foreign Ministry was the ministerial Party committee composed of the Foreign Minister, the vice ministers, ministerial assistants and department directors. Although secretary of the committee, Chen Yi came to the Ministry only on certain occasions. His duties as a member of the Politburo usually kept him at his offices in Zhongnanhai. In his place, it was Ji Pengfei, the deputy secretary and responsible vice minister, who presided over the routine meetings of the Party committee. After the seizure of power by the nucleus group the ministerial Party committee was deprived of directing political activities in the Ministry. The Ministry's personnel was then divided into two categories: one part of the staff was designated to take care of the Ministry's day-to-day work, while the larger portion of the personnel was engaged in 'carrying out the Cultural Revolution'.[19]

The liaison station was charged with the 'supervision' of the Ministry's work. With Zhou Enlai's approval, an organizational structure was created for this purpose; it functioned at two levels. First, for the Ministry as a whole, a supervisory group of about ten persons was established and assigned to work at vice minister level. Second, in each department – depending on its size – a supervisory group of three to five people was set up to oversee the activities of the department heads. These groups were required to read all incoming material and to countersign all outgoing documents.[20]

With Zhou's outspoken support, the rebels' clout had risen considerably and their ranks had increased substantially. Since the end of 1966, among the Ministry's staff of about 2,000, the number of persons participating in the rebel movement had expanded from roughly 100 at the very initial stage to about 1,700 in the summer of 1967.

Most of the Ministry's employees participated in the rebels' movement, but they were not a homogeneous entity. Zhou Enlai, though he repeatedly cautioned the liaison station about associating themselves with the red guards of the Foreign Affairs System so as to avoid the spill-over of their factional strifes into the Ministry, could not prevent the emergence of rival groups among the Foreign Ministry staff. Whereas the liaison station represented the majority of the staff, two conservative groups had also appeared, calling themselves respectively the 'general headquarters of the rebels' (*zhong bu*) and the 'climbing the dangerous peak corps' (*pan xian feng*). The former consisted mostly of drivers of the administrative department and the latter were staff from several area and functional departments.

A series of divergences existed between the liaison station and the other two organizations. Some of their differences could be traced back to the early stages of the Cultural Revolution, when many members of the latter groups had supported the ministerial Party committee and had put into practice the committee's policies against rank-and-file employees. Later they openly defended the Party committee, arguing that it had continuously followed Mao's revolutionary line. Other subjects of controversy surfaced during the campaigns against Chen Yi and in their attitude towards Zhou Enlai.

In the Chinese embassies abroad, factionalism also began to spread. At the start of the Cultural Revolution Zhou Enlai, Chen Yi and the Foreign Ministry's Party committee had decided that the Chinese embassies abroad should not get involved in the movement. Yet one single remark from the Chairman was sufficient to change this decision. Mao, early in September 1966,

12

had received a letter sent to him by a group of foreigners – stout supporters of his concept of the Cultural Revolution – who had participated in an international conference in Vienna. On that occasion they had observed Chinese government representatives and were struck by their 'bourgeois' appearance. The Chinese diplomats had shown up wearing high-quality clothes and in expensive cars. This incited the writers of the letter to complain to Mao that the Chinese diplomats had been corrupted by the Western bourgeois style of life. Mao apparently took this letter very seriously. On 9 September, he remarked that embassy staff needed to be revolutionized.[21] As soon as his remarks became known in the Foreign Ministry, its staff began to demand the return to the capital of Chinese ambassadors and of some of their senior cadres. They argued that, in their life abroad, the diplomats had become so divorced from the revolutionary process in their home country that they were unable to grasp the significance of the developments taking place there. Moreover the majority of the ambassadors, since they were also Party bureaucrats, were accused of acting like overlords towards their embassy staff and were resented as such by their subordinates. Given the strict hierarchical structure in Chinese bureaucracies, where a chief was really the master, this accusation might well have contained some truth. At the same time, the Cultural Revolution was spreading to Chinese missions abroad where, following the same lines as on the domestic scene, factions appeared among the staff and many ambassadors had become unable to exercise their functions normally.

All this created enough pressure on Zhou Enlai to compel him to order, in early 1967, the return to the capital of all Chinese ambassadors. At the same time between half and two-thirds of the embassies' personnel were also called back. The only exception was Huang Hua, the ambassador to Egypt who had been newly appointed and thus had not yet become subject to attacks from his staff.[22]

The objective of this measure was to oblige the ambassadors and their staff to participate in the Cultural Revolution. For this purpose an old condemned building belonging to the Foreign Ministry was put at their disposal where each embassy occupied one large room used to carry out the Cultural Revolution. In the process of discovering and criticizing bourgeois, reactionary and revisionist elements in each embassy most of the leading embassy personnel became targets. In any pyramidal structure such as an embassy, it was not difficult to single out autocratic superiors and to blame them for their 'revisionist line'.

Personal confrontations appeared to have been the major cause for the emergence of opposing factions inside embassies. The conservatives, who named themselves the 'united revolutionary rebels', were either of moderate disposition or on good terms with their ambassador, whereas those who, for one reason or another, had disagreements with their superiors and wanted to demonstrate their dissatisfaction, took the name of 'September 9th rebel corps'. This latter group was on good terms with the Foreign Ministry's liaison station. The majority faction within each embassy obtained the right to lead the Cultural Revolution there.[23]

Regardless of the faction they belonged to, the embassy rebels were known for their toughness and intransigence with respect to the 'target persons' they had selected. In some embassies this gave rise to violent in-fighting, with sometimes farcical consequences, as one faction might have selected the ambassador as their primary target whereas the other faction was hostile to the first counsellor who, in turn, might have been appreciated by the first faction because he happened to be on bad terms with the ambassador. In sum, total confusion reigned in the embassies.[24]

The case of Chen Yi

In the Foreign Ministry, the person who was most affected at that stage of the Cultural Revolution was the Foreign Minister himself. Chen Yi was a man of outstanding qualities and extraordinary disposition among the Chinese leaders. He was born in Sichuan in 1901. During the civil war, he commanded the Third Field Army and later became one of the ten marshals of the Peoples Liberation Army (PLA) nominated by Mao for their contribution to the victory of the revolution. At the beginning of the Cultural Revolution, he was a member of the Political Bureau of the Central Committee, vice chairman of the Central Military Commission, vice premier and Foreign Minister. But it was his personality which distinguished him from many other leaders. He was a soldier, but also a diplomat and a poet, and a person known for his humour, eloquence and frankness. Mao, who always kept Party leaders at a distance and whose contacts with members of the Politburo were usually limited to business, considered him as one of his few friends.[25]

This friendship, however, did not shield Chen Yi from Mao's political persecution. As noted earlier, according to a rule Mao had introduced, all leaders who had followed the Liu–Deng line during the initial stage of the Cultural Revolution were expected to make self-criticism in the presence of the 'masses' and win their pardon. If their self-criticism was accepted they would be considered 'liberated' and could resume their work. This rule particularly concerned the Foreign Minister Chen Yi who had approved the missions of eight work teams mandated to monitor different institutions of the Foreign Affairs System in June 1966. They had operated, for example, in the foreign languages institutes, in the Commission for Cultural Exchanges with Foreign Countries and in the Commission for Overseas Chinese Affairs.[26]

Since most of the vice prime ministers of the State Council had been involved in work team policies and thus needed to be reinstated after self-criticism, Zhou succeeded in persuading Chen Yi to be the first to submit to this procedure. Chen Yi read his self-criticism to 10,000 representatives of the masses of the Foreign Affairs System on 24 January 1967 in the Great Hall of the People. He admitted that he had promoted the bourgeois reactionary line and, on several occasions, had criticized the Cultural Revolution. He attributed his mistakes to his poor understanding of the substance of the Cultural Revolution initiated by the Great Leader Chairman Mao and he promised that he would make every effort to remould his world outlook and to conscientiously study Mao Zedong Thought so that he would be able to join hands with the revolutionary masses in promoting the Cultural Revolution to its end.[27] Since Chen's statement had been approved by Mao prior to the meeting, reading it to the meeting was a pure formality; it was readily accepted by the participants.

Zhou, in his speech to the meeting, declared that, since Chen's self criticism had been well received by the masses, he should be reinstated to all his former responsibilities within the Foreign Affairs System. Chen Boda, head of the CCRG, and a number of representatives of the masses also responded positively to Chen's speech, confirming that his self-criticism and repentance

15

were sincere. He was thus declared 'liberated' and was restored as the leader of the Foreign Affairs System and of the Cultural Revolution within that system. The Foreign Ministry staff was in favour of their Minister's return to his official functions. Despite his occasional critical remarks against the Revolution and the Ministry's rebels, Chen Yi enjoyed great popularity among his staff.[28]

However, notwithstanding self-criticism, Chen Yi continued to voice his own dissonant opinions about certain foreign policy questions. He was very critical, for example, about the 'Red Square Incident' of 25 January 1967 where Chinese students provoked Soviet authorities by aggressively defending Stalin and by religiously reciting Mao's words. Although Beijing, in a strong reaction in defence of the students, sent vehement notes to Moscow protesting against the Soviet handling of the situation,[29] Chen Yi disagreed with the official interpretation of the incident:

> The Chinese students took the lead in reading Chairman Mao's quotations in the Red Square. That was the beginning. Then people began to read them everywhere in the world. This means hitting in all directions and copying things (of the Cultural Revolution) in foreign countries. This gave rise to problems with the Soviet revisionists and the French imperialists. The imperialists, the revisionists and the reactionaries all fell upon us. We have landed ourselves in a passive position.

He also criticized the Chinese students' initiative of laying wreaths in Lenin's and Stalin's tombs and suggested that their real aim was to put themselves in the limelight.[30]

Chen Yi's 'liberation' was short-lived. He was a man of strong character and convictions, a soldier, and an eloquent politician whose speech was vivid and humorous. But the most outstanding feature of his personality was his outspoken frankness which forcefully manifested itself on the occasion of a meeting between members of the Standing Committee, the Politburo and the Central Cultural Revolution Group (CCRG) at Huairentang[31] in February 1967.

By that time, many were appalled by the attacks and humiliations directed at high-ranking leaders, by the general disorder in the country and by the danger of its spill-over into the army.

At the meeting a number of high-ranking leaders expressed their indignation about the excesses and the injustice of the Cultural Revolution. Among them, Chen Yi was one of the most outspoken critics of the recent radical policies.[32] This sealed his fate. Mao severely condemned the 'February Adverse Current' – as it was officially termed since it represented a course opposing Cultural Revolution policies. He also denounced Chen Yi as a major representative of this 'current' and gave him leave to again prepare his self-criticism. Between 25 February and 18 March, Chen was criticized at a number of enlarged meetings of the Politburo. At the same time, the CCRG leaked the news of the event of the February Adverse Current to radical red guards. In the following months, vigorous attacks – directed by the CCRG and carried out by red guard and rebel organizations – unfolded against the February Adverse Current. Of the seven Politburo members involved in this event, Chen Yi became a major target and was denigrated on numerous posters.[33] Radical red guards and rebels regarded him as the 'number one capitalist roader of the Foreign Affairs System', and as an 'anti-Party, anti-socialist, anti-Mao Zedong Thought element' (*sanfan fenzi*). They issued numerous statements demanding that he be 'smashed' and that he should 'come to the masses to submit to their criticism'.[34] The Foreign Ministry nucleus group, fearing that it might be suspected of procrastination, also tuned in after some debate about the matter. On 16 April, it issued a formal statement advancing the slogan 'Down with Chen Yi'.[35]

In the atmosphere of revolutionary fervour prevailing during the month of May, when the campaign against Chen Yi reached a peak, the two conservative organizations felt compelled to join in the criticism against the Foreign Minister. But they argued for greater moderation in the campaign, expressed by the slogan that Chen Yi should be 'first criticized and then protected'. In response to this, the rebels condemned them as 'royalists'. The liaison station did not recognize the groups and attempted to suppress them. But this was not easy because the conservatives, although outnumbered by the rebels, still counted large numbers of sympathizers among the staff. At the same time Chen's two closest collaborators, the vice ministers Ji Pengfei and Qiao Guanhua were also attacked. Though denounced as 'capitalist roaders', they continued in their functions. But this was not the case with ChenYi. While he had not been formally deprived of his ministerial duties, he was, nonetheless, unable to exercise them effectively again after his involvement with the February Adverse Current.

The varying degree of radicalization among the rebels began to manifest itself in their different reactions to Zhou Enlai. In spite of his support for the Ministry's rebels, Zhou had time and again shown signs of reservations about the Cultural Revolution. For example, during the Huairentang meeting, which produced the February Adverse Current, and which Zhou had chaired, he had neither joined in the criticism of the Cultural Revolution, nor did he clearly take a stand in its favour. This apparently ambivalent attitude had become publicly known. Some red guard groups in the Foreign Affairs System even began to assert that Zhou was the 'black boss' behind the February Adverse Current, and that it was he who had staged the entire event. Big character posters directed against Zhou Enlai appeared in the streets and on the campuses of Beijing. Undoubtedly influenced by this evolution of events, a number of members of the liaison station's nucleus group and some of the radical rebels at department level also began to express their dissatisfaction with Zhou's moderation and reproached him for not following conscientiously the policies promoted by the Central Cultural Revolution Group. They became more and more aggressive in their dealings with the premier.[36]

The campaign against Chen Yi gave rise to arguments between Zhou and the radical rebels in the Ministry. In order to organize the campaign, a 'liaison station to criticize Chen Yi' had been established within the Foreign Affairs System. This station was dominated by the radical red guards from the foreign languages institutes, especially the 'red flag rebel corps' and the extreme leftist 'June 16th' red guards. These groups had become particularly hostile towards Chen Yi during the early stages of the Cultural Revolution when they had been harassed by the work teams he had sent to their institutions. Soon after its establishment, the station began to organize a mass rally at Tiananmen Square, which was to take place on 11 May, and which was to demand that Chen Yi 'come to the masses' to make self-criticism and to listen to their denunciations.

In spite of the increasingly frenzied atmosphere, Zhou Enlai still attempted to continue his policy of dissociating the Foreign Ministry rebels from the zealous and disorderly radical red guards. He therefore advised the Foreign Ministry rebels not to join the anti-Chen Yi station. He was strongly opposed to the participation of Foreign Ministry staff, whether they were rebels or not, in the planned mass demonstration against the Foreign Minister. In spite of the strict instructions issued to that effect to the Ministry's liaison station, a minority of the most radical rebels of the Ministry took part in the rallies, thus creating the widespread impression that the Foreign Ministry was part of the anti-Chen alliance.[37]

It should be noted that the principle and the procedure of Chen Yi's self-criticism regarding his involvement in the February Adverse Current was no longer an issue. It had already been decided by the centre, i.e. by Mao Zedong, that Chen, like the other Politburo members involved in that phenomenon, had to subject himself to a procedure which often consisted of several stages. Chen had already confessed his 'mistakes' in front of the Politburo. In a second stage, he was expected to appear in front of the 'masses' of the Foreign Affairs System, an event which had to be properly organized.

Red guards and radicals had become increasingly suspicious that Chen Yi's self-criticism in front of the masses had been delayed on purpose. The rally at Tiananmen Square on 11 May was clearly intended as a means of pressuring Zhou Enlai to proceed with the organization of this event.

Zhou Enlai agreed to discuss Chen Yi's case with the red guard and rebel groups. For this purpose he convened a meeting with their representatives during the night of 11–12 May. During the discussions he made it a point to meet with the two opposing factions of the foreign affairs system separately. While he agreed that Chen Yi had committed a certain number of mistakes he also made it clear that Chen was not to be 'smashed'.[38]

In spite of his efforts, Zhou did not succeed in calming down the excited radical red guards who kept up their pressure on Zhou Enlai. On 13 May – though fully aware that Chen Yi was in Zhongnanhai – they forced their way into one of the Foreign Ministry buildings declaring that they had come to abduct the Foreign Minister. Once on the premises, they were confronted by Foreign Ministry staff who objected to their interference. It was only by the strength of their numbers that the Ministry staff succeeded in persuading them to leave the premises after-some minor scuffles.[39]

The attacks on Chen Yi became increasingly vociferous. Both factions of the Foreign Affairs System, the conservatives as well as the radicals, put forward the slogan: 'Down with Chen Yi'. Zhou Enlai again attempted to dilute these attacks. During the night of 14 May he convened yet another meeting to discuss Chen Yi's self-criticism with the two factions. He proposed that three different sessions, of 'small, medium and large size', should be organized. The small meeting was to be held at the Foreign Ministry, the medium-sized meeting would number about 10,000 participants and take place in the Great Hall of the People whereas about 100,000 people from the entire Foreign Affairs System would be invited to the large meeting to be held in an open sports forum. This proposal was generally accepted but, during the discussions, an additional complication surfaced with regard to the organization of the meetings. Although all factions had basically agreed to Zhou Enlai's suggestions, there was a conflict as to who should chair the meetings. As far as the small meeting was concerned, it was to take place in the Foreign Ministry where the radicals dominated to such an extent that their chairmanship was not disputed. This was not the case with respect to the medium and the large meetings where both factions competed for the presidency. The solution which was finally found was that the meetings would be chaired alternately by the radical and the conservative factions.[40]

The increasing difficulties Zhou encountered in his nego-tiations with red guards and rebels in the Foreign Affairs System was only one example of the problems he met with the similar groups in other administrative systems too. At the same time, public attacks directed against Zhou Enlai had escalated to such an extent that his political survival had become seriously threatened. Mao, in spite of his radicalism, could not afford a total collapse of the administration which – at this point – depended almost entirely on the premier's ability to maintain a minimum of order. He himself intervened, instructing Chen Boda to put a halt to the attacks. Chen Boda, in a public state-ment, declared that the red guards and rebels had overstepped their limits, and suggested that they proceed with a 'rectification campaign' analysing and criticizing their errors of opposing Zhou Enlai.[41]

After Chen Boda's confirmation of Zhou Enlai's position in the 'proletarian headquarters' of Mao Zedong, his critics became much more muted. In the Foreign Ministry, the rebels' liaison station was compelled to make self-criticism and was 'struggled against' by the rest of the Ministry's staff. This rectification led to a severe loss of status for the liaison station and especially for its more radical members. The two small rival organizations were particularly acrimonious in their accusations. The campaign lasted throughout the greater part of the month of July and, among other things, interrupted the negotiations on the organization of Chen Yi's self-criticism.[42]

However, the Wuhan event[43] – one of the most violent occurrences of that period – ended with a great victory for the revolutionary left of which the red guards of the Foreign Affairs System took immediate advantage. While the Ministry's rebels had not quite recovered from their own rectification, the red guards' attacks on Chen Yi escalated again. On 15 July the 'rebel corps' of the Beijing foreign languages college set up camp in front of one of the Foreign Ministry buildings, thus intensifying the pressure on Zhou Enlai to reactivate the procedure for Chen Yi's self-criticism. At the same time, the most radical 'June 16th' red guards of this college blocked the entrance to another Foreign Ministry building which was used for the reception of foreign guests. They, too, protested against what they considered an inappropriate postponement of the criticism meetings as they had been agreed upon with Zhou Enlai. On 4 August, these radical groups received the explicit support of two prominent members of the CCRG, Guan Feng and Qi Benyu, who told them that they had chosen the right course of action.[44]

Public criticism of Chen Yi could no longer be postponed. It had become unavoidable. The first small meeting was held in the Foreign Ministry on 7 August 1967. Liaison station rebels and department representatives had prepared speeches to criticize Chen Yi for his attitude towards the Cultural Revolution. Since there was not enough time for all the speakers to air their arguments, a second small meeting, to be convened at the same place, was scheduled for 26 August. Both meetings, presided over by the radical faction, were attended by about 100 participants seated in one of the Ministry's small auditoriums. Other Foreign Ministry employees were able to listen to the proceedings, broadcast in the large auditorium and in the corridors of the building. Zhou Enlai's presence at the meetings ensured their moderate tone and the omission of such slogans as 'Down with Chen Yi'.

On 11 August, the first medium-sized meeting was held in the Great Hall of the People. Chen Yi was accompanied to the meeting by Zhou Enlai and Xie Fuzhi, the Minister of Public Security whose presence assured that excesses would be avoided. As previously decided, the meeting was chaired by radical red guards and rebels from the Foreign Affairs System. The second part of the medium-sized session to be presided over by the conservative faction, was scheduled for 27 August, also at the Great Hall of the People. But before it would be convened, the second small meeting was held in the Foreign Ministry on 26 August. When it was about to start a large number of red guards and rebels from the 'criticizing Chen Yi station' – in an attempt to sabotage the 'medium-sized' meeting to be chaired by the conservative faction on the following day – forced their way into the Foreign Ministry building declaring that they had come to abduct Chen Yi. This time Zhou Enlai was not present but he instructed Yao Dengshan, who was then considered a famous 'red diplomat', and who was able to exercise some moderating influence over the radicals, to confront the rebels and to guarantee Chen Yi's safety. Chen Boda also intervened, arguing that the procedure previously decided upon had been accepted by Mao and ordering them to leave the premises. The meeting was interrupted, but Yao Dengshan, with the cooperation of the Ministry's nucleus group, succeeded in hiding the Foreign Minister in an office in accessible to the intruders. In the evening of that day, Chen was secretly escorted to the safety of Zhongnanhai.[45] With this event, the process of Chen Yi's criticism and 'liberation' came to an abrupt end. Due to the disturbances at the Foreign Ministry the planned 27 August meeting never took place, but neither did the large-scale meetings. In early September, the political atmosphere changed, red guard and rebel movements were increasingly criticized and finally suppressed. Chen Yi's 'case', however, was never brought to a conclusion as Zhou Enlai had hoped to achieve through the criticizing sessions, and which would have permitted Chen Yi's reinstatement as vice premier and Foreign Minister. He, and the other members of the Politburo implicated in the February

Adverse Current, never received their political clearance and remained deprived of the right to assume their professional roles.[46] From September 1967, Chen Yi's duties were taken over by Ji Pengfei who was nominated acting Foreign Minister. Only once again – in 1969, on the occasion of reassessing the international situation and China's security needs – was Chen Yi called upon by Mao to provide his expertise on foreign relations.[47] But the fact that he was called back for a specific purpose, where his expertise could be useful, did not avert his political fate. At the 12th plenary session of the 8th Central Committee in December 1968 which prepared the 9th Party Congress, the issue of the February Adverse Current was raised again by some members of the CCRG and by a number of military representatives close to Lin Biao. Once more, they attacked Chen Yi and his Politburo colleagues who were involved in the event. In discussing whether or not Chen Yi should be nominated as a delegate to the Congress, Mao ironically suggested that he could represent the right wing of the Party. At the 9th Congress in April 1969, Chen Yi was re-elected to the Central Committee but not to the Politburo. A few months later, when the national evacuation plan[48] was implemented in October 1969, Chen was sent to work in a factory in Shijia-zhuang in Hebei Province. In August 1970 he took part in the Central Committee meeting at Lushan, where he fell again into political disgrace. Having sided with Chen Boda on the issue of Mao's genius,[49] he was condemned by Mao as a 'sham-Marxist and an 'anti-Party careerist'. Kang Sheng accused him as a collaborator of Chen Boda against whom most accusations at the Lushan conferences were directed.[50]

Chen Yi was deeply depressed by his political setbacks. In early 1970, he developed an intestinal cancer of which he died in January 1972.

Wang Li's talk on 7 August 1967

However, the most serious disturbances within the Foreign Ministry were not created by the red guards' assaults, they were directly related to a talk given by Wang Li, on the evening of 7 August, to Yao Dengshan and to a number of representatives of the liaison station. Wang Li, a former deputy minister of the International Liaison Department of the Central Committee and a senior member of the Central Cultural Revolution Group, was at the height of his prestige after his return from Wuhan as a national revolutionary hero.[51] Yao Dengshan, who had returned to China from Indonesia as a much celebrated 'red diplomat', was one of the few senior Ministry staff who enjoyed high prestige among the Ministry rebels, so much so that he had been invited by Zhou Enlai to act as an adviser to the liaison station's nucleus group.[52]

In his talk Wang Li expressed his dissatisfaction with the manner in which the Cultural Revolution had been carried out in the Foreign Ministry. He reported that conservative groups in the Ministry had complained to the Central Cultural Revolution Group about the attitude of Yao Dengshan and the rebels towards Chen Yi. That they had dared to challenge the rebels, in Wang Li's view, was a clear indication that the rebels had been too lenient towards the conservatives and that they had failed to maintain a strong leftist stand. Wang expressed the opinion that the slogan 'Down with Chen Yi' was not only justified but also truly revolutionary. Moreover, he pointed out, the 'seizure of power' in the Ministry had been neither sufficiently thorough nor altogether complete. First, the supervision the rebels had been allowed to exercise within the Ministry was neither effective nor exhaustive. Wang emphasized that the rebels could become authoritative only by taking into their hands the administrative and personnel affairs of the Ministry. Only then would they be able to play a significant role in external relations.

Second, in reference to the continuing existence of the ministerial Party committee, Wang pointed out that the leadership of the Foreign Ministry should be reorganized. In comparison with the complicated problems among red guards, he said, there was nothing complicated about foreign affairs. Also, he stated that both Mao Zedong and Zhou Enlai had suggested that Wang should take into his hands matters concerning the Foreign Ministry. Finally, he pledged his full support to the Foreign Ministry rebels and urged them to be more active in the Cultural Revolution.[53]

Clearly, Wang Li's declarations were a direct affront to Zhou Enlai. They were in effect an invitation to circumvent the premier's instructions of keeping foreign relations and the Ministry's internal affairs in the hands of the central policy-makers. Wang's intervention was also an embodiment of the deep dissatisfaction

Jiang Qing and the Central Cultural Revolution Group felt *vis-à-vis* Zhou Enlai's policies within the Foreign Ministry. For one thing, the CCRG considered him too powerful and too independent in his handling of the Ministry's day-to-day affairs. For another, his approach to the Cultural Revolution in the Ministry and, in particular, his attitude towards its rebels left much to be desired. For the Central Cultural Revolution Group, Zhou displayed distinct signs of ambiguity in all these respects. While he ostensibly supported the rebels, he also maintained close contacts with the conservative groups and, to the dismay of the radicals, he insisted that the moderates should be included in the revolutionary activities within the Ministry.

The news of Wang Li's talk spread like wild fire not only through the Foreign Ministry but also through Beijing. In the Ministry it catalysed the revolutionary fervour of the radical rebels. After the setback they had suffered a few weeks earlier, the official support extended to the liaison station by an important member of the Central Cultural Revolution Group boosted their self-confidence. They were particularly satisfied with the unequivocal condemnation of their rivals as conservatives and were pleased with the stamp of approval they received regarding the genuineness of their own revolutionary spirit. The rebels lost no time. Acting quickly they launched a large-scale attack against the conservative organizations – an attack that put them completely on the defensive. One of them dissolved immediately, while members of the other went into hiding. At the same time, the nucleus group of the liaison station was reorganized and purged of all moderate elements. This invested the radicals with total control and gave rise to the widespread belief that Zhou Enlai was no longer in charge of the Cultural Revolution in the Foreign Ministry.

In response to Wang Li's call to increase their power status the liaison station nucleus group, on the evening of 13 August, held a discussion to consider the seizure of power in the political department.[54] Though not directly involved in foreign policy matters, this department was particularly important since it controlled matters related to personnel and had been a traditional stronghold of the conservatives. Though Wang Li did not explicitly demand the seizure of power in this department, the liaison station took it over on 14 August.[55]

Yao Dengshan, who had been present at Wang Li's talk, sud-

25

denly became a popular speaker. He was asked by several other government agencies to report – on the basis of his direct knowledge of Wang Li's revolutionary concepts – on the latest developments in the Cultural Revolution Group's thinking. His talks boosted the morale of the radicals, who did not hesitate to take revenge on their rivals. Following the Foreign Ministry's example the political departments in a number of other ministries were also taken over by radicals.

Wang Li's talk also had an important impact on the red guards of the foreign languages institutes. On 18 August about 90 of them arrived at the Ministry offering the rebels their help to seize more power from the Ministry's Party committee. The following morning, a group of students who had forced their way into one of the Ministry's buildings succeeded in sealing off the Party committee's office. On this occasion representatives of the nucleus group discussed the question of power seizure with them. The Foreign Ministry rebels argued that, without specific instructions from the premier, they could not accept the power the red guards thought they could 'hand over' to them. In fact, they clearly resented any attempt at outside interference in their own affairs.[56]

Wang Li's instruction to reorganize the leadership structure within the Foreign Ministry had to be taken seriously because, at that time, the word of a CCRG member carried as much weight as that of a Central Committee directive. On 19 August the liaison station nucleus group drafted two alternative plans for this reorganization. They proposed either to establish a revolutionary committee or to create a temporary group to direct the Ministry's work. On 23 August both plans were submitted to Zhou Enlai. Wang Li, an advocate of reorganization and supposedly partisan of taking over the Foreign Ministry himself, was also consulted. But he seemed no longer interested and evasively suggested that the Foreign Ministry liaison station should learn from the experiences of the Ministry of Coal and Coke. His attitude remained vague and mysterious.

Zhou Enlai rejected both reorganization plans. Instead, he proposed that Luo Guibo, Han Nianlong, Xu Yixin (vice ministers) and Yao Dengshan should be responsible for the administration of foreign affairs.[57]

In the last week of August a big character poster appeared on Tiananmen Square. It contained one single sentence expressing the 'firm demand that Yao Dengshan should become Foreign Minister'. A similar poster, written by a rebel, was put up in the Foreign Ministry. In the confusion that ensued some observers wrongly concluded that Yao Dengshan had indeed taken over the Foreign Ministry. In any event, the rumour about his having taken charge of the Foreign Ministry became an international fiction. Mao himself contributed to this. In his talk with the Ceylonese Prime Minister, Mrs Bandaranaike, on 28 June 1972, he declared that the Foreign Ministry had been out of his control for as long as one and a half months. When Yao Dengshan was interviewed in Beijing in March 1990, he expressed surprise at his international fame as – however temporary – Foreign Minister and confirmed that he never occupied this or any other comparable post even for a single day. Not only did Yao not become Foreign Minister, but even the group in which, according to Zhou's decision, he was to have participated to direct foreign affairs never really took off. Nonetheless, Yao had to pay a price. He spent years in custody where he was consistently interrogated about his role in August 1967, and was condemned to ten years of imprisonment, only to be officially rehabilitated in 1979.[58]

The Third Stage

During the summer of 1967, the Cultural Revolution had moved into a new phase of intense radicalization leading to more and more frequent incidents of violence, armed fighting among rival factions, paralysis of national and provincial government institutions and threats to the army. A *Red Flag* editorial of July, demanding purges of the PLA leadership – allegedly penetrated by numerous 'capitalist roaders' – resulted in the escalation of the Cultural Revolution within the army. But Mao, having become aware of the general disintegration of order within the country, decided that the time had come to restore order. During his talks with provincial leaders in August 1967, Mao made a number of remarks which signalled a change of political direction. While, in the beginning of that year, he had called for an 'all-round class struggle' he now appealed to rebels and red guards to abandon their differences, to unite and to establish 'great alliances'. Mao's apparent aim was to reorganize administrative structures of the country through 'revolutionary

27

committees' based on 'great alliances' between mass organizations, revolutionary cadres and the military.

He condemned the *Red Flag* editorial dealing with capitalist roaders in the army and characterized Wang Li's speech to the rebels in the Foreign Ministry as 'poisonous weed'. Also he ordered the arrest of Wang Li and Guan Feng, the author of the editorial. A third member of the CCRG, Qi Benyu, deeply involved with the red guard movement, was arrested later. The CCRG was thus purged of some of its most radical members, who were accused of promoting anarchism and excesses.[59]

This change of direction became public knowledge in early September 1967. The radical leaders of the Cultural Revolution, Chen Boda, Jiang Qing, Kang Sheng and even Lin Biao, the deputy commander of the Cultural Revolution after Mao Zedong, all began to assume a different posture. At two mass meetings, on 1 and 5 September, they distanced themselves from the excesses of the previous months, attributing them to ultra-leftism in mass organizations and inaugurating a new wave of criticism directed against this trend.[60]

The Purge of the Rebels

In the Foreign Ministry an abrupt change in the political outlook could also be noted. Wang Li's purge changed the configuration of forces within the Ministry. The previously dissolved conservative organization 'climbing the dangerous peak' (*pan xian feng*) resumed its activities and its membership suddenly increased remarkably. In a reversal of roles this group, together with the other conservative organization, (the 'general headquarters of the rebels' – *zhong bu*), launched severe attacks on the liaison station. During September and the first half of October the two small organizations, with the support of Zhou and Mao, continued their campaign denouncing the ultra-left policies of the main rebel organization. As the conservative factions reasserted themselves, the radical rebels felt increasingly insecure and their revolutionary fervour was considerably dampened. But the final blow to the radical faction was dealt by Zhou Enlai himself. On 18 October 1967 one of the vice ministers, Han Nianlong, called the entire staff to a meeting where he transmitted to them a message from the premier. The message claimed that the liaison station nucleus group 'has direct or indirect connections with the May 16th counter-revolutionary conspiracy clique'.[61] Zhou referred to an underground organization which was considered to be composed of extremely dangerous anti-revolutionary conspirators and which had been officially condemned by Mao himself.[62]

The accusation that the liaison station had connections with the May 16th group was extremely serious. It implied that it had lost the trust of the 'proletarian headquarters' of Mao Zedong since the Ministry had been infiltrated by the conspiratory group, which was blamed for the disorders that had previously occurred. The station was also held responsible for the escalation of the Hong Kong riots and especially for setting fire to the British mission.[63]

The liaison station nucleus group became paralysed and was finally dissolved. At departmental level, the rebel organizations disintegrated. Most of their members were reluctant to belong to an organization that was accused by the premier himself of having had dealings with a counter-revolutionary conspiratory clique. By the end of 1967, a 'committee of great unity' was established which received full support from Zhou Enlai. It was dominated by the Ministry's conservative rebel groups now calling themselves the 'proletarian revolutionaries' (*Wu Ge Pai*). Mao's grand-niece, Wang Hairong,[64] then a woman in her late 20s and an employee in the Foreign Ministry, had become the committee's *de facto* leader. Through her, the committee was assured of the support of Mao himself, since Wang was one of the few persons who, at that time, had access to the Chairman.[65]

In January 1968, the 'committee of great unity' started a campaign of 'criticizing ultra-leftism and uncovering bad elements' in which the rebels became a prime target. A number of people were singled out as 'bad elements' and were labelled class enemies to be subjected to the 'dictatorship of the masses'. In other words, they were to be detained in custody. Among them were, first of all, the 'red diplomat' Yao Dengshan and other cadres at department director level who had acted as advisers to the liaison station. Second, a number of middle-level cadres who allegedly had betrayed the Communist Party to the Guomindang authorities during the 1930s, were labelled 'alien class elements' and 'renegades'. As a part of the campaign against ultra-leftism, an increasing number of conservatives and veteran cadres began to re-evaluate Cultural Revolution policies and to accuse prominent members of the CCRG of having promoted ultra-leftist policies.

As the political clout of the conservatives became increasingly strong, 91 leading cadres, among them vice ministers, department heads and ambassadors, signed a big character poster which severely criticized ultra-leftism, defended the loyalty of the Ministry's cadres and challenged the accusations which had previously been levelled against Chen Yi. For them Chen Yi was a great revolutionary who had made important contributions to the Party and the state. The charges made against him, they declared, had no foundation and were due to ultra-leftist excesses.[66]

The poster, which appeared on 13 February 1968, was, however, ill-timed. Feeling personally threatened by this new wave of criticism against ultra-leftism, Jiang Qing and the CCRG struck back. Jiang Qing publicly declared that the purge of Wang Li, Guan Feng and Qi Benyu had fomented the rise of rightist conservatism; and Kang Sheng pointed to the 'current danger of right opportunism and splittism'.[67] All this did have an effect. In March, the campaign against ultra-leftism was suddenly halted and replaced by a campaign against the 'rightist deviationist wind' represented by the February Adverse Current. It was compounded by the much publicized purge of three important military leaders accused of conspiracy and collusion with the February Adverse Current.[68] The appearance of the Foreign Ministry poster in support of Chen Yi, at a time when right-wing revisionism was again under attack, became a national event. The writers of the poster could not have foreseen this sudden change in the political wind from ultra-leftism to revisionism. Clearly they had made an embarrassing tactical mistake. The poster was also disconcerting for both Zhou Enlai and Chen Yi. Zhou had to criticize it as a mistake in principle and an interference from the right;[69] and Chen, whom the poster was intended to rehabilitate, was forced to disavow it.[70]

In the summer of 1968, the campaign against right deviation gradually subsided. Since the leadership was preoccupied with the establishment of revolutionary committees, no new campaign was implemented for a few months. By the fall of 1968, revolutionary committees had been installed in the provinces and the major municipalities. Wherever they functioned efficaciously, they began to revive Party organizations. Since the overall political situation had become relatively calm, Mao decided to call the 12th Plenum of the 8th Party Congress before the end of 1968 to prepare the 9th Party Congress which had been delayed for thirteen years. The Plenum reiterated the criticism of rightist deviation in the form represented by veteran leaders, a move which culminated in the expulsion of Liu Shaoqi, the 'renegade, traitor and scab' as he was then referred to, from the Party 'forever'.[71]

The 9th Party Congress opened on 1 April 1969, with a high-sounding eulogy of Mao and of the Cultural Revolution. The Political Report presented by Lin Biao, especially, reviewed the achievements of the Cultural Revolution and insisted on the necessity for its continuation for two reasons: (1) 'the socialist transformation within the superstructure' had not yet been carried 'through to the end' and class struggle had 'by no means ceased in the ideological and political spheres'; (2) the revolution still had to accomplish 'a thousand and one tasks' such as implementing 'mass criticism and repudiation, purifying class ranks, consolidating the Party organization, simplifying the administrative structure, and sending office workers to workshops'.[72] Thus, in spite of Mao's intention to terminate the Cultural Revolution at the 9th Congress, its most important outcome was to prolong it. By insisting on the numerous tasks the Cultural Revolution still had to perform, it confirmed in fact the beginning of a new phase of political persecution which again was to affect large numbers of people of all walks of life.

In November 1969 this campaign entered a new phase. In accordance with Mao's instructions of 7 May 1966, cadres were sent to the countryside in order to be remoulded ideologically in May 7th Cadre Schools. Although all of the Foreign Ministry's employees were considered in need of such remoulding, one-third of the staff remained at the Ministry in order to ensure the continuity of its operations. The others were sent to the Cadre Schools, established in the provinces of Hunan and Jiangxi. Several thousand officials with their families, including people employed in Chinese missions abroad and by institutions belonging to the Foreign Affairs System, were thus transferred to the countryside.[73]

Ideological remoulding in effect meant involvement in a campaign against some designated target. This time, it took the form of an escalated campaign against rebels accused of being members of the May 16th group and anyone alleged to be a member was interrogated about his relations and dealings with the group. Under heavy pressure, such targets were compelled not only to confess their own involvement with the group, but also to implicate others. Each person who 'confessed', had to state who recruited him and what other members of the group were known to him. These tactics of forced confessions mixed with denunciations of others – a process drawn out over a number of years – led to accusations against hundreds of persons among the Foreign Ministry staff.

In May 1970, Ma Wengbo, the military representative in charge of the 'May 16th problem' in the Ministry submitted a report to Zhou Enlai according to which there were more than 1,000 people in the Ministry who had been involved with the May 16th group. Within that group, 304 persons had readily 'confessed' and should therefore be treated leniently. In the middle of the same year the total number of 'May 16th elements' had already reached 1,500. All former rebels and even a number of conservatives had been implicated in this conspiratory group. When the campaign expanded into the ranks of the 'proletarian revolutionaries', it began to falter. How far was it to go? The process of forcing denunciations from the 'target persons' had clearly backfired. Zhou tried to find a solution to this dilemma by advising the Foreign Ministry 'proletarian revolutionaries' not to focus on the problem of whether or not a person was a member of the May 16th group ('516' fenzi), but rather to concentrate on the political crimes he or she may have committed ('516' zuixing).[74]

Four major criteria were established as indicators for these crimes:

1 The participation in the counter-revolutionary 'seizure of power' following Wang Li's talk on 7 August. According to the version Mao later adopted about the events of August 1967, this had led to the loss of central control in the Ministry for a period between four days to one and a half months. Wang Li was now considered the ringleader of the '516' clique in the Foreign Ministry.

2 The support of the demand to 'bombard the proletarian headquarters' during the months of May and August. This referred to the attacks against Zhou Enlai which had appeared during

that time and which were now referred to as the 'black wind blown up by the May 16th elements'.

3 The disclosure of confidential documents. This referred to the request by Wang Li and Guan Feng to the Foreign Ministry in the name of the Cultural Revolution Group to provide them with examples of Liu Shaoqi's foreign policy of 'three capitulations and one elimination' (*san xiang yi mie*).[75]

4 The burning down of the British mission in Beijing. This was now considered as an outcome of the collaboration between '516' elements in and outside the Foreign Ministry.

From the second half of 1970 onwards, the authorities in the Cadre Schools no longer mentioned May 16 elements as such. Instead the focus of attention turned to those who had made 'May 16th mistakes'. The majority of those who had earlier been accused as May 16th elements, and had confessed accordingly, were quietly upgraded from 'class enemy' to people who had committed 'May 16th crimes'.

The campaign to purify class ranks came to an end in October 1972. One of the major reasons for this undoubtedly was that one of its most important components – the campaign against the May 16th group – had reached absurd proportions involving an unrealistically large number of people. Another cause was the transformations China's foreign relations had undergone since the early 1970s. The Chinese authorities were unprepared for the changing international environment. The establishment of diplomatic relations with many countries in a relatively short span of time required a large number of diplomatic personnel to staff the new embassies and to reinforce the Foreign Ministry, whose staff had been cut to less than one-third in 1969. To prepare for the new situation, people who were considered 'clean' were called back from the Cadre Schools. Most of these Schools were closed down.[76]

To terminate the campaign in the Foreign Ministry, a report was submitted to Zhou Enlai suggesting that fifty people should be officially labelled May 16th elements. This was a remarkable reduction from the record which had been presented only a few months earlier and which had contained 1,500 names. Zhou went even further and reduced the list to twenty names. During a series of meetings in late October 1972, the final list of twenty was confirmed. Among them were Yao Dengshan and two other

33

cadres at department director level who had acted as advisers to the liaison station. The others were carefully chosen from the liaison station's nucleus group at ministerial and departmental levels and from the rank and file of the radical rebel group. They were treated as class enemies, were deprived of their political rights and of their income, and subjected to manual labour under the supervision of the 'masses'.[77]

The Fourth Stage

In spite of the stronger focus on foreign affairs demanded by the new diplomatic requirements with which China was confronted, campaigns in the Foreign Ministry still continued to flourish. Although they did not attain the intensity of the earlier period they still created some ripples in the Ministry.

Zhou Enlai was now well in command, and with the disappearance of Lin Biao in September 1971, his prestige and power reached new heights that were surpassed only by Mao himself. Zhou's position within the hierarchical order of the Party and the state was at its peak. He was again mandated with the day-to-day affairs of the Party and the state, a privilege of which he had been deprived in the immediate aftermath of the February Adverse Current episode. Lin Biao's disappearance thus marked a major turning point for Zhou's political status.

But this did not last long. Zhou's pre-eminent position was challenged by Jiang Qing who was a fervent partisan of the Cultural Revolution. In effect, after the death of Lin Biao, a new power structure emerged at the apex of leadership, dominated on the one hand by Jiang Qing representing Cultural Revolution policies and on the other by Zhou Enlai who incarnated a more moderate political position and who was supported by the veteran revolutionaries who were slowly returning to their posts. This new and competing power structure was consolidated at the 10th Party Congress convened in Beijing in August 1973. It established a Central Committee, a Politburo and a Standing Committee, each clearly divided into two factions with diverging interests.

The 80-year-old Mao towered above the two factions, trying to balance them out or to mediate between them. But since the basic interests of the two groups were fundamentally different it was difficult to find a middle ground. The Cultural Revolution faction on the one hand had risen to power as a result of its support for radical leftist policies, which they desired to continue if not to reinforce. The veteran revolutionaries, on the other hand, had been victims of these policies. They had been humiliated in the name of the Cultural Revolution; their political careers had been jeopardized and, in many cases, their very survival had been threatened. It was in their interest to restrain the policies of the Cultural Revolution. This power structure, where the groups strove to out-manoeuvre each other, became the basis for mounting friction.[78]

The power struggle between the two factions coincided with the campaign that was launched against Lin Biao after his death. At first, it was directed against his supporters in the army, and later it was extended against him and his military career. Whatever defects Lin Biao may have had, his military record was flawless. So most of the attempts to downgrade his military achievements were unconvincing, and apparently fell on deaf ears. The campaign did not have the effect that its partisans had originally hoped for. In fact, it led into an impasse.

Zhou Enlai seized this opportunity to give the campaign a new impetus and a new direction. In his view, it should not focus only on Lin Biao's person but on the 'ultra-leftism' Lin had promoted during the first part of the Cultural Revolution. In this campaign, Zhou clearly aimed at the repudiation of radicalism and anarchism, and at the reinstatement of veteran revolutionaries to their previous positions. But this campaign also backfired and this time Zhou found Mao standing in his way. If Lin Biao's policies were ultra-left, then it would be a plausible conclusion that Lin, who had wielded widespread influence over the Cultural Revolution, had directed it on the wrong course. To negate the Cultural Revolution, together with Lin Biao, was only a further step in this direction. Mao, well aware of this danger, terminated the campaign against ultra-leftism by ruling that Lin's policies had not been ultra-left but ultra-right, since he had practised 'revisionism, conspiracy and betrayal, and had aimed at schism in the Party and the state.'[79]

Mao's confrontation with Zhou was not only due to Zhou's campaign against ultra-leftism though it was undoubtedly a weighty factor. It was also due to the fact that Zhou had acquired unprecedented prestige, both nationally and internationally: nationally because he had contributed to the stabilization of the domestic situation and internationally because he was perceived as the real architect of a new and moderate foreign policy. Psychologically insecure as Mao was, and over-sensitive and inclined to overreact as he had always been to other emerging competitive centres of power, it cannot be ruled out that he may have regarded Zhou's international prestige with envy. Zhou who had consistently accepted a secondary role was not a threat to Mao; and Mao did not have the intention of eliminating Zhou, whose administrative talents he needed. But he was determined at least to put him in his place and to teach him a lesson.

Mao's dissatisfaction with Zhou became increasingly evident as incidents of criticism of the premier began to multiply, and even spilled over on to some aspects of international affairs. In July 1973 Mao summoned Wang Hongwen, the Shanghai workers' leader and currently his designated heir, and Zhang Chunqiao, a Politburo member and radical leader, to his study to discuss foreign affairs. Mao told them that there were a few things he considered unsatisfactory in the Foreign Ministry. First, he disagreed with the Ministry's perception of the world situation.[80] In an internal paper, the Ministry had held the view that the current world situation was characterized by the collaboration between the US and the Soviet Union in an attempt to dominate the world. Mao was convinced that this was an unrealistic assessment which also departed from his perception of the world as being characterized by 'san da yi shen' (three bigs and one deepening), that was 'big upheaval, big splitting, big reorganization and the deepening of the revolutionary struggle'. By 'big splitting' and 'big reorganization', he referred to the socialist camp where China and the Soviet Union had split up; and to the Western bloc, where the US and France were disputing with each other. Second, he was convinced that the contention between the US and the USSR was a problem of primary importance, while their collaboration was secondary.[81]

Mao called the Foreign Ministry's memoranda 'shit papers' and ordered Wang and Zhang to learn some foreign languages so that they would be able to judge matters for themselves and thus avoid being taken in by the Foreign Ministry staff. In conclusion, he said that the Ministry staff, instead of discussing issues of major importance with him, continuously asked for instructions on minor matters. 'If it goes on like this', he added, the 'Ministry will surely become revisionist.'[82]

Mao's criticism of the Foreign Ministry was clearly directed against Zhou Enlai. In November 1973, the attacks against the premier became more pointed. In some cases they were directly linked to foreign affairs and especially to the process of establishing relations with the United States. In Zhou's talks with Henry Kissinger the Taiwan question was, of course, one of the major and most complicated issues. He argued that there were two solutions to this problem. It could be solved either by force or by peaceful means. But Mao took offence with this formulation and strongly disagreed with it. He considered that there was only one possibility and that was to fight. Referring to CCP policies in the late 1930s, when the Red Army was fighting in Shanxi, he said that even a small fortified village run by a despot refused to surrender unless it was forced to do so by the Red Army. He accused Zhou of being afraid of the US nuclear arsenal and ordered the Politburo to hold a session to criticize Zhou and to hear his self-criticism. Zhou's attitude towards the Taiwan question during his discussion with Kissinger was termed as 'capitulationist'.[83]

Mao's grand-niece also contributed to Mao's growing discontent with the premier. Wang Hairong was a radical with strong ties to the Cultural Revolution faction. From the Foreign Ministry, where she had been promoted to vice ministership, Wang reported that Zhou tended to practise the Confucian 'doctrine of the mean'.[84] This, in her view, had become obvious in his attitude towards the Cultural Revolution and thus, far from being supportive, he was motivated by caution and impartiality. Influenced by his own reservations against Zhou Enlai and by the critical assessments of his radical entourage, Mao had become persuaded that Zhou should be criticized in an official campaign.[85]

For this purpose, the campaign to criticize Lin Biao and Confucius, which had begun in early 1974, was now transformed into a movement to 'criticize Lin, Kong and Zhou Gong'.[86] The campaign was strongly promoted by Jiang Qing and her followers, who considered that the only remaining obstacle to their ascent to power would be removed if Zhou Enlai and his supporters could be eliminated. The campaign, which Mao had intended to use only as a critical lesson for Zhou, thus turned into a power struggle between two opposing factions at leadership level. This power struggle had immediate repercussions in the Foreign Ministry, where the conservative faction or 'proletarian revolutionaries' after having been united in their opposition to the rebels and in support of Zhou Enlai for years, began to disintegrate. A number of its members joined a new faction which had recently emerged in the Ministry and which was critical of Zhou. It had been established under the leadership of Wang Hairong and her friend Tang Wensheng. The latter, also known as Nancy Tang, had acted as Mao's interpreter on a number of important occasions. During the Cultural Revolution she had been promoted to the post of director of the Foreign Ministry's American and Oceanic department. Moreover, she had also been elected as an alternate member of the CCP Central Committee at the 10th National Party Congress in 1973.[87]

As was often the case in Chinese politics, and especially during the Cultural Revolution when campaigns against political leaders were easily launched, Wang and Tang's hostility against Zhou Enlai was more personal than political. It originated in a quarrel between Mao and his nurse Zhang Yufeng which caused Zhang to leave Mao's services. It was well known in Mao's entourage that he was deeply attached to Zhang whose services he appreciated. She was also one of the few people who were able to understand Mao's blurred speech and thus was called upon to interpret his words to the outside world.[88]

Her special position in Mao's entourage was bound to engender jealousies, especially those of his grand-niece who considered that Mao overvalued Zhang's importance. His quarrel with her prompted Wang and Tang to try to increase their own role in Mao's life. In their endeavour to promote themselves in Mao's eyes they criticized her. Mao considered this an unpardonable mistake which he resented to such an extent that he not only ordered his nurse back to his compound, but also ordered Zhou Enlai to replace Tang with another interpreter.[89] When Zhou followed Mao's instructions both Wang and Tang believed that it was Zhou's personal initiative which eliminated Tang as Mao's interpreter. Both resented this and took revenge by reporting negatively about Zhou to Mao. This was possible because Wang continued to be among the few persons who had access to Mao at that time.[90]

The nucleus of the new faction were five women. Besides the two already mentioned, they were Zhang Hanzhi, deputy director of the Asian department, Qi Zhonghua, deputy director of the Western European department and Luo Xu, deputy director of the African department. Since both Wang and Tang were, at that time, in their late 20s or early 30s, and since neither of them was married, their faction was known as the 'Mademoiselle faction'. It also went under the more colourful name of the 'five golden flowers'.[91]

For a period of time the 'Mademoiselle faction', boosted by Wang Hairong's easy access to Mao, dominated the power struggle in the Foreign Ministry. The removal of Ji Pengfei from his post as Foreign Minister was said to be its achievement. Ji was succeeded by Qiao Guanhua who was believed to have acquired this post under the influence of the 'Mademoiselle faction', and who was considered by a number of the Foreign Ministry staff as having betrayed Zhou Enlai, with whom he had worked since the 1940.[92] However, if such an association existed, it was only short-lived. Clearly, Qiao had no interest in opposing Zhou and, within a short time, the faction split. Wang and Tang continued to be hostile to Zhou Enlai and Qiao found it increasingly difficult to maintain good relations with Wang Hairong. Relying on the transmission through her person of 'orders from the highest authority', Wang attempted to dominate the Ministry. The situation was further complicated by Jiang Qing's interferences as she tried to take advantage of the split by supporting Qiao and by using him against Wang Hairong, whose easy access to Mao she resented.[93]

A central theme of Wang Hairong's activities was a 'Mao Zedong Thought study class' established to define the right methods of criticizing Lin Biao and Confucius at the Foreign Ministry. This class of about 100 participants was divided into several sub-groups staffed by persons from the different departments. The participants were believed to have the privilege of obtaining the most important insights from the power centre, and especially Mao's views and instructions. As soon as Mao's utterances against Zhou Enlai had become known to them they were ready to conform and to voice their own criticism against Zhou. During 1974 and 1975, Zhou Enlai's prestige at the Foreign Ministry declined to its lowest level ever.

Zhou was also gravely ill and confined to his hospital bed.

But the power struggle in the Foreign Ministry between the different factions continued. It was cut short only by the elimination of the 'Gang of Four' which officially terminated the Cultural Revolution. There was, however, an immediate aftermath to it in the form of a campaign to criticize the 'Gang of Four'. Within the Foreign Ministry this campaign soon began to overshadow all other quarrels. The controversy between Qiao Guanhua and Wang Hairong ended, as Qiao was removed from his post as Foreign Minister. He was accused of having had close connections with the Gang of Four, an accusation which he persistently denied.[94] Wang Hairong was also put under heavy pressure to justify her past activities against Zhou Enlai. Since she could not shift the responsibility for these actions to the Gang of Four, as she could have been too easily identified with them, Wang finally declared that she had acted under Mao's orders. She and Nancy Tang were finally removed from the Foreign Ministry staff.[95]

The events in the Foreign Ministry during the Cultural Revolution were a microcosm of what was happening in the country. But the Ministry, more than any other institution, at the central government level became a focus of national attention since two leading figures, Zhou Enlai and Chen Yi, were closely involved with the events at the Ministry.

Throughout this period, Zhou Enlai remained the dominant figure in the Foreign Ministry. Although he did not occupy the post of Foreign Minister after 1958, when Chen Yi was appointed to this position, he continued to manifest deep interest in the internal affairs of the Ministry as well as in the country's foreign affairs. During the Cultural Revolution Zhou's concern over the fluctuating developments in the Ministry was perhaps more intense and more conspicuous than was the case with other parts of the vast administration in his charge. He personally devoted a considerable amount of time and effort to controlling events in the Ministry and, during the earlier years, to save and protect Chen Yi. For this he had to endure several serious confrontations with rebels and red guards from the Foreign Affairs System.

In the course of the Cultural Revolution, Zhou appeared to have accumulated considerable resentment against the radical rebel groups in the Ministry who in the end became victims of a backlash he organized in the form of several campaigns.

Since a majority of the Foreign Ministry personnel at one stage or another had belonged to the rebel group, the composition of the leadership and the staff changed significantly in the later stages of the Cultural Revolution. A relatively large group of people, many of whom had been trained as experts in foreign affairs by Zhou Enlai himself, were dispersed. When it was realized that a competent staff was needed to deal with China's increasing involvement on the international and diplomatic scene, the Foreign Ministry had to face the situation with depleted ranks. It was for this reason that, for several years, China hesitated to join a number of specialized UN agencies feeling it was not sufficiently equipped to deal with the technical problems which membership would have involved.

2

PERCEPTIONS, IDEOLOGY AND DECISION-MAKING

Perceptions of the outside world, in most countries, constitute a significant determinant of foreign policy. The People's Republic of the 1960s and early 1970s, in comparison with most other nations, was unusually isolated. Under such circumstances perceptions, even though they did not necessarily reflect realities, played a distinctive role in policy-making. Chinese views of the outside world were largely dominated by Mao's ideological and strategic thinking. The visions of China's venerated leader became the convictions of the entire country and the most significant determinant of Chinese foreign policy.

Ideology and perceptions

Mao's earliest views of the world after the Second World War were spelled out in his talk with the American correspondent Anna Louise Strong in August 1946. As he perceived it, the US and the USSR were locked in a confrontation which dominated the world and in which the US was scrambling for control of the intermediate zone between them, a zone which comprised capitalist countries in Europe and Latin America as well as colonies in Asia and Africa.[1] In this conflictual situation, where the intermediate zone did not play a significant role, China had to choose her stand. After the founding of the People's Republic Mao – in spite of his past differences with Stalin over a number of issues pertaining to the Chinese Revolution – pledged solidarity with the Soviet Union. The Soviet Union was the only country to which he could turn to avoid China's complete isolation. This was particularly true after his timid attempts to win over the United States to his cause had failed. On 1 July 1949, Mao announced publicly that China had opted for a policy of 'leaning to one side'. He wrote:

> You are leaning on one side.... The forty years' experience of Sun Yat-sen and the twenty-eight years' experience of the Communist Party have taught us to lean on one side, and we are firmly convinced that in order to win victory, and consolidate it, we must lean on one side. In the light of the experiences accumulated in these forty years and these twenty eight years, all Chinese without exception must lean either to the side of imperialism or to the side of socialism.[2]

Leaning to one side also implied seeking allies among socialist countries and with the people of all other nations who were believed to aspire to socialist revolutions.[3]

As a result Mao closed China's doors to the Western world, a policy which had immediate repercussions on the status of foreign powers in China. The Chinese authorities refused, as Mao described it, 'to recognize the legal status of any foreign diplomatic establishment and personnel dating from the Guomindang period'. This was called 'starting from scratch' (linqi luzao). Mao also expressed his reluctance to 'hurriedly seek diplomatic recognition by "imperialist countries" '. With this policy he aimed at abolition of foreign political, economic and cultural influence in China, a measure referred to as 'cleaning the house before inviting the guests' (dasao ganjing wuzi zai qingke).[4]

In September 1956, the CCP convened its first National Congress since 1945. On this occasion, Liu Shaoqi reiterated the basic principles of foreign policy according to which China should continue to strengthen unity and friendship with the Soviet Union and the socialist countries and to oppose imperialism under the leadership of the US. It also introduced a few new elements into foreign policy, one of which was support for national movements against colonialism and for independence. The most important innovation was the official introduction of the 'five principles of peaceful coexistence' which implied a willingness to establish normal relations with countries which had different social systems.[5] These principles had first been formulated in the Sino-Indian agreement of 1954 and reiterated in the Sino-Burmese agreement of the same year. During the Bandung conference of April 1955, Zhou Enlai stressed the importance of the 'five principles' and laboured personally to have them included in the final resolution of the conference.[6] The promotion of these principles was due to the changed international environment. It was no longer possible to divide the international scene into a bi-polar world of friend and foe. First, the course of the events of the Korean War had not followed Chinese expectations. The Soviet Union had failed to provide the military aid that China had hoped to obtain in her crusade against US imperialism. This, and the American determination to follow its policy of containment in Asia, had led to a stalemate in the Korean War which could only be solved after difficult negotiations and considerable diplomatic initiatives undertaken by the Chinese government. Second, the emergence from colonial systems of an increasing number of non-aligned states operating under nationalist aspirations had transformed the configuration of forces on the international scene, thus requiring a more realistic approach to world politics.

The most important change in Chinese foreign policy concepts, however, occurred after the 20th Congress of the Soviet Communist Party in 1956 and the subsequent events in Poland and Hungary.[7] In the wake of these events, Chinese perceptions of the Soviet Union contributed significantly to the shaping of her outlook on the world in general. First, Mao's views on Soviet revisionism and later, his growing apprehension of a Soviet military threat determined a number of momentous domestic and external policy decisions.

Khrushchev's criticism of Stalin at the 20th Congress of the Soviet Communist Party caused bemusement within the Chinese leadership. Although Beijing publicly endorsed Khrushchev's repudiation of Stalin on most points, the Chinese authorities insisted that Stalin, in spite of his errors, was a great Marxist-Leninist.[8] Not long after the Soviet Party Congress, however, Mao, in a talk with Mikoyan, expressed a different view about Stalin which he reiterated later that year to the Soviet Ambassador in Beijing. 'Stalin deserves to be criticized', he said, 'but we do not agree with this [Khrushchev's] method.'[9] To Mao, challenging the leadership of Stalin bore the inherent threat that his own primary role in the Chinese Revolution might at some time also be questioned. Since, in his view, he himself was

44

the incarnation of the Chinese Revolution and the saviour of the nation, he automatically equated any diverging views with revisionism. As a Chinese historian expressed it, 'the more it proved impossible to put his ideas into practice, the more he saw this as a reflection of a class struggle . . . and of the emergence of "counter-revolutionary revisionist elements" '.[10]

A series of 'real' issues, pertaining mainly to territorial differences and to questions of strategy and security, were to become the basis for the conflict with the Soviet Union. However the ideological dimension of the controversies should not be underestimated. Mao was extremely serious when he criticized the ideological errors of the Soviet party. Over the next few years, this type of dispute between China and the Soviet Union continuously escalated. Chinese perceptions of Soviet ideological errors led to more disagreements on internal and international political issues.

A *Red Flag* editorial of April 1960 which, for the first time, brought the controversies out into the open, argued that renouncing the belief in the inevitability of war was a 'naive illusion', that peaceful coexistence was impossible, and that Khrushchev's foreign policy rejected class struggle and went out for 'peace at any price'. Stressing Mao's argument – expressed at the 1957 Moscow conference of communist parties – that a Third World War would benefit the world socialist movement, the article rejected the Soviet view that a nuclear war would be disastrous for everyone involved.[11]

However, the most significant aspect of these evolving perceptions was Mao's conviction that revisionism was expanding in the Soviet Union and in other countries belonging to the socialist camp, and that Khrushchev was the major proponent of this trend. This conviction was a significant factor leading to the radicalization of Mao's thinking on internal and international affairs. According to Mao's concept, as he defined it in 1962, although in several countries socialist revolutions had overthrown reactionary and bourgeois governments, they had not been able to eliminate the class system in their societies. Different classes continued to exist, to defend different and incompatible interests, a situation which inevitably would lead to conflicts and to class struggle among those groups. Mao believed a fierce struggle would occur within society, in particular between capitalism and socialism, containing the inherent threat of a capitalist restoration.[12]

The Chinese perception of the world reached a new peak of radicalization in 1965 when Mao became convinced that it was China's unshakeable duty to take over the leadership of world revolution. Since the early 1950s, Mao had considered the promotion of world revolution as China's cardinal role, with Moscow at the centre of the international communist movement. In 1960 already, he had rejected the Soviet view that, in the struggle for independence in colonial countries, socialists and the 'national bourgeoisie' should cooperate. The Soviets had argued that such cooperation would finally pave the way for a transition to socialism. This course of action, the *People's Daily* countered, had also been recommended to the Chinese communists by Stalin and history had proven that is was completely erroneous. Even more so was Khrushchev's view that, under certain circumstances, the transition to power of socialist parties could be achieved by parliamentary means.[13] Mao thus considered it imperative that the centre of world revolution should shift from Moscow to Beijing.

The Chinese authorities deemed it necessary to publicize their views on these issues which they considered to be of the highest importance to the contemporary world. This was done on three occasions during that year. The first was a speech by Peng Zhen at the celebration of the anniversary of the Indonesian Communist Party in May where he emphasized that the principle contradiction in the world existed between the oppressed nations of Africa, Asia and Latin America, and the imperialist countries headed by the United States.[14] This speech was followed in September by a long article signed by Lin Biao and entitled 'Long Live the Victory of the People's War', and by a press conference held by Chen Yi in September 1965.

From these statements it could be gauged that the Chinese leaders looked at the world in terms of four fundamental contradictions.

1 the contradiction between the socialist camp and the imperialist camp;
2 the contradiction between the proletariat and the bourgeoisie in the capitalist countries;

3 the contradiction between the oppressed nations and imperialism;

4 the contradiction among imperialist countries and among monopoly capitalist groups.[15]

Lin Biao's article was important in two aspects. It was a manifesto on world revolution calling upon the people of the oppressed nations to take up arms and to fight a people's war against US imperialism. According to Lin, the US was 'the most rabid aggressor in human history and the most ferocious common enemy of the people of the world';[16] and Asia, Africa and Latin America were 'the main battlefield of the fierce struggle between the people of the world on the one side and US imperialism and its lackeys on the other'.[17] Another major aspect of Lin's speech was the application, to the international scene, of Mao's theory on the encirclement of the cities as the most efficacious method of successful revolution. In this scenario, North America and Western Europe were considered as 'the cities of the world' destined to be 'encircled' by revolutionary Asian, African and Latin American nations.[18]

Chen Yi's major foreign policy statement of September 1965 also addressed 'US imperialism' as the major threat. He announced China's determination 'to make all necessary sacrifices to defeat US imperialism' and he declared that if the US intended to launch a war against China they should do it sooner than they had intended. China, he said, was ready for an American attack from the south and for a Soviet attack from the north. And he added: 'let the Indian reactionaries, the British imperialists, and the Japanese militarists come along with them'.[19]

At the commencement of the Cultural Revolution, China's perception of the Soviet Union had reversed entirely. Though the 11th Plenum in August 1966 continued to characterize 'US imperialism' as 'the most ferocious common enemy of the peoples of the world', the Soviet Union was not far behind. In fact, it was attributed second position on the list of China's enemies. It was accused of pursuing revisionism, of 'safeguarding imperialist and colonialist domination of the capitalist world and of restoring capitalism in the socialist world'[20] and it was viewed as the traitor *par excellence* of the socialist cause. The Soviets, for their part, condemned the Chinese Cultural

Revolution as a 'great tragedy for all true Chinese communists'.[21] The Chinese leaders perceived this as a provocative
statement in support of Liu Shaoqi and his followers. The official
Soviet press had indeed asserted that:

> Mao Zedong and his group chose the road of defamation
> and destruction of Party cadres, or the best representatives
> of the working class and the intellectuals, using for this
> purpose a section of the students and school children and
> the military and administrative apparatus . . .[22]

In spite of its militant and revolutionary rhetoric, China showed
great prudence in its activities in foreign countries. Mao knew
his country's military limitations and the risks of military
involvement abroad. Although verbally supporting the promotion of revolutions abroad, his main concern was national
security. This can be gauged from his preoccupation with a
possible nuclear war. In May 1964 he declared that, in the era
of atomic weapons, it was necessary to develop rear areas for
military defence. In this connection, he issued instructions to
classify different regions of China into first, second and third
lines of defence according to their strategic importance and to
establish an industrial base of national defence in the third-line
area – mostly located in inland provinces.[23] In October 1965, he
emphasized that China must prepare for war, and suggested
that every province should build its own third-line region so
that, in case of war, it would be able to fight autonomously.[24]

By the end of the 1960s, security issues had clearly come to
overshadow ideological preoccupations. While the US officially
remained the 'most ferocious enemy', it was generally acknowledged in Chinese foreign service circles that, from the late 1960s,
the United States was not the primary threat to China and the
Soviet Union was perceived as constituting the major risk to
China's security.[25]

Perceptions of the Soviet threat as being far more important
than the hazards represented by the US involvement in Vietnam
led Mao to reconsider China's position in the world-wide configuration of forces. The ensuing normalization of Sino-
American relations, the seating of the People's Republic in the
United Nations and the establishment of diplomatic relations
with an increasing number of Western powers eventually –
though not immediately – ushered in a sea-change in China's

foreign policy. Clearly, the Chinese contribution to these developments was influenced by cool reflections on power politics
and *raisons d'état* rather than ideological considerations. The
Chinese outlook on the world, especially the Western world,
continued to be subjected to ideological polemics. All the
changes taking place in 1971 and 1972 were construed by
the Chinese leaders as the success of its long-standing foreign
policy, a success symbolized by the fact that the outside world
– represented by Richard Nixon – was coming towards China.
In the official Chinese view, China's entry into the United
Nations and the 'immediate expulsion of the representative of
the Chiang Kai-shek clique from the UN and all organizations
related to it' was an indication of the 'bankruptcy of the policy
depriving China of her legitimate rights ... obdurately pursued
by US imperialism over the past 20 years and more of the
US imperialistic scheme to create "two Chinas" in the United
Nations'.[26]

The change of attitude that the West, and especially the United
States, had undergone with regard to China was also perceived
by its leadership as a 'victory of Chairman Mao Tse-tung's
proletarian revolutionary line in foreign affairs'.[27] The establishment of diplomatic relations with West European countries in
the early 1970s was seen in the same light. The diplomatic
opening towards the West did not change the Chinese perception of it – a fact that was manifest at the 10th Party Congress
in August 1973. The Political Report presented by Zhou Enlai
to the Congress did not contain a new approach to world affairs.
According to Zhou, the world was 'still in the era of imperialism
and of proletarian revolution' where the international situation
was 'characterized by great disorder on earth' (*tianxia daluan*), a
disorder which was 'favourable to the people'.[28] Attaching great
importance to 'the awakening and the growth of the Third
World' he repeated the view, already enunciated by the first
Chinese delegation to the UN, that 'revolution is the main trend
in the world today',[29] and that 'countries want independence,
nations want liberation and the people want revolution'.[30] Zhou
summed up the world situation by a sentence from a Tang
poem stating that 'the wind sweeping through the tower heralds
a rising storm in the mountains' (*Shanyu yulai fengmanlou*)
implying the approach of a world-wide revolutionary storm. As
for the two superpowers, they were, according to Zhou, in a

sorry state. Another verse was quoted to describe their plight: 'Flowers wilt no matter what one does' (*Wuke naihe hua louqu*)[31] which implied that they were on the loser's side in spite of all their efforts.[32]

The theory of the persistent danger of a new world war also continued to be announced on the grounds that 'the imperialist camp is split; the revisionist bloc is falling apart; and the reactionary countries are sitting on thorns'.[33] Whereas up to the early 1970s, Western Europe was hardly acknowledged as anything but an area of contention between the superpowers, this region and Japan were now considered as rivals to the United States in their 'scrambles for markets and raw material'.[34] The Soviet Union also was viewed as 'working feverishly' to fight off competition and to expand its own spheres of influence all over the world.

The new emphasis on the importance of Europe and Japan in the world configuration of forces found its expression in the Three Worlds Theory formulated by Mao in February 1974 and presented by Deng Xiaoping to the UN General Assembly in April 1974.[35] This theory was a variation of the doctrine of 'encirclement of the cities' which Lin Biao had enunciated in 1965 and which had stipulated that North America and Western Europe (the cities) would be encircled by Asia, Africa and Latin America (the rural areas). The Three World Theory claims that the superpowers, defined as the 'biggest international exploiters, oppressors and aggressors'[36] belong to the First World and are the targets of revolution. The Western industrialized countries and Japan, previously regarded as accomplices of US imperialism became the Second World which was subjected to the oppression of the superpowers. They represented potential allies to be won over in the fight against the superpowers. The Third World – formed by the socialist countries and the 'oppressed nations' – made up the main force of combat against the superpowers whose policies were characterized by colonialism, imperialism and hegemonism. China identified itself with the Third World and expressed its readiness to form a united front with it to combat the superpowers and to give 'support and impetus ... to the workers' movement in the developed countries'.[37] China thus continued to view the superpowers as its adversaries. Its *rapprochement* with the United States nonetheless found its manifestation in a subtle differentiation between the

50

two. It was stressed that among the superpowers, the Soviet Union was the more dangerous and the more likely to become the cause of a world war. It was argued that 'Soviet social-imperialism', being inferior in economic strength, 'must rely chiefly on its military power and have recourse to threats of war in order to expand'.[38]

In the first half of the 1970s, and even after Mao's disappearance, ideology continued to play a guiding role in foreign policy, especially as long as it was centred around an anti-Soviet stance. For much of that period, China's potential partners were accepted or rejected according to the position they took on Soviet policies. But ideology had been adapted over time to the changing international environment and to changing perceptions and, in due course, was gradually shed as a policy determinant.

Decision-making

Chinese traditions permitted central authorities to keep a tight grip over interactions with foreign countries and individuals. This was all the more true for Mao's China where, as a rule, the concentration of foreign policy decisions in the hands of the paramount leader reached such a pitch that it even excluded much of the political elite which was involved in decision-making on domestic policy issues. This rule applies above all to the task of defining goals of foreign policy as well as to general principles or to the 'political line' directing foreign policy decisions. It becomes somewhat less pertinent with respect to the execution of foreign policy, which involves a greater number of people.

Parallel to this, the Chinese political system, characterized by a firmly controlled and personalized hierarchy – produced weak institutions which, at their apex, were dominated by the paramount leader, Mao Zedong. The decision-making process, too, was influenced by the personality factor rather than by institutions. This became particularly evident during the Cultural Revolution when Mao demonstrated his ability to shake this system and even to destroy it. Mao's powerful personality combined with political flair and his marked voluntarism which refused to admit the impossible, had allowed him to contribute to the Chinese communist movement in a significant manner.

Over the course of many years of revolutionary activity he had been able to establish a unique position for himself within the power structure of the Chinese Communist Party. Mao's great prominence began to emerge during the Long March. It was reinforced during the Yannan period when his policies were recognized by his peers as the most efficient path to a successful revolution. Surrounded by a group of supportive revolutionary cadres, Mao took on the role of the undisputed leader at the summit of the political structure. This role became institutionalized in 1943 when – in a move with far-reaching consequences – the leadership resolved to grant Mao the final veto on Party decisions.[39] In 1945, with the inauguration of Mao Zedong Thought as the official ideology of the Party, the cult of his personality began to develop in continuously growing proportions. Liu Shaoqi, in his speech to the 7th Party Congress asserted that Mao Zedong Thought contained a complete analysis of the world situation and provided a conceptual basis for the problems facing the Chinese leadership. The years of civil war against the Guomindang were again marked by Mao's efficacious strategies. On the eve of the establishment of the People's Republic, he emerged not only as the most prestigious leader of modern China but also as the saviour of China's 600 million people.[40] His strong personality dominated political processes not only domestically but also in the domain of foreign affairs. In his own words, he himself made all the major decisions on foreign policy whereas Zhou Enlai was charged with their execution.[41]

Zhou Enlai was the second person intimately involved in China's foreign relations. From the 1930s, he had taken charge of the external affairs of the Party. After the founding of the People's Republic, he created the country's Foreign Ministry. Although his role in formulating foreign policy principles undoubtedly was less important than that of Mao, the execution of such policies was strongly marked by his personality. His charm, his diplomatic talents, his detailed knowledge of dossiers, his negotiating skills and his organizational capacities were legendary. They earned him the respect and admiration of a large number of diplomats and politicians throughout the world.

Scholars have attempted to analyse different attitudes towards foreign policy among the Chinese elite. The changing perspective of the Chinese government towards the Soviet Union and the United States (the superpowers), for example, was attributed to the differences over foreign policy between certain elite groups.[42] It has been argued that the opening towards the United States had become possible only after Lin Biao – perceived as a defender of Sino-Soviet *rapprochement* – had been eliminated.[43] In fact, Chinese foreign policy experts unanimously contend that opposition to Mao's foreign policy concepts and decisions, especially during the Cultural Revolution, could hardly have been voiced and even less could they have been effectively implemented. Under Mao's rule, debates on the political 'line' or fundamental principles of foreign policy were rare and usually confined to the application of such principles.[44]

In his talk with Nixon, Mao hinted that Lin Biao had opposed his decision to normalize relations with the United States.[45] There is, however, no evidence to support this accusation. Lin Biao had little interest in or understanding of international affairs. He had such a strong aversion against foreigners that he tried to avoid any contact with them. Most of the time, he saw foreign visitors only in the presence of Mao. His own meetings with foreigners were extremely rare. During the Cultural Revolution, he met the North Vietnamese Prime Minister and one of that country's leading generals, who persistently had demanded to be received by the legendary Chinese general.[46] Another occasion was a meeting with Begir Balluku, the Albanian Minister of Defence who visited China after the Soviet invasion of Czechoslovakia. He also requested to see Lin Biao to express his solidarity to the Chinese defence minister. But Lin, pretending to be sick, at first refused to see him. Only after the Albanian Minister of Defence repeatedly insisted and declared that the major reason for the meeting would be to have his picture taken with Lin Biao, did the latter agree to a short meeting of five minutes at the Great Hall of the People. After returning to his residence, Lin declared that he had felt unable, hitherto, to deal with foreigners.[47]

Furthermore, Sino-American contacts began to develop after the 1970 Lushan conference, when Lin's relations with Mao had already so seriously deteriorated that Lin appears to have been entirely concerned with his own political and physical survival. It can be safely assumed that he would not have attempted to antagonize Mao on any foreign policy issue.

Institutional framework

According to the constitution of the CCP, the highest organ of decision making in the Chinese government and Party structure is the Central Committee (CC) which embodies the political leadership of the country. During the ten years before the Cultural Revolution, from 1956 to 1966, the Plenary of the CC held ten sessions. During the intervals between the meetings, its functions were exercised by the Politburo and its Standing Committee.

Although many records of Politburo discussions on domestic issues, during the first 17 years of the People's Republic, have been made available to the public relatively little is known about its debates on foreign affairs. Only a few instances of such discussions have been publicized, among them the meetings over the problem of China's participation in the Korean War, or over the issues arising after the 20th Congress of the Soviet Communist Party. If such public records of Politburo meetings are at all significant, these occasions have occurred only rarely. But it can be assumed that such important issues as the shelling of Quemoy, which involved the risk of a direct confrontation with the US in 1958, or the split with the Soviet Union in the early 1960s, or the Sino-Indian border war, were on the Politburo's agenda.[48] When the Vietnam War escalated in the autumn of 1965 and Sino-Soviet relations further deteriorated, the Minister of Foreign Affairs, Chen Yi, made a major foreign policy statement at a press conference – later known to have been based on a discussion of the Standing Committee.[49] Nevertheless, there are no indications which might lead to the assumption that the Politburo and its Standing Committee regularly and frequently discussed foreign policy issues. This can be explained, first, by the high degree of concentration of decision-making on foreign policy issues. Second, China's involvement in foreign affairs was limited since it was rather secluded from the world, maintained diplomatic relations only with a few countries and was not represented in most of the international organizations.

The administration of foreign affairs was divided into several groups of activities which were dealt with either through government or Party channels. First, there were the state-to-state relations. They were handled by the State Council headed by Zhou Enlai who had been in charge of foreign affairs of the CCP since the late 1930s. As vice chairman of the Party, member of the Standing Committee of the Politburo and Prime Minister of the State Council, numerous issues fell within his jurisdiction. When, in his view, a problem was important enough to require a collective decision, he would refer it to the three persons who were involved in major policy decisions with his own recommendation for action. They were Liu Shaoqi, vice chairman of the Party in charge of the day-to-day work of the Politburo, Deng Xiaoping, general secretary of the central secretariat, and Peng Zhen, mayor of Beijing and *de facto* deputy general secretary of the Party. This procedure was, however, not always followed. It was left to Zhou's discretion and judgement whether or not to bring an issue to their attention. If he considered that he had to deal with problems of major importance he would submit them to Mao Zedong. There were also cases when matters would be decided directly between Mao and Zhou, who later informed the other three leaders.[50]

Day-to-day foreign affairs were directed mainly by the State Council with a number of institutions under its jurisdiction among which the Ministry of Foreign Affairs was, of course, the most involved. Though the Minister of Foreign Affairs repeatedly insisted that 'in foreign affairs, very limited authority is delegated' to the staff and that 'the power of decision-making belonged to the centre'[51], the Ministry's impact on decision-making was, nevertheless, not insignificant. It was an integral part of a consultation mechanism which, under the leadership of Zhou Enlai, formulated policy recommendations on major issues. The procedure usually went as follows: suggestions from ministerial departments were sent to the vice minister who then submitted them to Chen Yi. The Foreign Minister, in turn, forwarded them to Zhou Enlai who finally decided how to handle the recommendation.[52]

Under the State Council, several other offices dealt with international relations, among them the Ministry of Trade Relations with Foreign Countries, the Commission for Cultural Relations with Foreign Countries, the Commission for Overseas Chinese. The activities of all these offices were coordinated by the Foreign Affairs Office (*Waishi bangongshi*) of the State Council headed by Chen Yi.[53]

A certain number of institutions were affiliated to the Ministry of Foreign Affairs. The Institute of Foreign Affairs (*Zhongguo renmin waijiao xuehui*), for example, dealt with foreign non-communist parties; the College of Foreign Affairs (*Waijiao xueyuan*) and the Beijing Institute of Foreign Languages[54] were established for the training of young diplomats; there were also the Bureau of Services for Foreign Diplomats and the World Affairs Press.

The second area was party-to-party relations. They were dealt with by the Party Secretariat, the executive body of the Politburo of the Central Committee. In the late 1950s and early 1960s, the Secretariat's greatest concern was relations between the Chinese Communist Party and its Soviet counterpart. Apart from Mao, Liu Shaoqi and Zhou Enlai, Deng Xiaoping and Peng Zhen were the two men most deeply involved in the handling of the Sino-Soviet conflict. Both had direct talks with the Soviets about their divergences; and both directed the polemics against the Soviet Party in accordance with the guidelines established by Mao. Also they organized a group of people who – based on their reputation as the best polemicists – were chosen to produce articles, letters and documents to be used in these attacks. They operated out of headquarters especially assigned to them, at the state guest house Diaoyutai in Beijing.[55]

Under the Secretariat, a number of offices were involved in foreign affairs, the most important of which was the Central Committee international liaison department. Its main responsibility was to manage relations with communist and left-wing parties in foreign countries and to inform the leadership about their policies. The office operated in close cooperation with the Chinese Foreign Ministry and frequently provided staff for Chinese embassies abroad.

The second office was the propaganda department under the Central Committee which had as one of its responsibilities the international diffusion of Chinese propaganda. Its main organs were the New China News Agency, the *People's Daily* and the Foreign Languages Publication Bureau.

The third was the CC investigation department (*Zhonggong zhongyang diaochabu*) which was an intelligence agency. While this department's task was to gather information about foreign countries, its focus of attention was Hong Kong and Taiwan. The existence of this department was not publicized, and only a small group of persons involved in foreign policy were aware of its activities, for it belonged to the category of '*bao midanwei*' (a work unit to be kept secret). The investigation department regularly dispatched a number of their staff abroad, either as newspaper reporters or as part of embassy staff. They also placed their people in Chinese institutions dealing with foreign countries, as for example the Chinese Academy of Sciences.[56]

Like the State Council, the Party apparatus also had established an office for the coordination of international affairs, the Foreign Affairs Group (*Waishi xiao zu*) of the Central Committee. This group, established in 1958 at the same time as the Foreign Affairs Office of the State Council and also headed by the Foreign Minister, was in charge of overall supervision of Chinese foreign relations.[57] It remained almost totally invisible, and little is known about its composition and activities.

Repercussions of the Cultural Revolution on decision-making

Though the People's Republic, since it began, had gone through a number of fluctuating political movements, none of them had had any real impact on the country's foreign policy. The two areas had consistently been kept separate from each other. It was therefore generally assumed that the Cultural Revolution would likewise not interfere with foreign policy. This was confirmed as a policy principle in a directive issued by the Central Committee in early June 1966 which stipulated that 'a clear distinction should be made between internal and external matters' (*Bixu fenqing neiwai*).[58] To ensure an uninterrupted course in foreign affairs, Zhou, on the basis of this directive, informed the Chinese ambassadors that the staff should be kept informed about relevant documents concerning the Cultural Revolution, but that the Cultural Revolution should not be carried out in the embassies.[59]

Another Party decision stipulated that 'the focus of the Cultural Revolution is the cultural and educational departments of the CC and Party and government organs'.[60] Furthermore, since Mao had emphasized that schools and literary circles had become dominated by bourgeois intellectuals and had suffered from 'the dictatorship of a black anti-party and anti-socialist line', it was generally assumed by Zhou Enlai and Chen Yi that foreign policy would be excluded from the Cultural Revolution. Chen Yi had repeatedly emphasized this point to the staff of the Foreign Ministry, clearly declaring that foreign policy should not be questioned, since it had been formulated by Chairman Mao himself. If problems occurred, in his view, they were due to its implementation. Therefore, he concluded that the Cultural Revolution did not require a review or a change of foreign policy, but rather an improvement in the style of work.[61]

This position, which suited Zhou Enlai and the moderate faction of the Chinese leadership, could not be maintained very long. It soon became evident that Zhou's attempts to dissociate foreign policy from the Cultural Revolution were in vain, and a spill-over onto Chinese relations with other countries became unavoidable. Two major factors contributed to this change: the first was the radicalization of Mao's thinking on class struggle in Chinese society which was comparable to a similar trend in the outside world. In a general manner, he linked the Cultural Revolution directly to the cause of the international communist movement, of which he was clearly laying claim to leadership. Mao's animosity towards Khrushchev had led him to distrust the Soviet Union as a possible leader of world communism. This trend reached such proportions that a *People's Daily* article characterized the Cultural Revolution as the fundamental historical force instrumental for the establishment of world communism.[62]

The second factor was the transformation of the Chinese leadership structure which had taken place from the very outset of the Cultural Revolution. Following the purge of Peng Zhen, one of the first to be eliminated, the 11th Plenum of the Central Committee, acting under Mao's instructions, removed Liu Shaoqi and Deng Xiaoping from power in August 1966, a decision which led to the complete paralysis of the Central Secretariat. Replacing to some extent the demoted Secretariat the Politburo took charge, under Zhou Enlai's direction, of the daily routine of political, including foreign, affairs. At the same time, the power of the Politburo began to dwindle in favour of the Central Cultural Revolution Group which was increasingly a force in its dealings. Although many of its members did not belong to the Politburo and even less to its Standing Committee, in accordance with Mao's instructions Group members participated in 'enlarged' meetings of both the Politburo and of the Standing Committee.[63] Consequently, they were able to take part in decision-making at the highest level.

The secretarial role of the Politburo, too, was soon completely terminated and superseded by the CCRG. When most of the members of the Politburo became targets of criticism, after the February Adverse Current in February 1967, Mao decided that the CCRG should function as the Secretariat of the Central Committee. As a result the CCRG's power extended to all fields and it became the most powerful unit in the country.

Noticeable conceptual differences on foreign policy issues existed between professionals like Zhou Enlai and Chen Yi, on the one hand, and the new Cultural Revolution faction on the other. According to Zhou and Chen, 'diplomacy should cover up for the Cultural Revolution' (*waijiao yingdang yanhu wenhua dageming*), an expression which signified that China would need a 'peaceful international environment' to permit its leadership to concentrate on the Cultural Revolution. Zhou Enlai and Chen Yi thus continued to maintain the premise that Mao's 'red line' had always been dominant in foreign affairs. The rising radical faction represented by Kang Sheng and Jiang Qing, eager to consolidate their newly acquired power status, contended that foreign policy had been subjected to the reactionary Liu–Deng line. In the hands of Kang Sheng, a policy proposal of 1962 – directly linked to the dramatic consequences of the Great Leap Forward – became the striking example for the 'reactionary Liu–Deng line'. In 1962, the Chinese economy, as a result of the Great Leap Forward, was in a state of collapse forcing the leadership to carry out a policy of drastic retrenchment and readjustment in all sectors. Wang Jiaxiang believed that a readjustment in foreign policy had also become necessary. He submitted a recommendation to Zhou Enlai, Deng Xiaoping and Chen Yi suggesting:

1 that a foreign policy statement be issued to confirm that China's foreign policy was a policy of peace;
2 that, in order to gain time in the process of economic recovery, a policy of relaxation towards the outside world should be adopted;
3 that China should display prudence, adroitness and flexibility in its relations with the outside world. In this connection, he recommended showing particular care regarding the United States in order to avoid a possible concentration of American forces near China; to make efforts to break the stalemate on the Sino-Indian border; and to develop a high degree of vigil-

ance towards Khrushchev who had tried to isolate China and who might want to break off relations with it;

4 that aid to other countries and to revolutionary movements should be provided according to China's economic capacity. Utmost care was needed to avoid overstatements and over-extension.[64]

It is not known how Zhou Enlai, Deng Xiaoping and Chen Yi reacted to these proposals. In any case they were never implemented. By early 1964, Mao himself came out with a clear position on these proposals, construing them as an international programme of revisionist officials and condemning them as a policy of '*san he yi shao*' by which he meant that they advocated peace towards imperialists, reactionaries and modern revisionists (*san he*), and the reduction of assistance to the revolutionary struggle of other peoples (*yi shao*).[65]

During the Cultural Revolution, Kang Sheng escalated the attack on this policy recommendation and dubbed it '*san xiang yi mie*', namely surrender to imperialists, Soviet revisionists and foreign reactionaries (*san xiang*); and elimination of the revolutionary struggle of the suppressed people of the world (*yi mie*).[66] Attributing such policy to Liu Shaoqi, Kang Sheng claimed that it had interfered with Mao's foreign policy. At a meeting with red guard and rebel organizations, in early June 1967, he reiterated his condemnation of this policy. On 13 August the CCRG – convinced that Liu Shaoqi was guilty of applying the principle of '*san xiang yi mie*' – requested archives from the Foreign Ministry in order to prove their case. The material was duly compiled and sent to the CCRG office and to the members of the Standing Committee.

With their newly acquired power status, the radicals were able to exercise increasing influence over foreign affairs. Since they were in a position which allowed them to play a role in the decision-making process at the highest level they succeeded, in due time, to impose what they considered should be the primary goal of foreign policy, namely the dissemination of Mao Zedong Thought throughout the world.[67] With the mass media under their control, they frequently published editorials which were intended as guidelines for foreign affairs. In their view, 'the world had entered a new era of Mao Zedong Thought'. They also did not hesitate to by-pass Zhou Enlai and to issue instructions directly to the Foreign Ministry. Zhou Enlai's inviolable domain thus became open to encroachment.

The administration of the Foreign Affairs System, though not paralysed, was very much weakened. Zhou Enlai's position had become fragile since the beginning of the Cultural Revolution. The Foreign Minister, Chen Yi, first involved in Liu Shaoqi's work team policies and then in the February Adverse Current, had become the main target of attack within the Foreign Affairs System, being assaulted by the CCRG from above and by the red guards of the System from below. As a result, his ability to carry out his duties as Foreign Minister were virtually neutralized. Zhou's deputies at the State Council Foreign Affairs Office, Liao Chengzhi, Zhang Yan and others who assisted him in the coordination of the activities of the various departments dealing with foreign affairs, also were affected by their involvement in Liu Shaoqi's work team policies and were not allowed to function normally. Within the Foreign Ministry itself, the work of most vice ministers was disrupted by the Cultural Revolution. The first vice minister, Zhang Hanfu had been put under custody by a special case group of the Party centre because he was suspected of having turned into a traitor during his imprisonment by the Guomindang in the 1930s. The vice ministers Ji Pengfei and Qiao Guanhua became major targets of attack by the red guards and rebels because of their close association with Zhou Enlai and Chen Yi. Two other vice ministers, Wang Bingnan and Chen Jiakang had been under examination since the beginning of the Cultural Revolution for their allegedly bourgeois lifestyle and working methods. The few remaining vice ministers who were not under political attack had only sectoral responsibilities. None was in a position to exercise effective leadership over the Ministry as a whole.[68]

All the directors of Foreign Ministry departments and some of their deputies had been accused of having followed the 'bourgeois reactionary line' in their relationship with their subordinates. This accusation, which was in effect a 'verdict', had forced them to interrupt their professional activities and to 'stand aside' (kao bian zhan). Only a few among them, namely those considered free from this line and close to the rebels, were allowed to continue their normal activities.[69]

During this period of the Cultural Revolution, China's foreign relations were marked by distortions and increasing tension for which the frequent meddling of CCRG members in foreign policy issues was at least partially responsible. Another factor contributing to the confusion was the emergence of red guards and rebel organizations and the seizure of power in all ministries – including the Foreign Ministry. These provocative groups were instrumental in the staging of demonstrations against foreign embassies in Beijing. Since they were strongly supported by the radicals of the CCRG, they did not bear the sole responsibility for these actions. But, once in the streets, they became uncontrollable and – in defiance of instructions – resorted to violent actions, as in the case of their attacks against the Indian, Burmese and Indonesian embassies, and the British Mission.[70]

Although the rebels of the Foreign Ministry – most of them rank and file – had a direct effect on the performance of foreign policy, the importance of their role should not be overestimated. After their power seizure in January 1967 – a process which Mao had approved as part of the power seizure throughout the country – Zhou granted them the responsibility of supervising activities within the Foreign Ministry. This implied that they had the right to make policy proposals concerning the Ministry's dealings with other countries. Influenced by the heated revolutionary atmosphere their proposals tended to be very radical. This was evident in their response to the reactions of foreign countries to the provocative Chinese practices abroad, where embassy personnel was engaged in distributing Mao's *Little Red Book*, his works and Mao badges. Since the rebels were acting as supervisors their views could not be ignored.

The veteran officials, including Zhou Enlai, were under continuous pressure from the CCRG radicals and from the rebels. On several occasions, Zhou himself had been forced to admit his 'poor understanding of the Cultural Revolution'. There was very little he could do to fend off the popular fanaticism against foreign countries. Under the circumstances he was forced to compromise on many of the proposals emanating from the domestic left-wingers and to sanction, one after the other, suggestions from the rebel-dominated Foreign Ministry to lodge the 'strongest and most vehement protest' against foreign countries when relatively minor incidents had occurred. He approved plans to hold mass rallies against the Soviet Union, Indonesia, India, Burma and the British authorities in Hong Kong which – under normal conditions – he would have carefully avoided.[71]

By the end of 1968 the situation had changed. Mao had succeeded in eliminating those whom he perceived as his ideological and political adversaries. But, in the process, he had destroyed large parts of the state and Party organization, brought the economy into a state of collapse and the country to the brink of civil war. In a reversal of radical policies he called the country back to order. In the Foreign Ministry and in the Foreign Affairs System, as elsewhere in government and administration, rebels and red guards had been neutralized. As has been discussed, large contingents of the Ministry were moved to the countryside, in 1969, where special case groups ferreted out 'politically undesirable elements' among the staff. Only about 30 per cent of the Foreign Ministry staff – and even those on a rotation basis – remained in Beijing to handle the routine affairs of the Ministry.

It was during this period of reduced efficiency of the foreign policy apparatus that major changes took place in China's foreign policy. This can be taken as another example of the dominance of Mao Zedong's direct leadership in foreign affairs. That Mao responded positively to the changing American attitude towards China, and proceeded with the normalization of relations with the United States, was a direct result of his perceptions of China's security requirements. In Mao's view the Soviet threat – at that time – greatly outweighed the peril of American involvement in Vietnam.

This view was reinforced after the Sino-Soviet border clashes in early March 1969. They compelled Mao to thoroughly examine China's security alternatives and, in this process, he practically ignored the Foreign Ministry. Instead he postulated that the four Marshals Ye Jianying, Chen Yi, Xu Xiangqian and Nie Rongzhen should be consulted. They were asked to form a study group to examine China's security problems. The generals produced a number of operational reports, among them a general appraisal about the threat of War.[72] Although they did not altogether exclude the possibility of a Soviet war against China, they considered it more likely that, in the short run, the border skirmishes would continue. They also expressed doubts about the Soviet military capacities to attack China. In their view the Soviets had over-extended themselves by mobilizing 20 divisions – about half a million troops – in the invasion of Czechoslovakia in 1968 and by stationing twice as many divisions along the endless Sino-Soviet border. Although the concentration of troops at the border represented a threat, the marshals estimated that the Soviet Union would need at least 100 divisions to wage a major war on China. In their view, it would be problematic for the Soviets to mobilize such a large number of soldiers.[73]

In another report the Marshals argued against the possibility – often invoked by official Chinese propaganda – that the Soviets might cooperate with the United States in a joint war against China. They had become aware of certain subtle changes in the attitude of the United States towards China since the Nixon administration had come to power and suggested that the Warsaw talks should be resumed. They also suggested that – in view of the tense situation on China's northern border – it would be in its interest to become more active on the international and diplomatic scene.[74]

Considering the frenzied anti-American rhetoric prevalent at that time, these were bold ideas. But the suggestions to improve relations with the United States obviously corresponded to Mao's thinking on the matter and thus established the basis which allowed Zhou Enlai to respond positively to American signals aimed at normalizing relations between the two countries. Nevertheless, when it came to deciding on concrete steps, Zhou did not take any initiative without consulting Mao. The ping-pong policy – which made a considerable contribution to the thawing of relations between China and the United States – is a good example. The question of issuing an invitation to an American table tennis team to visit China involved a decision that implied a new course in Sino-American relations. Zhou Enlai, who was too prudent to take upon himself such an initiative, referred the dossier to Mao who instructed the Foreign Ministry to proceed with the invitation.[75]

Kissinger attributed the success of the ping-pong policy to Zhou Enlai[76] but the decision had been entirely Mao's. Zhou Enlai, years later, observed that he had not made the right judgement in this case.[77] The decision concerning the resumption of China's seat at the United Nations followed a similar path. Although for many years Zhou had regularly sent letters to the UN protesting against the presence of Taiwan at the UN and claiming its seat for the People's Republic, he now hesitated to accept U Thant's invitation to participate in the ongoing 26th

General Assembly.[78] In his discussions of this matter with the Foreign Ministry staff the prevailing view was predominantly shaped by ideological considerations. The overall consensus was that the General Assembly was a bourgeois institution controlled by the superpowers and thus ill-suited to represent oppressed nations and peoples. Thus the Ministry's suggestion – which Zhou at first supported – was that China should not participate in the General Assembly for the time being. In accepting this view, Zhou clearly wanted to avoid giving the impression that China was eager to become a part of the 'bourgeois' world organization.[79]

Internal considerations also prompted Zhou to adopt a prudent attitude. As he had done in the case of ping-pong diplomacy, Zhou took into account the radical faction's belligerent views represented by Jiang Qing which, after the disappearance of Lin Biao in September 1971, had gained a new – if only temporary – height of power. Zhou could not afford to openly antagonize her. Whenever major policy changes were involved, he was careful to avoid decisions until Mao personally had pronounced himself on the issue. Once more, Mao overruled Zhou's decision. Once more, he himself was taking a major foreign policy decision. 'We should go there' (to the UN), he declared. 'It was the black brothers of Africa who carried us into the UN. We will divorce ourselves from the masses if we refuse to go there.'[80]

3

REVOLUTIONARY DIPLOMACY
Spill-over of the Cultural Revolution on to International Affairs

In its early stages, the Cultural Revolution ushered in a major change in Chinese foreign policy. Encouraged by the CCRG, revolutionary fanaticism mixed with rampant xenophobia became widespread throughout China. It stimulated the idea of promoting the Cultural Revolution outside China – an idea which red guards were all too ready to advance – and fomented unprecedented hostilities against all foreigners who were hesitant to embrace left-wing policies. During the first year of the Cultural Revolution, foreign policy lost whatever sophistication it might have had in the past. China lived in autarchic self-reliance and in increasing isolation from international realities. Its foreign policy, already limited in scope, became even more so and began to focus on the dissemination of Mao Zedong Thought which Mao's radical coterie declared to be the major goal of foreign relations.[1]

Kang Sheng and other CCRG members frequently interfered in foreign affairs by instructing Chinese embassies, trade missions and individuals working on foreign relations to contribute to the propagation of Mao Zedong Thought, and to distribute Mao badges and his quotations wherever possible. The profuse and indiscriminate distribution of these items became a major part of Chinese activities abroad.

Chinese revolutionary activities in foreign countries provoked negative reactions from their governments. Within a year, from mid-1966 to mid-1967, China had disputes with more than thirty out of roughly forty countries with which it had diplomatic relations. Provoked by Chinese proselytizing, a series of diplomatic incidents occurred in several countries. They began with the events in the Portuguese colony of Macao in November

1966, which – originally involving a simple matter of obtaining the permission of the Portuguese authorities for the construction of a school – escalated into riots setting local Maoists against moderates in which several people were killed. On 29 January 1967, the Portuguese governor of Macao felt compelled to sign an agreement which all but formally turned over political power to Macao's Maoists.[2]

The already tarnished relations between China and the Soviet Union deteriorated even further. From the end of August, red guards repeatedly demonstrated in front of the Soviet embassy in Beijing and renamed the street where it was located as 'Anti-Revisionist Street'. But the situation worsened even further after the so-called Red Square incident in Moscow on 25 January 1967, when 69 Chinese students, returning from Europe, proceeded to visit Lenin's and Stalin's tombs. According to Mao's interpretation, capitalism had been restored in the Soviet Union ever since Khrushchev's rise to power and his denunciation of Stalin in 1956. The students, to demonstrate their hatred for the capitalist system and their admiration of Stalin, publicly read two pieces of Mao's quotations. The first read: 'The socialist system will eventually replace the capitalist system . . .' and 'Stalin was the true friend of the cause of liberation of the Chinese people. No attempt to sow dissension, no lies and calumnies, can affect the Chinese people's wholehearted love and respect for Stalin and our genuine friendship for the Soviet Union.'[3] The demonstration of the Chinese students was suppressed by the Soviet police who, according to Chinese accounts, injured about 30 of them.[4]

As on similar occasions, the Chinese authorities over-reacted to this incident. The next day the Foreign Ministry lodged the 'strongest and most vehement protest' with the Soviet government. In its official note, sanctioned by Zhou Enlai himself, the Soviet leadership was castigated for the 'sanguinary atrocities' against the Chinese students. The note expressed the belief that the 'Soviet People will rise in rebellion against the revisionist rulers, dismiss them from office, seize power from them and smash the revisionist rule.'[5]

Moreover, Zhou Enlai cabled a message to the Chinese students in Moscow conveying to them Mao Zedong's and Lin Biao's 'warm regards'. In Moscow, the Chinese Embassy lodged a strongly formulated protest with the Soviet Foreign Ministry.[6]

The official press denounced the Soviet Union, terming it a 'filthy . . . revisionist swine',[7] thus encouraging further the wave of xenophobia which began to spread through Beijing. Within a few days of the Red Square incident, millions of people demonstrated at the Soviet embassy to protest at the treatment of the Chinese students. The Soviets retaliated by sending some 160 people to the Chinese embassy in Moscow who, on 3 February, destroyed the embassy's news display cases. A number of Chinese diplomats, including the Chargé d'Affaires, were manhandled and even injured by the demonstrators.[8]

In response to these incidents, Zhou Enlai approved a suggestion by the Foreign Ministry to condemn the 'Soviet revisionists' fascist outrage' in an official government statement on 5 February. In the wake of this declaration, the central authorities issued orders to all provinces to organize anti-Soviet demonstrations. On 11 February a mass rally, attended by Zhou Enlai, Chen Boda and other leaders, was held in Beijing where Chen Yi delivered the main speech condemning the Soviet revisionists.[9]

Parallel incidents occurred in other countries. In France, for example, Chinese students protested against the Red Square incident in front of the Soviet embassy. Some students were physically maltreated as the police attempted to break up the demonstration. The Chinese embassy protested strongly to the French authorities and, on 31 January, Chen Yi sent a cable to the students expressing his 'support and sympathy'.[10]

In connection with these incidents, the French ambassador in Beijing was summoned to the Chinese Foreign Ministry to be handed an official protest note. On this occasion, one of the rebel leaders was present in his function as supervisor of Foreign Ministry activities. When the ambassador refused to accept the note and rose to take leave, the rebel representative blocked the door, declaring that the ambassador would not be allowed to leave unless he accepted the note. This almost escalated into another unnecessary diplomatic incident, barely avoided by the vice minister who was present. Very much embarrassed, he explained to his 'supervisor' that his actions were contrary to diplomatic usage.[11]

At the same time, a display case in front of the Chinese embassy in Paris, which showed photos of Mao Zedong and of events linked to the Cultural Revolution, was destroyed. On 28 February, Chen Yi protested against this act of vandalism, and a massive demonstration was held in front of the French embassy in Beijing to denounce the 'criminal police action of tearing up Chairman Mao's portrait and trampling on "Quotations" '.[12] The events were followed by yet another deterioration of Chinese relations with another country. Press articles on France – which hitherto had been relatively friendly – changed in tone. Instead of emphasizing French resistance to British entry into the Common Market and of supporting its 'struggle' against the United States, France was reproached for its 'imperialism' and for 'standing on the side of US-Israeli aggressors' in the Middle East.[13]

The Hong Kong riots

Relations with Great Britain also deteriorated considerably at that time. From May 1967 onwards they revolved around con-frontations in Hong Kong. This started with a labour dispute at the Sanpokony Branch of the Hong Kong artificial flower factory where, on 1 May, demonstrating workers clashed with the police. In a manifestation of solidarity with them, groups of left-wing workers, students and teachers, all influenced by the Cultural Revolution, took to the streets. The dispute escalated into bloody conflicts between the Hong Kong riot police and the demonstrators. By 15 May, the Chinese Foreign Ministry was involved in the conflict, publishing a statement of protest against the 'persecution' of Chinese residents in Hong Kong, which it characterized as 'sanguinary atrocities . . . perpetrated by the British authorities'.[14] It reminded the British authorities that 700 million Chinese supported the struggle in Hong Kong and demanded that the British authorities 'immediately and unconditionally' accept a 5-point request by the Chinese govern-ment asking for punishment of those responsible for the bloody clashes, for apologies to the victims and for guarantees against the recurrence of similar incidents.[15] From that point onwards, more than 1 million people demonstrated in front of the British Mission in Beijing. On 18 May, a rally with 100,000 people was held in the presence of Zhou Enlai, Chen Boda, Chen Yi and other leaders. Xie Fuzhi, vice premier and chairman of the Beijing revolutionary committee made the major speech, in which he declared that 'all activities carried out by our compat-riots in Hong Kong in studying, propagating, applying and defending Mao Tse-tung's Thought are their absolute, sacred and inviolable right. There is no ground whatsoever for the British authorities in Hong Kong to interfere'.[16]

On 3 June, the *People's Daily* published an editorial drafted under Chen Boda's direction, which issued a call to 'patriotic compatriots' in Hong Kong to 'be ready at any time to respond to the call of the great motherland and to smash the reactionary rule of British imperialism!'

These exhortations and manifestations were part of a general plan which the Foreign Ministry had devised with the aim of destabilizing Hong Kong and which Zhou Enlai had approved. But the call issued by the *People's Daily* was more extreme than Zhou Enlai's policies and created much confusion, since it gave the impression that, if the requests contained in the 5 points were not fulfilled, the Chinese government would be willing to go as far in its support for the Hong Kong riots as to take over the colony by force.[17]

By the middle of June, Zhou Enlai was in a dilemma. China's internal situation was so chaotic that he already had his hands full with the most basic problems of administering the country. Moreover, foreign relations – much against his own preferences – had continuously deteriorated. At the same time, the Hong Kong problem was being systematically escalated by a series of actions instigated through the influence of Chinese radicals.[18]

Large-scale strikes were organized in Hong Kong by left-wing trade unions following orders from Beijing. Confrontations between the police and the demonstrators became increasingly violent and escalated during the summer months. The demonstrators, many of whom were injured, expected more than rhetorical support from Beijing. But Zhou, on the one hand, refused to provide any level of material support which might endanger the status quo of the British colony, and on the other, he sanctioned an ultimatum to the British authorities which led to the burning of the British Mission in Beijing. The ultimatum was a Foreign Ministry note of 20 August to the office of the British Chargé d'Affaires demanding – within 48 hours – the cancellation of a ban of three pro-mainland newspapers and the release of 19 Chinese journalists who had been arrested during the riots in Hong Kong.[19]

When the note was made public by the *People's Daily*[20] an organization named 'anti-imperialist and anti-revisionist liaison station' planned a demonstration in front of the British Mission, while radical red guards from the Institute of Foreign Languages, and others, were determined to storm the Mission if the ultimatum was not met within the specified time. During the afternoon of 22 August huge crowds gathered in front of the Mission's building. The Beijing garrison, aware of the explosiveness of the situation, sent troops to protect the building. A number of Foreign Ministry officials also went to try to persuade the red guard student leaders to abstain from violent action. Chen Boda, upon Zhou Enlai's request, sent a message to the demonstrators urging them to stay outside the buildings. But the atmosphere of fanatic revolutionary fervour, which prevailed in Beijing at that time, frustrated all attempts at moderation. When the ultimatum expired after 48 hours the demonstrators broke into the building and set it on fire.[21]

Zhou Enlai reacted to these events with the utmost outrage. He summoned Foreign Ministry officials and Beijing garrison officers to his office at Zhongnanhai for a briefing about the details of the events. He apologized for having approved of the ultimatum, saying that he had not carefully considered the note because he was exhausted when it was presented to him. Mao also criticized the actions of the red guards, saying that the burning of the British Mission was done either by bad or by naive people.[22] But the officially published reaction to this event was defensive. It merely mentioned that enraged red guards, in 'justified indignation . . . took strong action against the Office of the British Chargé d'Affaires'.[23]

Clearly, the British authorities were not ready to give in to any Chinese demands. And the Chinese authorities, short of intervening militarily in Hong Kong, were thus powerless. It appeared that not only Zhou Enlai but also Mao, once he realized the ultimate consequences of such actions, wanted to avoid a more serious confrontation with the United Kingdom. Therefore, the only option was to de-escalate the conflict. This was possible in early September, when the political atmosphere in China radically changed. Two members of the CCGR, Wang Li and Guan Feng, were arrested and ultra-left excesses were severely criticized, which allowed Zhou to phase out the Hong Kong problem by the end of the year.[24]

Conflicts with Third World countries

Indonesia

Soon after the Red Square incident a conflict broke out between China and Indonesia. The Chinese embassy in Indonesia had received an invitation from the 'People's Provisional Consultative Congress' which had been addressed not to the 'People's Republic of China' but to the 'Republic of China'. This mistake was interpreted as a plot on behalf of the Indonesians to play the 'two China game', and the Chinese embassy launched a vehement protest with the Indonesian Foreign Ministry on this matter.[25]

The relations between the two countries had already deteriorated since October 1965, after the aborted *coup d'état* by the Indonesian Communist Party and the toppling of Sukarno's government by General Suharto. Although there appears to be no convincing evidence that the Chinese government was involved in the attempted coup,[26] it had extended its official support to Sukarno and the Indonesian Communist Party. Furthermore, ethnic Chinese residing in Indonesia, most of whom had also supported the Communist Party's attempt to take over, were submitted to increasing harassment and even violent persecution. The Chinese authorities blamed 'Indonesian rightists' for the attacks against Chinese and Indonesian communists, accusing them of 'catering to the needs of US imperialism and its lackeys'.[27] When it became increasingly evident that the army was determined to weaken the Indonesian Communist Party and refused to show any signs of friendliness towards the Chinese government, Beijing's denunciation of the Indonesian army, and the new government it had helped to install, became increasingly vociferous. On 16 April 1966, the *People's Daily* published an article comparing the anti-Chinese activities in Djakarta with the behaviour of 'Hitlerite hordes', who engineered a 'counter-revolutionary military *coup d'état*' aided by 'US imperialism and Japanese reactionaries'.[28] These provocations culminated in an attack on 22 and 23 April against the Chinese diplomatic mission in Djakarta, when Indonesian troops and police encircled the embassy and a clash with Chinese diplomatic personnel ensued. On 24 April the Chargé d'Affaires,

Yao Dengshan, and the Consul General Xu Ren, were declared *'personae non grata'* and ordered to leave the country.[29]

The Chinese reaction towards the 'Indonesian right-wing military clique' was again vehement. The Chinese authorities lodged 'the strongest and most emphatic protest against the reactionary Indonesian government' and, on 27 April, staged demonstrations condemning Indonesia for its anti-Chinese 'crimes'. When Yao Dengshan and Xu Ren arrived in Beijing, on 30 April, they were received by a large group of leaders headed by Zhou Enlai who bestowed the title of 'red diplomat fighter' on them.[30] In the evening of 1 May, both were invited to the rostrum at Tiananmen, where Yao received the honour of having his picture taken with Mao and Jiang Qing, a picture which was published the next day on the front page of all newspapers.[31] In October, official relations between the two countries were suspended; both China and Indonesia closed down their respective embassies.[32]

India

The case of India was similar to Indonesia in the sense that it involved a deterioration of formerly friendly relations. However, a number of issues had ushered in a process of disaffection between the two countries over the years before the Cultural Revolution, the first of them being the question of Tibet and, in particular, India's readiness to grant asylum to Tibetan refugees. In the early 1960s the friction between the two countries increased with the border disputes, leading to military engagement, and with the improving relations between India and China's two great enemies, the Soviet Union and the United States. The question of whether anti-imperialism, as advocated by China – or non-alignment, which India propagated, should be the leading ideology for cooperation among Third World countries also became an issue of disagreement. But it was again during the first year of the Cultural Revolution that verbal abuse, hitherto unknown, became symptomatic of Sino-Indian relations. In March 1967, an official Chinese comment on the re-election of the Congress Party stated that:

> The Indian people's opposition to the Congress Party is growing stronger ... and the crisis in which Indian reac-

tionary rule finds itself is more acute than ever. The whole of India is today littered with dry faggots. It is certain that revolutionary flames will rage throughout the vast territory of India.[33]

In July 1967, the Chinese press singled out an armed peasant upheaval against landlords in the Darjeeling area of West Bengal as a characteristic example for the rise of Indian revolutionary fervour which – marked by the superior influence of Mao Zedong Thought – would lead the entire country onto a road of ultimate national liberation.[34]

Burma

By the mid-1960s the Burmese government had been engaged, for several years, with a series of insurrections in its hinterland. They were carried out by several revolutionary organizations including a pro-Beijing one which called itself the 'White Flag'. Though it was Beijing's acknowledged policy to support revolutionary movements in Asia and other Third World countries, the Chinese authorities refrained from interference in the Burmese situation and developed a policy of friendly relations with the Burmese government. The Chinese press did not mention and even less endorse the revolutionary movement in Burma. On the contrary, there were accounts of the friendly visits between Chinese and Burmese officials, including Zhou Enlai, Chen Yi and General Ne Win, the Burmese Head of State.[35] But within a year after the launching of the Cultural Revolution, the situation was reversed. In June 1967, the Burmese authorities began to implement a policy of harassment against Chinese nationals in Burma. The conflict started when students began to wear Mao badges and to propagate Mao Zedong Thought at school – a practice which the Burmese government attempted to prevent. During the suppression of these activities at least 100 Chinese residents were killed, and the official Chinese mission in Rangoon came under attack.[36] Beijing's reaction followed the same pattern as before. A government statement of 29 June denounced the 'fascist atrocities' committed by the Burmese government against the Chinese, a million people demonstrated for four consecutive days in front to the Burmese embassy in Beijing, and an official rally gathering 100,000 people was staged on 3 July to condemn the Ne Win Regime.[37] The Chinese embassy in Rangoon sent a diplomatic note to the Burmese foreign ministry on 11 July which stated that:

Chairman Mao is the very red sun that shines most brightly in our hearts and Mao Tse-tung's Thought is our lifeline. We must warn you that we will fight to the end against anyone who dares to oppose Chairman Mao and Mao Tse-tung's Thought. Anyone who dares to oppose Chairman Mao and Mao Tse-tung's Thought is hitting his head against a brick wall and inviting his own destruction.[38]

Other countries

In July 1967, the news display of the Chinese embassy in Nepal was destroyed and the Nepalese government – much to the satisfaction of the Chinese Foreign Ministry – apologized for the event. Kang Sheng insisted that China 'should wage a resolute struggle and not fear to break relations' with Nepal.[39] The strong Chinese protest which was lodged with the Nepalese government resulted in a situation of great tension.

Another series of protests was lodged against the Mongolian and Soviet Embassies in Beijing for having insulted the picture of Mao.[40] Copies of Mao's works, which were being transported aboard a Chinese ship, were destroyed by the Ceylonese authorities, resulting in a protest by the Chinese embassy in Ceylon as well.[41]

In Kenya, the news display cases in front of the Chinese embassy were destroyed and the vice president of Kenya accused the Chinese embassy of distributing Maoist propaganda to Kenyan citizens, which again provoked a strong protest from Chinese officials.[42]

On 23 August, the Chinese Council for the Promotion of International Trade issued a statement protesting against the Italian authorities, who had stopped a Chinese freighter from posting Mao's quotations.[43] On 15 September, the Chinese embassy in Tunisia protested against President Bourgiba's 'frenzied vilification of Chairman Mao'. The relations between the two countries deteriorated to such an extent that, a few weeks later, China closed down its embassy in Tunisia.[44]

These events and the over-reaction of the Chinese government to them had the same pattern everywhere. They were paralleled by gross exaggerations of the significance of the Cultural Revolution by the mass media. The official press affirmed that the Cultural Revolution was 'shaking the entire world like an earthquake', and that 'all other major developments in the world today are pale in comparison'. According to its formulation, China was 'the bastion of world revolution', the Chinese revolution:

> fundamentally defeated US imperialism and its global counter-revolutionary strategy and prevented a big reverse and a big retrogression in world history; it reopened the channel leading to communism that was blocked by modern revisionism, and advanced the international communist movement and world revolution to a brand new stage.[45]

This corresponded to Mao's conviction about world revolution, which he believed was about to enter a new stage. In his view, 'revolutionary upheaval in Asia, Africa and Latin America was sure to deal the old world a decisive and crushing blow'.[46] But on the European scene, too, Beijing believed in the emergence of a new revolutionary era, and it developed a two-pronged strategy to foster radical movements on the West European political scene. The first part consisted in promoting the establishment of secessionist organizations which broke with the established communist parties, whom they considered to have become unfit to represent Marxism-Leninism. Some of the splinter parties had already been set up before the Cultural Revolution in the course of the ideological and political rivalry between China and the Soviet Union. But most of those 'Maoist' parties gained impetus after the start of the Cultural Revolution, a period during which China took even greater interest than before in their formation and growth. The Chinese press, for example, tended to attribute an importance to them which was out of proportion with their actual political clout. 'The Marxist-Leninist parties', wrote the *People's Daily*, 'are growing in strength. We are convinced that these parties and organizations, under the guidance of Marxism-Leninism, Mao Zedong's Thought and by rallying and leading the working class and other laboring people of Europe, will surely be able to overthrow the reactionary rule of imperialism, capitalism and revisionism and achieve their own complete emancipation'.[47]

Many of these splinter groups were further split into different contending factions. The pro-Maoist Belgian Communist Party, for example, which was founded in 1963, went through as many as five splits in two years. The most important among them was provoked by its party secretary, Jacques Grippa who fell out with the CCP over his support for Liu Shaoqi.[48]

The second aspect of Chinese policies in Western Europe was support of the student uprising of 1968 which was perceived as a left-wing revolutionary revolt. The Chinese began to organize massive demonstrations in support of the 'progressive student movements in Europe and North America'.[49] During the month of May 20 million people in Beijing, Shanghai, Tianjin, Wuhan and Nanjing were reported to have manifested their support for the French students.[50] The Chinese press also expressed lively interest in these developments, criticizing the French Communist Party as a 'revisionist clique' which had failed to transform the revolt into a fully-fledged revolution and praising the students who 'stood at the forefront of this revolutionary struggle'.[51]

Obviously, the Chinese interest in the student movement in Western Europe was primarily focused on the instability they produced in West European societies. Although many of the ideals the student demonstrations aimed at realizing in their society were inspired by leaders such as Che Guevara rather than by Mao Zedong, the Chinese press nonetheless attributed the emergence of such revolts to the strong influence of Mao's revolutionary thinking on the minds of the young people. As the People's Daily declared on 27 May, it was 'the extensive dissemination of Mao Zedong's thoughts throughout the world' which 'has spurred the development in depth of the contemporary world revolution. The tremendous victory of China's Great Proletarian Cultural Revolution has inspired the people of all countries.'

In spite of the fact that many Western intellectuals at that time admired Mao Zedong and the Cultural Revolution, the impact of Mao Zedong Thought on Western societies was, in fact, non-existent. The student movement was short-lived, and the new pro-Beijing parties were marginal.

During the second half of 1967 the political atmosphere in

China began to change, turning towards greater moderation. This transformation could also be felt in the leadership's perception of external relations. Since most of China's conflicts with foreign nations had arisen from the Chinese attempt to spread Maoist ideology abroad, Mao decided to change this course. On 17 March 1968, he issued an instruction postulating a 'resolute and systematic reform in external propaganda'. In a number of written statements, throughout the year, he forbade the printing of his 'quotations' on the packages of goods destined as foreign aid and the distribution of Mao badges to foreigners. He emphasized that the focus of Beijing as the 'centre of world revolution' was self-styled and mistaken and he repeatedly warned against the imposition of Chinese ideology on outsiders. After reviewing a document of the international liaison department, he issued an instruction that 'from now on, such self-praising terms as "Mao Zedong Thought" should be omitted from all documents and articles related to foreign affairs'. He also warned the same department to adopt greater care when producing propaganda for international use, instructing them to 'avoid the impression that you are imposing your views on others'.[52]

Mao applied the same principles to a *People's Daily* editorial in September 1968 from which he removed such statements as: 'the great and all conquering Mao Zedong Thought is the new development of Marxism-Leninism in the contemporary era'; 'our era has Mao Zedong Thought as its banner, and Mao Zedong Thought is the synthesis of the revolutionary practices of all countries. Mao Zedong Thought is widely spreading in Asia, Africa, Latin America and in all other parts of the world.'[53]

During the same months the Foreign Ministry drafted a plan for the reception of a Pakistani government delegation in which top priority was given to the 'propagation of the great Mao Zedong Thought and its current instructions'. Mao again removed the passage. But it was clear that in this period, when the cult of Mao was raging feverishly in China, it was only Mao himself who could attempt to dampen the prevailing fanaticism.

4

NATIONAL SECURITY POLICIES

If ideology and revolutionary ambitions had influenced China's external relations in the early stages of the Cultural Revolution, by the second half of the 1960s they had given way to cool calculations of *raisons d'état*. With the unprecedented threat by the Soviet Union from the north and by the United States from the south, concerns about national security had increasingly overshadowed most other determinants of Chinese foreign policy.

This does not imply, however, that Mao's perceptions of the outside world had changed. He continued to view the superpowers and the Western world through the same eyes as before. On the domestic scene he periodically vacillated between moderate policies, directed at repairing some of the damage created by excessive 'leftist' policies, and promoting hard Cultural Revolution concepts, of which one of the most striking manifestations was the absurd defence policy of 'third line construction'.[1]

While polemical rhetoric against the superpowers continued unabashed throughout the 1960s and a large part of the 1970s, Chinese operational politics underwent a substantial transformation. Considerations of security as the dominant factor eventually did have far-reaching consequences on China's foreign policy behaviour. Its *rapprochement* with the United States, the normalization of relations with other Western countries and Japan, its presence at the United Nations and especially in the Security Council, ended the People's Republic's diplomatic isolation, inevitably transforming it into one of the most important actors on the international scene.

This chapter will examine the evolution of bilateral relations between China and her most important interlocutors (Vietnam, the Soviet Union, the United States, and Japan). China's relations with Vietnam are examined first because they represent a case of what could be considered as something between revolutionary and security policies whereas in the other cases, the security aspect is dominant. Since these topics have been dealt with in numerous studies, it would seem redundant to explore them again. However, what is proposed here is to group them and to analyse China's policies with these countries against the backdrop of domestic events dominated by the Cultural Revolution.

Sino-Vietnamese relations

From the early 1950s, China supported Vietnam's struggle for independence. This was particularly obvious at the 1954 Geneva conference, where Zhou Enlai played a significant role and which resulted in the Indochina agreement and in the end of French rule in Vietnam. From then onward the relations between China and Vietnam developed rapidly. There were several reasons for China's interest in Vietnam. First, as a promoter of revolutionary struggles in the Third World, China supported the revolutionary struggle of the Vietnamese Communist Party, all the more so as the struggle was taking place in a neighbouring country. Second, the Sino-Soviet conflict engendered major competition between the two rivals to draw other communist parties to their side. This naturally incited Beijing to focus on Vietnam, which was already showing signs of a pro-Soviet bias. The Chinese revolutionary commitment to Vietnam became even more marked during the Cultural Revolution. Though revolutionary euphoria had much to do with China's support of Vietnam, the security dimension slowly began to emerge as a non-negligible determinant in Chinese diplomatic behaviour. The escalation of the conflict was no longer perceived only in revolutionary terms, but also in terms of the threat it represented to China's national security. Though, in response to the expansion of US military presence in the south, revolutionary rallies and calls from the streets of China proliferated, Beijing's overall reaction was more complex. First of all there was an intensification of bilateral consultations and military assistance.

In the summer of 1962, a North Vietnamese delegation led by Ho Chi Minh arrived in Beijing to discuss the situation with the Chinese leadership. According to the Vietnamese assessment, the expansion of the US military presence in South Vietnam increased the likelihood of a US military intervention in North Vietnam. The meetings resulted in the agreement that China would provide, free of charge, enough armament to North Vietnam to equip 230 infantry battalions.[2] Throughout 1963 and 1964 high-level Chinese missions to Vietnam, whose message was substantiated by Mao, confirmed the Chinese military commitment.

In March 1963, a Chinese military delegation led by Luo Ruijing, General Chief of Staff, arrived in Hanoi to discuss the military situation and the modalities of Chinese military aid to Vietnam. On that occasion, the Chinese expressed their readiness to assist North Vietnam militarily in case of an attack by the South.

In May, Liu Shaoqi visited Saigon, where he reaffirmed the solidarity of the Chinese government with North Vietnam. In his talks with the Hanoi leadership he emphasized that China was on their side. 'Should a war break out' he said, 'you could take China as your rear area.'[3] In August, Mao issued a sharp statement condemning the 'aggression by the US-Ngo Dinh Dien clique against South Vietnam and the slaughter of its people'.[4] This was an unusual gesture since Mao was not in the habit of making public speeches or of publishing articles in his name. He obviously intended to demonstrate the seriousness of China's concern about the US intervention in Vietnam.

At a meeting with the Vietnamese Chief of Staff in June 1964, Mao reiterated his concern about the Vietnamese situation, telling the Vietnamese general: 'What matters to you, also matters to us'; and he emphasized that the two countries 'should unconditionally join hands in fighting the enemy'.[5] The Tonkin Gulf incident in early August 1964 triggered a strong verbal and military response from the Chinese. Mao used it to launch a movement: 'Resist America and Assist Vietnam', inciting 20 million people throughout China to demonstrate against the American threat.[6] Airforce units and anti-aircraft artillery were moved to the areas bordering Vietnam and the construction of two new air fields in Guanxi was started.[7]

With the arrival, in March 1965, of 3,500 US marines in Da

Nang, the American involvement in Vietnam further escalated. The Chinese government responded with a statement by Zhou Enlai making it amply clear that: 'China will send the people of South Vietnam all the necessary material aid, including arms and all other war material'. He declared that China was prepared: 'to send our own men whenever the South Vietnamese want them, to fight together with the South Vietnamese people'.[8] This statement symbolized the readiness of the Chinese government to again confront the US on the battlefield. Moreover, this time Zhou's warning was far more explicit than the one he had made in 1950 before the Chinese forces crossed the Yalu River.

Following an agreement between China and North Vietnam, signed in April 1965, China sent a total of 320,000 soldiers to North Vietnam who were able to handle surface-to-air missiles, anti-aircraft guns, military engineering, railway communications, mine sweeping and logistics.[9] In the peak year, which was 1967, 170,000 Chinese troops were engaged in logistics and military operations. At the same time the first wave of third-line construction, moving vulnerable industries from the coastal areas to the centre of China and improving infrastructure in the central regions, had begun to materialize with the construction of new railway links between Chengdu and Kunming, Sichuan and Guizhou, Yunnan and Guizhou.[10]

At this time US military aircraft began to violate Chinese airspace over Hainan Island, Yunnan and Guanxi, dropping bombs and launching missiles over these areas and killing and wounding Chinese soldiers and crews.[11] To this, the Chinese government responded by sending a message – via the Pakistani President Agha Mohammad Yahya Khan – to President Johnson of the United States which emphasized that China will not 'provoke a war with the United States', but it will come to the help of any country which 'meets with aggression by the imperialists headed by the United States'. If as a consequence of such action the United States should impose a war on China, 'the United States will not be able to pull out, however many men it may send over and whatever weapons it may use, nuclear weapons included'.[12]

This warning was followed by military action and by another agreement with North Vietnam on military assistance. An order of 11 January instructed the Chinese airforce to monitor the movements of American aircraft over Chinese airspace and, after some incidents of penetration into Chinese airspace, Mao ordered on 9 April that the Chinese air units should strike back.[13]

Chinese aid to North Vietnam continued to be substantial throughout the major part of the Cultural Revolution. It was provided in three forms. First, the 'Chinese People's Volunteer Engineering Force', established in 1965, played a major role in the construction of defence installations, airfields, railways and roads in North Vietnam. Second, Chinese anti-aircraft artillery units were used to defend targets in North Vietnam and to provide cover for engineering troops. Third, weapons and other military equipment were provided, as well as items such as soap, food, uniforms and cigarettes.[14]

In sum, the aid that was extended to Vietnam from the early 1950s to the late 1970s, by far exceeded that to any other country. Over this period it totalled $20 billion, including arms and other military material, enough to equip 2 million soldiers, 35,000 trucks, 4 million tons of food grain, 2 million tons of oil, $635 million in hard currency, etc. Most of this aid was provided free of charge. Among the military and civilian personnel sent to Vietnam, some 5,000 were killed in the war, of which 1,000 were buried in Vietnam.[15] After the end of the Vietnam War in 1975 Le Duan, First Secretary of the Vietnamese Workers' Party, visited Beijing. Meeting with Mao he emphasized that the North Vietnamese victory would have been impossible without the assistance extended by China to the Vietnamese people. 'We have always believed that it was China who has been able to provide us with the most urgent life-and-death assistance', he said.[16]

While formally continuing to support the North Vietnamese, two major developments constrained Beijing to take a more prudent course at the height of the Cultural Revolution. The first, clearly, was the scenario of a direct Sino-American confrontation. China began to show signs of concern at the prospect of an escalation of Sino-American tensions as a result of which a direct conflict might become unavoidable. This prudence was signalled to the US through Yahya Khan in the above-mentioned message indicating that China 'will not provoke a war'. But perhaps the most important indication of this growing preoccupation was the signal sent to the US through an interview which Mao gave to Edgar Snow in February 1965 that China had no intention of intervening in Vietnam as long as the Americans abstained from doing so in China.[17] The second development was the gradual improvement of relations between Moscow and Hanoi which maintained a stance of neutrality in the Sino-Soviet conflict and which received increasing political and military support from the Soviet Union. A new situation had thus developed, particularly at a time when the Chinese leadership was losing control of the turbulent domestic situation affecting the transport of military equipment from the Soviet Union to North Vietnam.[18] Shipments of army equipment were frequently interrupted by factional fighting in key communication centres such as Zhengzhou in Hunan and Liuzhou in the Guangxi Autonomous Region. During the summer of 1968, the interruptions of transportation and the looting of war material destined to Vietnam in Chinese cities close to the Vietnamese border (Liuzhou, Guilin and Nanning for example) became so serious that tough measures had to be taken to ensure their continuity. The authorities condemned as 'counter-revolutionaries' the factions involved in the stoppages and the looting of trains. But it was only after the intervention of the PLA, who disarmed the contending groups, that the harassment of military transports was terminated.[19]

By 1968 the gap between China and North Vietnam had considerably widened. This became obvious over the issue of Hanoi's peace talks with the United States and Saigon in Paris, about which the Chinese had major reservations. Beijing clearly had lost influence over North Vietnam's policy decisions. Moreover, by the end of the 1960s Beijing was confronted with serious economic disruptions which discouraged massive military aid. Between 1968 and 1970, all engineering units and anti-aircraft troops had left Vietnam, and while assistance in military and other equipment continued, its quantity began to decrease.[20]

By the early 1970s China had shifted its foreign policy priorities from promoting world revolution to national security. With the start of the process of *détente* with the US, Beijing was also faced with different strategic options, allowing it to forego any compromise in the triangular relationship between China, the Soviet Union and Vietnam which had proven to be a major obstacle to normal Sino-Vietnamese relations. When the war ended, China – disappointed by the Vietnamese attitude and hard-pressed by domestic economic problems – decided to cut its aid to Vietnam. But the Vietnamese, in 1975, insisted upon the continuation of Chinese aid, on the grounds that Vietnam had made major contributions and great sacrifices to the common cause of resisting the American foe. Zhou Enlai, however, argued that China had done its utmost in helping Vietnam and that it needed some breathing space, since it still had to cope with difficult economic problems engendered by the Cultural Revolution.[21] While Vietnam showed little understanding for the Chinese arguments, its relations with the Soviets, who were ready to provide Vietnam with economic aid, improved continuously. At the same time Vietnam, much to the dismay of the Chinese, was expanding its influence in Indochina. In June 1976, Vietnamese troops occupied the Cambodian Way Island, an action which, in the Chinese view, was incomprehensible for a country like Vietnam which had fought so long for its independence. Three years later, when Vietnam invaded Cambodia, China responded with a military attack in the north of Vietnam 'to teach Hanoi a lesson'.

Sino-Soviet relations

Sino-Soviet relations were based on a complicated 'friendship' between the two socialist giants, an interaction where ideological controversies and conflictual politics had frequently interfered. Although Mao had adopted the principle of 'leaning to one side', frictions between the two countries appeared at a very early stage after the establishment of the People's Republic. The first disagreement between them surfaced over Soviet air cover for Chinese forces during the Korean War. It was followed by a series of controversies over foreign policy issues related to Khrushchev's efforts at de-Stalinization, his attempts to improve relations with the United States, his neutrality in the Sino-Indian border dispute, and the Soviet repudiation, in 1959, of the agreement on nuclear armament signed only two years earlier.[22]

These policy controversies played an important role in the deterioration of relations between China and the Soviet Union, but so did ideological disputes. Mao's evaluation of Khrushchev's ideology – which was examined in more detail in Chapter 2 – significantly contributed to the radicalization of his thinking on revisionism within the international communist movement and to the strengthening of his determination to launch the Cultural Revolution.

As the Cultural Revolution unfolded, relations between China and the Soviet Union deteriorated seriously. The ideological fanaticism aroused by the Cultural Revolution led to mutual accusations of ideological impurity. From August 1966 onwards, the Chinese authorities began to accuse the Soviet Party of heading the modern revisionists and of having betrayed the revolutionary cause, the Soviet people and socialism.[23]

The Soviet invasion of Czechoslovakia in August 1968 added a new dimension to the controversies between the two communist giants. Although the Chinese leadership had supported Soviet repression of the Hungarian revolt, it strongly condemned the invasion of Czechoslovakia as: 'the most barefaced and typical specimen of fascist power politics played by the Soviet revisionist clique against its so-called allies'.[24] The theory of 'limited sovereignty' which Brezhnev announced on 12 November 1968 to justify the invasion, gave rise to even more serious concern. Chinese leaders believed that the Soviets were preparing public opinion for further armed interventions in other countries, including China. In their view, the Brezhnev doctrine marked a new stage of Soviet external adventurism which eventually would lead to the overthrow of the Soviet leadership, a 'clique . . . of a handful of renegades', by the people of the Soviet Union.[25]

The Chinese concern with Soviet hostility was compounded by the military incidents occurring on the Sino-Soviet border. All this was perceived by Beijing as a serious threat to national security, so much so that the Soviet request for talks about the situation was met with deep distrust by the Chinese. Indeed they saw it as a 'smokescreen' behind which the Soviets were hiding their real intention, namely to attack China.

Sino-Soviet border clashes

According to Chinese statistics, 4,189 incidents had taken place in the border area between October 1964 and March 1969. Both China and the Soviet Union had augmented the frequency of their patrols in the area, a measure which resulted in a considerable increase of the number of incidents between border guards in 1967 and 1968, finally culminating in armed clashes on Zhenbao Island on 2 and 15 March 1969.[26]

The increased frequency of incidents at the northern border

alarmed the Central Military Commission (CMC). On 24 January 1968, it issued instructions to the Shengyang and Beijing military regions to strengthen the deployment of border guards along the eastern section of the border. The instructions also specified how the border guards should react in case of a Soviet provocation: as in many cases, Soviet and Chinese soldiers were merely armed with clubs the instructions stipulated that if the Soviets attempted to beat the Chinese soldiers, they should strike back; if the Soviets attacked the Chinese with armoured cars, then the Chinese should try to explode the cars and hit the soldiers with their clubs; if the Russians opened fire, the Chinese should lodge a protest and fire warning shots. To open fire was allowed only in self-defence, if the Russians ignored the Chinese warnings. It was emphasized that border disputes should not be considered as military disputes, but as a political and diplomatic problem which had to be handled directly by Beijing. Before taking any military action precise instructions would have to be sought.[27]

The Heilongjiang military authorities, after detecting increased military activity on the northern bank of the Ussuri River, submitted a plan to the Shenyang military region headquarters requesting permission to react to the Soviet activities. They submitted a plan of operations suggesting the deployment of three companies to confront the Russians on Zhenbao Island. Part of the forces would patrol the island and another part would wait in ambush and would come to the soldiers' rescue in case of a Russian attack. The plan was approved by the Shenyang military region, but it was suggested that the temperature might be so low as to make it too cold for the troops to wait in ambush. On 19 February, 1969, the plan was also approved by the Headquarters of the General Staff and by the Ministry of Foreign Affairs in Beijing. The General Staff emphasized that, though the border guards should avoid giving an impression of weakness, they should not initiate provocation, and use arms only in self-defence. Zhenbao Island should become 'a center of self-defense and counter-attack'.[28]

In spite of all these precautions, the incidents of March 1969 brought the two countries virtually to the brink of war. On 2 March, the first armed confrontation took place on the island. China and the Soviet Union gave different versions of the event. According to Chinese reports, two groups of frontier guards were sent to patrol Zhenbao Island in the morning. When the first group arrived, it was met by about 70 Soviet frontier guards who, unlike in the past when they were carrying clubs, were fully armed. The Chinese group decided to retreat, while the Soviets pushed them back, using some of their soldiers to flank the Chinese patrol. The second Chinese group suddenly emerged in front of the Russians and attempted to protect the first Chinese team. The Soviets opened fire, killing and wounding six Chinese soldiers. As the Chinese fired back Soviet armoured cars began to open fire, to which a Chinese company, lying in ambush on the river bank, responded. The fighting lasted one hour. The Chinese killed 38 Russians, wounded about 30 of them, and destroyed one armoured car, a command vehicle and a truck. On the Chinese side, 17 soldiers were killed, 35 were wounded, and one messenger disappeared.[29]

The Soviet version claims that about 300 Chinese soldiers had crossed the frozen river during the night of 1–2 March, and lay in ambush on Damansky Island. In the early morning, about 30 more Chinese approached the island and, when Soviet soldiers moved towards them in order to protest, they opened fire without warning. At the same time, Chinese troops on the river bank opened fire on another group of Soviet soldiers. With the help of reinforcements from a neighbouring post, the Soviet troops succeeded in expelling the intruders after a two-hour battle in which 31 Russians, including one officer, were killed and 14 were wounded.[30]

After the confrontation, the Central Military Commission ordered the Shenyang military region to send reinforcements to Zhenbao Island. A considerable force consisting of infantry, artillery, anti-aircraft and anti-tank detachments was concentrated in the area.

On 15 March fighting between Soviet and Chinese troops broke out on a large scale. According to the Chinese version of the event, more than ten Soviet armoured cars landed on the island in the early morning and the Soviets were the first to open fire. Fighting continued for more than two hours, at which point the Soviets received reinforcements of more tanks and armoured cars. During several hours of that afternoon, Soviet artillery shelled Chinese positions. The Chinese soldiers, in an attempt to destroy their opponents' armoured cars and tanks, divided into two groups. Since they were covered by Chinese artillery positioned on the river bank, they succeeded in forcing the Soviet troops to withdraw from the island. The clashes had lasted altogether nine hours, killing 60 Soviet soldiers, including a colonel, and wounding 80. Thirteen tanks and armoured cars were destroyed. The Chinese lost 12 frontier guards and counted 27 wounded.[31]

The Soviet military spokesman, General Lobanov, told the press on 16 March that the Chinese infantry in regimental strength – up to 2,000 men – had repeatedly attacked the island under cover of artillery and mortar fire from the river bank. After seven hours of fighting the Chinese were driven back, with the aid of reserve units and frontier guards from neighbouring posts.[32]

Following the first border clash on 2 March, the Foreign Ministry lodged a strong protest against the Soviet government, which was again followed by officially encouraged rallies and demonstrations. On 3 March, 400,000 people gathered in the streets of Beijing to 'condemn the towering crimes committed by the Soviet revisionist renegade clique'.[33] The following day, 1 million people demonstrated in front of the Soviet embassy. By 5 March an estimated 5 million people had taken part in anti-Soviet demonstrations all over the country.[34]

On 21 March, the Soviet Premier, Kosygin, requested a telephone communication with Chinese leaders to discuss the tension on their common border. The Chinese leadership refused to accept this demand on the grounds that: 'in view of the present relations between China and the Soviet Union, it is unsuitable to communicate by telephone. If the Soviet government has anything to say, it is asked to use official diplomatic channels.'[35] Two Soviet notes – sent on 29 March and 11 April – though claiming sovereignty over Damansky Island, proposed the resumption of border talks which had been broken off.[36]

The Chinese leadership, however, appeared more inclined to risk further military confrontation rather than to resume their talks with the Soviets. Mao especially seemed to be prepared for armed conflict. On 15 March, he spoke to a CCRG meeting about the possibility of war. At the 9th National Congress, which opened on 1 April, Mao, in high spirits, devoted most of his long speech to the battle of Zhenbao Island, describing the events in detail. Emphasizing Chinese bravery during the border clashes, he compared the equipment used by the Soviet and the

Chinese soldiers, pointing out that although the Chinese troops' equipment was inferior, this inferiority was compensated by their daring spirit and their excellent performance. The decisive factor in this battle, Mao declared, was the soldiers' bravery. He awarded Sun Yuguo, the young officer who had commanded the Chinese troops at Zhenbao Island, the title of 'combat hero' and asked him to speak to the Congress.[37]

At the first Plenary of the 9th Central Committee on 28 April, Mao talked again about the possibility of war, emphasizing that China must prepare morally and materially for it.[38] As a result, the Central Military Commission, in June, submitted a defence budget which proposed to increase military expenses by 34 per cent in 1969.[39]

While Mao concerned himself with preparations for a war with the Soviet Union, Zhou Enlai supervised the release of protests on the diplomatic front. Polemics between the two parties continued to flourish. The Chinese accused the Soviet Party of having turned into a 'revisionist and fascist Party',[40] of having 'totally undermined the socialist economic base',[41] of having 'turned the homeland of the Soviet working people into a land of terror'.[42] They also denounced the Soviets as 'social imperialists', 'new Tsars',[43] and accused them of colluding with the United States, Japan and Taiwan.[44] The Russians, for their part, contended that the Chinese had eroded the very 'foundation of socialism'.[45] Each thus excluded the other from the socialist camp.

During the same period, border clashes in different areas became increasingly frequent. In June, they occurred in Xinjiang and Heilongjiang; in July, armed fighting took place in the area of Pacha Island on the Heilongjiang River; in August, more clashes occurred in Xinjiang. Both countries reinforced their troops in their border areas not only at the Ussuri River but also along the eastern and western frontiers.[46]

The sense of an emergency was heightened when the news spread that the Soviet Union was considering a pre-emptive nuclear strike on Chinese nuclear installations.[47] All this reinforced the unwillingness of the Chinese leadership to consider talks with the Soviet Union. Starting with Mao, they believed that the Soviets, though they persisted in demanding discussion of the issues, could not be trusted. Their apparent desire for conciliation was, in the Chinese view, nothing but a *now realstre this threat assembly?*

façade which they used to hide their inherent aggressiveness. On 28 August the Central Committee issued an order to the provinces and municipalities, the PLA, and to the Chinese people to be fully prepared to fight a war against foreign aggression. The order emphatically stressed the necessity to expect a surprise attack on China.[48] The central authorities established a 'leading group of people's air defence'. All local governments were requested to install similar organs to take charge of local air defence. Moreover, people in cities of a certain size were organized to dig air-raid tunnels and this became a major operation during the summer and the fall of 1969.[49]

The Chinese refusal to discuss their differences with the Soviets left them facing a dilemma after the death of the Vietnamese President, Ho Chi Minh, in September 1969. Zhou Enlai was expected to lead a delegation to Hanoi to attend the funeral. Since he wanted to avoid encountering the Soviets, he decided to fly to Vietnam on 4 September to pay his last respects to Ho Chi Minh and return to Beijing the same day, well before any other foreign delegation would reach Hanoi. It was planned that a second delegation, headed by Vice Premier Li Xiannian, would attend the funeral on 8 September and should avoid any contact with the Soviets.[50] Kosygin, however, intended to use the occasion to talk to the Chinese. On 10 September he informed the Chinese ambassador in Hanoi that he would like to meet Zhou Enlai in Beijing. Mao decided that Zhou should receive Kosygin but, to demonstrate the Chinese anger about the Soviet threats of war, their encounter should take place at the airport and not in the city.[51]

airport meeting

In his talk with Kosygin, Zhou Enlai expressed Mao's view that the polemics on principles and theories between the two parties might continue for many years to come but that relations between the two countries should not be affected by them. As for the Russian allegations that China wanted to go to war, Zhou pointed out that the Chinese leadership had enough problems to deal with at home and thus did not want to fight. He emphasized that China's territory was already so vast that she did not envisage any further expansion. Unlike the Soviet Union, China stationed no troops in foreign countries and did not intend to follow the Soviet example of invading others. Moreover, Zhou accused Kosygin of having threatened to destroy Chinese nuclear bases through a pre-emptive strike. If the Soviets carried out such a threat, Zhou said, then China would view this as aggression, it would declare war and resist the aggressor to the end. Finally, Zhou emphasized, no war should be fought over border problems; these should be solved through talks, which ought take place in an atmosphere free of tensions and threats.[52]

According to Kosygin a great number of problems existed between the two nations and an exhaustive discussion of these problems, in his view, would take at least three months. In the current period of tension this would be much too long. Both Zhou and Kosygin agreed that the two sides should first concentrate on the most urgent problem, namely, the border question. Zhou expressed the belief that it would also take time to find a solution to this question. He thus proposed to take provisional measures to maintain the status quo along the border, to avoid armed conflict and to disengage the armed forces from the disputed border area. In Zhou's view, this would be the basis for constructive border talks.[53] Kosygin suggested a fourth measure which stipulated that, in case any new conflict broke out, the local border authorities should meet and seek a solution through talks.[54]

The two premiers reached an agreement on the meaning of 'status quo', but they disagreed on the question of 'disputed areas', which the Chinese defined as those territories which, in their view, belonged to China but which were occupied by the Russians. The Soviets rejected this definition. Finally, they agreed on the Soviet definition that 'disputed areas refer to areas you claim as yours and we claim as ours'. They also concurred that border talks at vice minister level should be held between the two governments.[55]

The third-line construction

In spite of Kosygin's relatively conciliatory attitude during his talks with Zhou Enlai, and in spite of the ensuing relaxation of tensions on the Sino-Soviet border, the Chinese leadership remained sceptical of the intentions of the Soviet Union. They even believed that the Soviet threat had increased rather than diminished. The Soviet Premier's insistence on pursuing the discussions with the Chinese government and on resuming border talks were viewed as a cunning Soviet manoeuvre to divert the Chinese attention from their planned surprise attack.

3rd Front

Mao, especially, continued to be suspicious. The 76-year-old Chairman believed that the Soviets were devious and, in reality, were trying to deceive China as Japan had deceived the United States with their attack on Pearl Harbor. Mao was convinced that he had to prepare for a similar eventuality.

Already, in 1964, he had announced his intention to develop a military rear area which would preserve China's military potential in an era of atomic weapons. Mao's decision was taken shortly after the incident in the Gulf of Tonkin on 4 August 1964 when American bombers were sent to North Vietnam in retaliation for an attack, by Vietnamese torpedo boats, on US destroyers. Perceiving an increased threat to China's security from the south, he decided to divide the country into three distinctive strategic areas. The regions in the north, the north-east and north-west adjacent to the Soviet Union, and in the east and south-east along the coast – all considered highly vulnerable – were classified as the 'first line' or 'first front'. The regions in the heartland of China in the south-west and north-west – including such provinces as Yunnan, Guizhou, Sichuan, Jiangxi, Shanxi, Shaanxi, Gansu and Hunan – constituted the 'third line'. Situated between the two areas was the strategically less important 'second line'. Since provinces belonging to the third-line area were located far from the vulnerable front line, they were determined to be China's strategic rear areas where important military industries should be relocated or be newly established.[56] As Mao saw it, the remoteness of their location, the ruggedness of the terrain in primarily mountainous areas, and the difficulties of transport made this region ideal for his purpose of organizing a secure basis of industrial and military production. Third-line construction was started in 1965 but, due to the disturbances of the early period of the Cultural Revolution, it soon slowed down considerably. In the wake of the armed clashes at the Sino-Soviet border, however, the project received a new impetus. Having called on the nation 'to prepare for war',[57] Mao decided to accelerate the expansion of war industries with third-line construction as its focal point.[58] Between 1969 and 1971 this policy was carried out on a massive scale, absorbing large quantities of investment and human resources.[59]

Parallel to these developments, at the end of September, Lin Biao issued a directive to the army according to which all military activities should be guided by the imminent threat of a war.[60] The headquarters of the General Chief of Staff held meetings to discuss military operations and, on 30 September, a few weeks before the start of the border talks, Lin Biao put the air force under first degree alert. Thinking it likely that the Soviet Union might take advantage of the celebration of the National Day on 1 October to launch an air attack on China, he instructed 1,683 aircraft to prepare for active duty, while more than twice as many planes – 3,900 – were evacuated into caves and remote airfields; and he ordered road blocks to be installed on the runways of major airfields in the North.[61]

Lin Biao also suggested draining all big water reservoirs in the area of Beijing on which the capital, being located in a zone of drought, heavily depends for its water supply. Lin considered that the enemy, were he to succeed in occupying the city, would not be able to survive without a water supply. Zhou, claiming that such drainage would raise considerable technical problems, was able to successfully oppose this.[62] As the Sino-Soviet border talks approached, war preparations became increasingly hectic. The ministries in Beijing were told to expect an attack at any day and any moment. Mao decided that the Chinese leadership, including those who had already been purged and were under arrest, should be evacuated. He even specified the destination for each of them. Liu Shaoqi and Marshall Xu Xiangqian were to be moved to Kaifeng in Henan Province, Zhu De and Li Fuchun to Conghua in Guangdong Province, Chen Yun and Deng Xiaoping to Nanchang in Jiangxi Province and Chen Yi to Shijiazhuang in Hebei Province.[63] Among those of the leadership who were still active, Zhou Enlai was assigned to remain in a secret place in Beijing from where he would direct government affairs. Mao himself decided to move to Wuhan, whereas Lin Biao was ordered to proceed to Suzhou in Jiangxi Province.

The plan to evacuate the leadership accelerated the implementation of another decision which had been taken earlier and which concerned the evacuation of city dwellers to the country and the reduction of functions of governmental and other departments.[64] This measure, originally perceived as a means of remoulding the minds of office workers and intellectuals, by sending them to the countryside to learn from the peasants, was now complemented by a security connotation. Each ministry and government institution retained only a small number of staff, the majority of the employees and their families left for various provinces. Out of roughly 2,000 professionals working in the Ministry of Foreign Affairs, for example, roughly 300–400 remained in Beijing. The rest were sent to the hastily set up May 7th Cadre Schools to do manual labour as well as to conduct political campaigns. Mass meetings were held to inform people about their imminent departure. They were told that war might break out at any time. Each family was allowed to take only a minimum of necessities. Furniture and any other possessions requiring heavy transport had to be sold or simply abandoned. Apartments had to be returned to the government. Trains were allocated to each ministry to transport their people to their destinations. From the second half of October, Beijing and other major cities were involved in a spectacular population movement which was both efficiently organized and highly disciplined.[65]

By October the entire army was in a state of alert. From Suzhou, Lin Biao issued an order to the Chief of Staff, General Huang Yongsheng, who had remained in Beijing with Zhou Enlai. The order stated that, in view of the fact that the Soviet negotiation team was due to arrive in Beijing within a few days, vigilance should be particularly strong. As a precaution against a Soviet surprise attack 'under the smokescreen of negotiations' – an expression Mao had coined during a recent Politburo meeting – the entire army should immediately evacuate their bases and barracks and move to the fields. Important military installations and equipment should be camouflaged; communications between army units should be reinforced; defence industries should intensify their production of weapons and ammunition.[66]

After Sino-Soviet talks resumed in Beijing on 20 October the surprise attack, which the Chinese leadership had so extensively prepared for, did not take place and the tension gradually relaxed. A month later Lin Biao gave the order to call off the army's state of emergency.[67]

Sino-Soviet border talks

Although a preliminary basis had been established between the Chinese and the Soviet prime ministers for the border talks, further discussions between the two parties started off with considerable difficulty. From the very beginning, the Chinese found that the Soviet delegation – composed of Vice Foreign Minister Vasily Kuznetsov and his deputy, Major-General Vadim Matrosov – had adopted a perspective which was considerably different from Kosygin's stance in his talk with Zhou. While Kosygin had demonstrated readiness to make concessions to the Chinese, on the contrary, the members of the Soviet delegation showed a lesser degree of flexibility. This became clear when the Chinese delegation presented a draft document on provisional measures, based on the agreement reached between the two premiers. The Soviet delegation refused to acknowledge that such an agreement had ever been reached.[68] Zhou Enlai was indignant about this incident. What was the use of border talks, he commented angrily, if the Soviets were brushing aside the agreement reached between himself and Kosygin? Mao, after receiving Zhou's report about the Soviet attitude, ordered the Chinese delegation to press the issue. The Chinese delegation proceeded by quoting the minutes of the meeting of the two premiers. This forced the Soviets to talk about the provisional measures but they nonetheless refused to admit that a binding agreement had been reached. When the talks switched to the border question, the gap between the two delegations remained as wide as before. During these negotiations heated debates took place, in particular on the issue of 'disputed areas' – the existence of which the Soviet representatives refused to admit.[69] The negotiations became deadlocked and were finally adjourned on 14 December without having reached any result.

By the end of the year the tension between the two governments increased again. On 31 December the Chinese embassy in Moscow received a harsh 'note of emergency' from the Soviet government accusing China of having invaded and occupied Qilixin and Zhenbao islands, thus violating the existing boundary. The note warned the Chinese government about the 'serious consequences' of this action. In the Chinese view, the two islands were Chinese territory since, according to the rules of international law, they were located on the Chinese side of the central line of the main channel of the river. Zhou Enlai received the note with bemusement as no conflicts had taken place on these islands since the beginning of the border negotiations. At midnight, the same day, he called a meeting to discuss the Soviet note. The deliberations focused on the meaning of 'serious consequences' mentioned in the Soviet note and on the possibility of a total breakdown of the negotiations. Most participants expressed the view that the Soviet warning was a bluff without substance. Zhou did not form any conclusion but issued an order to increase vigilance at the frontier.[70] On 2 January 1970 the chief Soviet negotiator, Kuznetsov, returned to Beijing for further consultations which, again, yielded no results.

During the 1 May celebrations at Tiananmen Square, Mao made a friendly gesture towards the Soviets by talking to the deputy head of the Soviet negotiation team. 'We should do a good job in our negotiations, so that good neighborly relations can be established', Mao said. He added, 'Be patient. Debate should be carried out by reasoning, not by force.'[71] However, this encouragement did not get the negotiations off the ground. Neither did the change of the Soviet head of delegation, in August 1970, give new impetus to the negotiations, which remained at a stalemate.

On 15 January 1971, the Soviet delegation repeated an earlier proposal suggesting that the two countries should sign a treaty renouncing the use of force against each other. Commenting: 'How can tension be reduced by an empty declaration of intent when large contingents of soldiers are present along the border?'[72] Zhou rejected the Soviet proposal. The Chinese response to a later proposal – put forward in June 1973 – concerning a non-aggression pact was similar. In Zhou's view there was no need for such an agreement since there 'still exists a treaty of friendship, alliance and mutual assistance between us'. Moreover, 'why should they talk so profusely about a pact' he asked, 'when they refuse to accept an agreement to maintain the status quo along the border, to avert armed conflicts and to disengage troops from the disputed areas?'[73] The Chinese government thus rejected the Soviet proposal and reiterated its desire to sign an agreement about the three points identified in the original meeting between Zhou Enlai and Kosygin. However, the negotiations continued to drag on until December 1979, when Soviet military forces entered Afghanistan. This event led the Chinese government to abandon the negotiations.[74]

97

Sino-American relations

The United States had become China's arch enemy since the founding of the People's Republic. The reasons for this are complex, but Washington's refusal to recognize the People's Republic and the open support for the Guomindang, compounded by the Cold War, can be considered as the main factors that kept the two countries at loggerheads. After its establishment the People's Republic corroborated the Soviet views on the bipolarity of the international system, made itself heavily dependent on Soviet economic and technical assistance, and inaugurated a harsh polemical campaign against the United States which, with such epithets as 'rotten imperialist nation' or the 'headquarters of reactionary degeneracy in the whole world'. To this open condemnation of the US were added the harassment of American citizens in China, the denial of exit permits – except after payment of large sums of money – and the seizure of American property. Relations between the two countries deteriorated even further during and after the Korean War, a period dominated by the rapid growth of McCarthyism in the United States which perceived China as aggressively expansionist. The US blocked China's entrance into the UN, pressed its allies not to recognize China, cut off all commercial and cultural relations and expanded its military alliances in Asia. What China considered perhaps as the most provocative act was the American decision to foster its relations with Taiwan and to conclude, in 1964, a mutual defence treaty with the island state.

Even at the height of Sino-Soviet tensions in the 1960s, when Moscow was formally declared China's greatest enemy, anti-American rhetoric remained strong. In fact, it increased with American involvement in the Vietnam War. However, the Sino-Soviet border clashes in March 1969 prompted Mao to reconsider China's relations with the United States. He perceived the Chinese strategic situation as unfavourable, since China was threatened by the Soviet Union in the north and by the United States in the south. In his view, the Soviet threat was more serious than the American engagement in Vietnam, since the Soviets had amassed a huge number of troops on the northern Chinese border, and had repeatedly demonstrated their expansionist policies, within the socialist bloc and elsewhere. All this pushed Mao to adopt a more flexible attitude towards the United States which was reinforced by a changing American attitude towards China, exemplified by numerous signals sent out by the newly elected Nixon administration.[75]

Thus during the height of the Cultural Revolution when the streets of China were full of millions of people denouncing both 'American imperialism' and 'Soviet revisionism', the Chinese leadership already had begun to orient its policies in the direction of seeking an understanding with the US. In sum, Chinese diplomacy was being slowly delinked from domestic considerations.

This pattern of thinking became even more evident with the 1969 recommendation of the four marshals to improve relations with the United States, obviously in keeping with Mao's thinking. The first measure the Chinese government took in this direction was to watch developments in the United States with greater attention than ever before. Zhou Enlai personally issued instructions to all departments involved in American affairs to closely monitor American policy towards China. He demanded to be kept informed continuously of all aspects of the American attitude towards China.

A minor incident signalled the change – albeit a cautious one – in the Chinese approach towards the United States. On 15 July 1969, the Guangdong security bureau arrested two American citizens whose boat had penetrated Chinese territorial waters near Hong Kong. The local authorities asked Beijing for instructions on how to handle the situation. Under the circumstances, the case was considered important enough to be referred to Zhou Enlai.[76]

Indeed, the arrest of the Americans became a political issue. Zhou summoned a meeting of officials from the Ministry of Foreign Affairs and the Ministry of Public Security for 10 o'clock the same morning to examine the situation. The time of the meeting vouched for the importance Zhou attached to it, for, according to his daily routine – which was adapted to Mao's insomnia – Zhou usually worked throughout the night until 6 o'clock in the morning when he slept. He rose shortly before midday – a time when he often scheduled the first meeting with his colleagues and/or subordinates. In this particular case, the routine was broken and his first instructions were to avoid any publicity, and to refrain from any open denounciation of the

99

Americans as 'agents of the CIA', undoubtedly an attitude of restraint in the midst of the Cultural Revolution. After some investigation, they were found to be students and Zhou ordered their release.[77]

This was a gesture towards the Nixon administration which, in addition to a number of statements indicating its willingness to end hostilities between the two nations, was also in a process of relaxing trade and travel restrictions with China.[78]

The most unambiguous public signal towards China was made by Nixon. In his first foreign policy report in February 1969 he declared:

> The Chinese are a great and vital people who should not remain isolated from the international community. . . . The principles underlying our relations with communist China are similar to those governing our policy towards the USSR. United States policy is not likely soon to have much impact on China's behaviour, let alone its ideological outlook. But it is certainly in our interest, and in the interest of peace and stability in Asia and the world, that we take what steps we can toward improved practical relations with Beijing.[79]

During the second half of 1969, Washington passed several messages to China. At a press conference in Guam on 25 July 1969, Nixon enunciated what the press termed the 'Nixon Doctrine', stating that non-communist Asian countries should take greater responsibility for their own defence, and that, in the future, the United States would give greater emphasis to economic rather than military aid to them. But, more important, Nixon suggested the 'Vietnamization' of the war, thus implying a possible disengagement of the United States from a war they no longer expected to win.[80] Moreover, through Pakistan and Romania, which Nixon visited in August, the Chinese leaders were informed that the US neither supported the Soviet proposal to establish an Asian collective security system nor had any intention of isolating China, nor of joining hands with the Soviet Union against China.[81] In November, the US announced that they would no longer patrol the Taiwan Straits.[82]

To reciprocate this gesture, Zhou ordered the release of two other Americans who had been arrested in February, when their yacht was found in Chinese territorial waters with wireless communication equipment on board which, in Chinese eyes, made them suspect as spies.[83] But the relationship of the two countries, it should be noted, remained at a level of gestures in the early stages of the Nixon administration; no direct contact took place between the two governments. Even the ambassadorial talks in Warsaw had been suspended again.[84]

The first American attempt to establish direct contact with a Chinese official took place at a diplomatic reception in Warsaw on 3 December, 1969. On this occasion, the American Ambassador to Poland, Mr Walter Stoessel, sought to approach the Chinese Chargé d'Affaires, Lei Yang, obviously in an attempt to speak to him. But, during the Cultural Revolution, it was inconceivable for a Chinese diplomat to have any contact with an American official unless he had received specific instructions to this effect. Lei Yang tried to avoid the contact by moving away. As Stoessel, instead of being discouraged, appeared determined to talk to him, he hastily took leave from his host and quickly left the building. Chasing after Lei Yang, Stoessel declared in Polish that the US was interested in resuming the Warsaw talks.[85] Zhou Enlai, albeit amused by the incident, was critical of the Foreign Ministry for having failed to keep the Chinese envoys informed of the subtle changes in the Chinese government's approach to the United States. He instructed Lei Yang to invite the American ambassador to the Chinese mission 'for a chat'.[86]

The meeting between the two envoys took place on 11 December 1969. It led to the resumption, on 20 January, of the 135th Sino-American ambassadorial talks. On this occasion, the American ambassador declared that the US 'would be prepared to consider sending a representative to Beijing for direct discussions with your officials or receiving a representative from your government in Washington for more thorough exploration of subjects of mutual interest'.[87] At the next meeting, held on 20 February, the Chinese representative agreed to the American suggestion to receive an American emissary in Beijing.[88]

But the Chinese government suddenly cancelled the next ambassadorial talks scheduled for 20 May. The reason advanced for this cancellation was the American intervention in Cambodia. Anti-American rhetoric resounded again in the official press which – among other vitriolic declarations – published a statement by Mao calling for the 'people of the whole world [to] unite and to repulse the US aggressors and all their lackeys'.[89] The Chinese government nonetheless remained committed to its new policy of *rapprochement*, a commitment which it attempted to signal to the US by inviting Edgar Snow and his wife to stand beside Mao on the Tiananmen Gate tower during the celebrations for National Day on 1 October. The front page of the following day's *People's Daily* was arranged by Zhou Enlai himself and was largely occupied by the picture of Mao and the Snows. The picture was technically processed in such a way that only Mao, the Snows and an interpreter appeared in it.[90] However, the message was ignored by the Nixon administration. As Kissinger later recalled, 'unfortunately, they [the Chinese] overestimated our subtlety, for what they conveyed was so oblique that our crude occidental mind completely missed the point'.[91]

In October, President Nixon declared in an interview with *Time Magazine* that if there was something he would like to do, before his death, it would be to go to China. If he were unable to do that, he would like his children to go.[92] This was taken by the Chinese leaders as a public declaration of intent by the US President.[93]

In November, the President of Pakistan, Yahya Khan passed a message from Nixon to Zhou Enlai expressing his willingness to send one or two high-level emissaries to Beijing to discuss the situation with Zhou at any time and any place. Zhou replied that the key question of Sino-American relations was the stationing of American troops in Taiwan and in the Taiwan Straits. The Chinese government would welcome an American envoy in Beijing, if the US President had the desire and the means to solve this problem.[94] Similar messages were sent to China through Romania, to which Zhou Enlai replied that President Nixon would be welcome in Beijing if he wished to make the visit.[95]

On 28 December, Mao received Edgar Snow for a five-hour interview during which he stated that he had lost interest in the Sino-American ambassadorial talks in Warsaw. In his view, it would be better to talk to Nixon if problems between the United States and China were to be solved. He would be willing to talk to Nixon, he said, either to achieve something or to achieve nothing. Nixon might come to China either as a tourist or as president, Mao added.[96]

Ping-pong policy

Some aspects of Sino-American exchanges became public knowledge after the Chinese invitation to an American ping-pong team, in April 1971. Under the guise of sportsmanship, this was a major political gesture which China was extending to the United States.

During the world table tennis championship in Nagoya in April 1971, the Chinese world champion of table tennis, Zhuan Zedong, was approached in a friendly manner by Glenn Cowan, a player on the American team. According to Chinese reports Zhuan, in a spontaneous response and without official instructions,[97] invited Cowan to an outing of the Chinese players and later exchanged presents with him. After this friendly encounter the Chinese delegation reported to Beijing that a number of foreign teams, including the American team, had expressed the wish to play in Beijing. Zhuan's actions were later praised by the Chinese authorities as a positive contribution to China's opening towards the United States.[98]

The Chinese Foreign Ministry and the Commission for Physical Culture and Sports advised Zhou Enlai that it would be inappropriate to invite the American team because of US involvement in Vietnam and Cambodia as well as their relations with Taiwan. Zhou, who was too prudent to take any major initiative apt to change China's foreign policy, agreed with the recommendation and added that a letter should be sent to the American team which was to specify that the Chinese people oppose the plots of the 'two Chinas' or 'one China and one Taiwan' policy.[99] But he did not take the final decision on this issue. The entire dossier was submitted to Mao who, at first, failed to express his view on the matter. Since the tournament in Nagoya was soon to end, the Foreign Ministry informed the Chinese team that the time was not ripe to receive an American team in China.[100] But Mao disagreed, changing the instructions of the Foreign Ministry and asking Zhou to inform the Chinese delegation in Nagoya to invite the American team to China.[101]

Since Mao had made this decision, Zhou Enlai executed it with his usual minute care, personally overseeing detailed arrangements concerning the American guests. He himself checked the schedule of their activities, their food and accommodations, and issued precise instructions to the press regarding reporting about the team. He ordered the re-opening of the Imperial Palace for the American visitors – upon his orders, the palace had been closed in 1966 to save it from the destructiveness of red guards. He also instructed the Chinese players, who were a superior team, to let the Americans win a number of games.[102] On 14 April, Zhou received the American visitors in person, stressing that their visit to China 'opened the door for friendly contacts between the people of the two countries'.[103]

The visit of the American sports team was followed by a series of other initiatives which, through the mediation of the Pakistani government, finally led to Henry Kissinger's meeting with Zhou Enlai in July 1971. Their talks paved the way for Nixon's epoch-making visit to China.[104]

The evolution of the contacts between Kissinger and Zhou ushered in an entirely new phase of China's role on the international scene. But, at first, the new course of China's foreign policy remained a secret confined to a restricted number of people among China's highest leadership. Officials at lesser level, as well as the Chinese people, were not informed and, even less, prepared for the major change in Chinese foreign policy symbolized by Nixon's visit. During the secret contacts between Kissinger and Zhou Enlai the Chinese media continued its anti-American rhetoric and, for most government officials, it continued to be unthinkable that a high-ranking US representative would be received by the People's Republic. Only in late May 1971, upon Zhou's advice to Mao, leading members of ministries and of the PLA were informed about the changing relations between the two countries.[105] A working group under the direction of Ye Jianying was established to prepare for Kissinger's visit.[106]

While the Chinese leaders were very hesitant about informing even their own inner circle about the changing relations with the United States, they considered it necessary to inform their closest allies beforehand about Kissinger's pending arrival in Beijing. For this purpose Zhou Enlai paid a secret visit to both Pyongyang and Hanoi to inform the Korean and Vietnamese governments about this unprecedented event. Both governments expressed their understanding concerning the Chinese desire to improve its relations with the Americans. Only one of China's allies, Albania, which was also informed, reacted negatively. The Politburo of the Albanian party expressed its strong disapproval of China's new attitude towards the US.[107] The US government, for their part, had decided to maintain secrecy about Kissinger's visit to China.[108] This decision created suspicion among the Chinese leaders who did not understand the need for it.

Kissinger arrived in Beijing on 9 July 1971 in the midst of an internal crisis within the highest echelons of the Chinese government. It had erupted a year earlier at the 2nd Plenum of the 9th Central Committee at Lushan as a power struggle between the Cultural Revolution faction and the military faction, represented respectively by Mao's wife, Jiang Qing and by Mao's designated successor, Lin Biao. The immediate result of this power struggle – which Mao arbitrated in favour of Jiang Qing and against the Lin Biao group – was the elimination of a number of Lin Biao's supporters in the army and especially of Chen Boda, against whom a political campaign was started. In the course of the year since Lushan, it had become increasingly clear that Mao not only used the events of that conference to remove some of Lin Biao's supporters but that his ultimate target was Lin Biao himself, whose political status he was systematically destroying.[109]

Mao continued to be seriously preoccupied with the repercussions of the Lushan conference. When Zhou – accompanied by Xiong Xianghui, a foreign relations specialist at the headquarters of the General Chief of Staff – appeared at Mao's study to relate his first discussions with Kissinger on 9 July 1971, Mao gave priority to information about the campaign against Chen Boda and the military which he discussed for more than an hour. Only then did he listen to Zhou's report about his encounter with the US envoy.[110]

Talks between Kissinger and Zhou Enlai had commenced harmoniously. Both sides – at least at that stage – appeared to have been more interested in highlighting understanding rather than in pressing controversial issues. But it was clear that no progress would be made in the *rapprochement* between the two countries unless some agreement on the issues of Indochina and Taiwan could be reached. According to Chinese accounts, Kissinger had promised:

1 the withdrawal from Taiwan of two-thirds of the US forces stationed on the island after the termination of the war in

Indochina and the gradual reduction of the remaining troops during the process of Sino-American normalization;

2 American opposition to the concept of 'two Chinas' or of 'one China, one Taiwan', while the People's Republic would commit herself to solve the Taiwan question by peaceful means;

3 recognition that Taiwan was a part of China; he also proposed that

4 the mutual defence treaty between the United States and Taiwan should find a solution through history; and

5 that the United States would support China's admission to the United Nations and its organizations but would oppose the expulsion of Taiwan from them.[111]

Zhou Enlai, in his statement, emphasized that differences between the two countries should not jeopardize their common efforts to find an equal and friendly basis for their relations. Elaborating on the Taiwan question, he demanded that the mutual defence treaty between the United States and Taiwan should be abrogated and that all US troops should be withdrawn from Taiwan over a certain fixed period of time. On the question of Indochina, he insisted upon an immediate and complete withdrawal of US forces from that area.[112]

After listening to Zhou's report about his first contacts with Kissinger, Mao issued a few – rather vague – instructions regarding US presence in Taiwan and in South East Asia. Regarding the presence of US forces on Taiwan, he commented: 'the monkey fails to evolve to man, he still has a tail'. (This referred to the troops to be left over, the tail, in Taiwan.) Concerning the questions of Vietnam and Indochina, Mao commented that Vietnam was the primary problem. There was no hurry concerning Taiwan, he said. The important issue was the US withdrawal from Vietnam, but 'the domino will not fall without knocking on it'.[113]

Mao then started ruminating about 'world revolution' instructing Zhou to convey to Kissinger and his aides some basics about the subject. He insisted especially that Zhou expound Mao's views on 'great disorder under heaven', the 'situation is excellent', that 'we are prepared for the US, the Soviet Union and Japan to come and carve up China', and any other related subject.[114] Zhou faithfully carried out these instructions during his second meeting with Kissinger, lecturing his American guests on the world situation characterized by chaos and conflicts, the upsurge of revolutionary struggle, the readiness of the People's Republic to face collusion of the superpowers against her, to fight a protracted people's war against the aggressors and similar rhetoric.

Kissinger seemed to have been taken somewhat by surprise by this tirade, pronounced by the hitherto so genial and urbane Zhou Enlai and which, according to Kissinger, was 'put forward with little rhetorical flourish'.[115] He began to refute Zhou's views concerning American aggressiveness against China, a rebuttal which Zhou soon interrupted with a reminder that lunch would be served. At lunch over Peking duck the atmosphere relaxed again.[116] Chinese accounts have it that Mao was especially impressed with one particular point in Kissinger's argument: the American emissary had assured Zhou that the US had no plan to start a war with China, which should set her mind at rest and which should permit Beijing to move all its troops to the north.[117]

But differences with the Chinese emerged regarding the draft of the communiqué concerning Nixon's visit to China. The question was who initiated the visit. In his recollection, Kissinger mentioned that 'in best Middle Kingdom tradition, it [the draft communiqué] suggested that Nixon had solicited the invitation'.[118] Drafted by two high-ranking Foreign Ministry officials, Huang Hua and Zhang Wenjin, under the influence of long periods of anti-American rhetoric which had been further intensified by the Cultural Revolution, this was precisely what they wanted the communiqué to express. Mao overruled this wording saying: 'none took the initiative, both sides took the initiative' ('*shui ye by zhudong, shuangfang dou zhudong*'). The wording which was finally accepted by both parties was, as Kissinger confirms, the first version presented by the Chinese which he had found adequate 'with a change of only one word'.[119] It reads: 'Knowing of President Nixon's expressed desire to visit the People's Republic of China, Premier Zhou Enlai, on behalf of the Government of the People's Republic of China, has extended an invitation to President Nixon to visit China at an appropriate date before May 1972. President Nixon has accepted the invitation with pleasure.'[120] By mutual consent, this statement was made public simultaneously in the United States and in China on 15 July.[121]

The announcement of the impending visit of the US President to China stunned the world. Its immediate impact was a UN General Assembly vote, on 25 October, to admit the People's Republic into its midst.

The vote in favour of the seating of the People's Republic in the UN and the forthcoming visit of President Nixon boosted the Chinese leadership's morale which was still under the shock of Lin Biao's sudden defection. Although it was a decision of strategic significance made by Mao himself, the official presentation to the public of this epoch-making event posed a number of problems to the Chinese leadership. Nixon's visit became a major subject in Zhou Enlai's talks with Chinese subordinates, and a few chosen foreign visitors, and was usually presented as an event which had been solicited by the United States. Under the circumstances, with the domestic situation still mired in the Cultural Revolution, with the censorious image of the United States firmly implanted in the popular mind, it was hardly possible to publicly advance any other argumentation. It was all right to invite a US ping-pong team or even to release two Americans, but to invite Nixon to come to China was a major political act, which could have hardly gone across well with the partisans of the Cultural Revolution. So the brunt of the explanation had to be that Nixon wanted it. It was almost like the olden times when foreign dignitaries came to pay homage to the Middle Kingdom.

On 20 November 1971, Zhou told Neville Maxwell that: 'President Nixon himself knocked at the door, expressing his wish to come to Beijing for talks. . . . Since he wants to come, we will talk to him.'[122] In a speech on foreign policy issues in December, Zhou used a vulgar Chinese expression to describe Nixon's visit: like a woman without morals who would 'dress up elaborately and present herself at the door' (*shuzhuang daban, songshang menlai*), Nixon, in Zhou's words, 'eagerly requested to visit China'.[123] This eagerness, according to Zhou, could be explained by the external and domestic difficulties Nixon was facing. Concerning the international scene, Zhou said:

> the US got stuck in Vietnam; the Soviet revisionists caught the opportunity to expand their sphere of influence in

Europe and in the Middle East. The US imperialists have no choice but to improve their relations with China in order to counteract the Soviet imperialists.[124]

Internally, Zhou suggested, Nixon was 'under immense pressure engendered by the request of the people in the US to improve Sino-American relations. . . . When he comes, he has to bring something in his pocket'. The visit would also give China the opportunity to make use of 'the contradictions between the US and the USSR and to magnify them'.[125]

Whatever might have been Zhou Enlai's public explanation for Nixon's visit to China, he nonetheless gave his full attention to every detail of the organization of his stay. During the preparations for the visit, he encountered difficulties with Jiang Qing and her coterie, who took exception to several aspects of his arrangements. This was a period of the Cultural Revolution when the 'newly born things' fostered by the Cultural Revolution faction were again in full swing. The Minister of Culture, for example, disapproved of the playing of the song: 'America the Beautiful' which Zhou had chosen for a banquet in Nixon's honour. Jiang Qing objected to the activities of American broadcasting companies who wanted to film Nixon's visit in China, on the grounds that they were 'doing propaganda for Nixon on Chinese soil'.[126]

A major question which remained to be solved was whether Mao himself would be able to receive Nixon. Only a few persons were aware of Mao's state of health. In January 1972 he had suffered a stroke, but his illness was kept a top secret of which not even all Politburo members were informed.[127] His doctor wrote that three weeks before Nixon's arrival, Mao's illness became 'so serious that a recovery was out of the question' and that he was 'so weak that he could hardly speak'.[128] However, he did apparently recover, for he received Nixon.

At that period of his life, Mao had the habit of deciding at the last moment whether or not he wanted to meet foreign visitors. For Nixon's visit he ordered a new suit and a new pair of shoes made for him. But it was unforeseeable when he would be able to meet the American President.[129] Mao kept himself closely informed about Nixon's arrival and his activities in Beijing. Only a few hours after Nixon had reached the city, Mao suddenly decided to receive him and informed Zhou Enlai accordingly. On very short notice the US President, together with Kissinger and Winston Lord,[130] were ushered to Mao's study on the very first day of the American President's visit.[131]

During Kissinger's second visit to China in October 1971, the communiqué to be signed during Nixon's visit to China again became a subject of discussion. Kissinger himself criticized the American draft handed to Zhou Enlai as one which 'followed the conventional style, highlighting fuzzy areas of agreement and obscuring differences with platitudinous generalizations'.[132] While Zhou was ready to accept the American draft as a basis of negotiation, Mao desired a communiqué similar to the 'October 10th Agreement' of 1945 between the Chinese Communist Party and the Guomindang in which the two parties had set forth their agreements and differences. This was meant to demonstrate to the world that China, which for years had unequivocally emphasized Sino-American differences, was not seeking conciliation with the US at the expense of basic principles, especially since she had accused the Soviet 'revisionists' of committing this very mistake. The Shanghai communiqué, signed on 28 February 1972 by Nixon and Zhou Enlai, reflected this particular need. It clearly stated the differences between the two parties on the problems of Vietnam, Korea, Japan, and South Asia.[133]

The issue of Taiwan remained the thorniest question between the two parties. Since it had been the major source of contention between them, the Chinese viewed it as a matter of direct concern of their sovereignty, it called for more than a statement of differing opinions. The wording which was finally agreed upon reads as follows:

> The United States acknowledges that all Chinese on either side of the Taiwan Strait maintain there is but one China and Taiwan is a part of China. The United States does not challenge this position. It reaffirms its interest in a peaceful settlement of the Taiwan question by the Chinese themselves. With this prospect in mind, it affirms the ultimate objective of the withdrawal of all US forces and military installations from Taiwan. In the meantime, it will progressively reduce its forces and military installations on Taiwan as the tension in the area diminishes.[134]

This wording reflects both the American and the Chinese viewpoints. The Chinese insisted on the withdrawal of US forces from Taiwan, while the Americans desired to link their withdrawal to the decrease of tensions in the area. But it also mirrors the determination of both parties to avoid the obvious impasse which lay in the path of normalizing their relations. Apparently, the Americans were willing to obscure their official 'two Chinas' policy, if the Chinese would gloss over the question of sovereignty with such ambivalent language.

Relations between the two countries thereafter developed rapidly on a working level through the American and Chinese embassies in Paris and Ottawa. In February 1973, Kissinger raised the issue of a more direct exchange with Zhou Enlai, proposing trade representations, consulates, or liaison offices in Beijing and in Washington. As a counter-offer, he promised the withdrawal of all remaining US forces from Taiwan and the abandoning of official ties with Taiwan. Kissinger did not expect his proposal to be readily accepted by the Chinese since they had repeatedly declared that they would not establish any official representation in a country where a Taiwanese embassy was accredited. But, in spite of the continuing official presence of the United States in Taiwan, the Chinese agreed to establish liaison offices in their respective capitals. In a joint communiqué, both parties announced that 'the time was appropriate for accelerating the normalization of relations'.[135]

A year later, however, the normalization process slowed down. Kissinger, who continued to travel to China about twice a year, recalls that since November 1973 his visits 'either were downright chilly or were holding actions'.[136] The timing coincides with Mao's disapproval of the Foreign Ministry and the campaign against Zhou Enlai ('criticize Lin, Confucius and Zhou Gong') who, as was described in an earlier chapter, had come under sustained criticism from Mao and the Cultural Revolution faction. Zhou's handling of Sino-American relations, and especially the unresolved Taiwan issue, were significant elements of the campaign, which accused him of 'capitulation' to the United States and forced him to make self-criticism to the Politburo.[137]

The Taiwan issue had indeed remained unresolved. The American hope that it would be acceptable to China to continue the process of normalization while the United States would maintain some kind of official relations with Taiwan, perhaps even avoid the abrogation of the mutual defence treaty, did not materialize. On the contrary, the Chinese showed increasing signs of dissatisfaction with the American attitude, a reaction which was compounded by the slow pace of retreat of American troops from Taiwan.[138] Another issue which complicated Sino-American relations in that period was the policy of *détente* between the West and the Soviet Union. According to Kissinger, Chinese perceptions of the danger inherent in such policies carried more weight than the Taiwan question.[139]

Sino-Japanese relations

Since the 1950s, none of China's neighbours had received more attention than Japan, in spite of the fact that there were no diplomatic relations between the two countries. The reasons for the unusual interest were multiple, including historical, cultural, economic, political, as well as strategic considerations.

For over a thousand years the civilizations of the two countries have been linked. Communications across the sea had permitted repeated cultural contacts over many centuries. The result, however, was not one of mutual and equal cultural interaction but rather asymmetrical with a strong Chinese impact on Japanese civilization: the writing system, architecture, philosophy and religion, all of them right up to today, bear the Chinese imprint. Political and economic interaction on the other hand was non-existent. Neither of the two countries were really interested. It was only the incursion of Western powers in the nineteenth century which forced both countries to abandon their autarchic systems and led to the development of a different kind of relationship between them.

Under the impact of Western industrial civilization the two countries reacted differently. While China – convinced of the superiority of her cultural, social and political values – resisted all foreign impact on its civilization, Japan assimilated what it considered useful for its own technical and social development. This process – which led China into a state of semi-colonialism, and which transformed Japan into a modern country – also changed the relations between them. The tables had turned. It was Chinese reformers and the Chinese elite who were interested in Japan and who sought to emulate the new Japanese model.

But the modernization of Japan had made it expansionist with China as one of its principal victims. In several waves of aggression, beginning with the establishment of Japanese control over the Ryukyus Islands in 1870 and the annexation of Taiwan after the Sino-Japanese war of 1894, and ending with the declaration of war on China in 1937, Japan established its claims over Chinese territories.

The allied victory after the Second World War transformed the political constellation in Asia. Japan was defeated, while China emerged as a victor in the international sphere. Ever since the founding of the People's Republic, China had attributed great importance to Japan but relations between the two countries were complicated by several factors. First, the presence of the superpowers in the region, especially the commanding position of the United States which had established its power base in Japan, was viewed as a threat to China's security. The security pact which Japan had signed with the United States in 1951 was considered a clear manifestation of this threat. Moreover, during the following year, Japan had concluded a peace treaty and established diplomatic relations with the Taiwanese government, another act which the Chinese authorities condemned as extremely serious and as a flagrant provocation against the People's Republic.[140] Second, the historical opprobrium attached to Japanese conduct during the Sino-Japanese war was far from overcome.

In spite of these complications the Chinese government began to develop a well-organized programme of relations with Japanese non-governmental organizations in which a number of institutions of the Foreign Affairs System were involved. The Chinese People's Institute of Foreign Affairs devoted a considerable amount of time and energy to receiving Japanese politicians, both from the ruling and the opposition parties. Japanese left-wing parties, both communist and socialist – were particularly responsive to the Chinese initiatives and even constituted powerful pressure groups for the amelioration of relations. The Chinese Commission for the Promotion of International Trade worked on the expansion of trade relations with Japan. In 1952 it succeeded in signing a trade agreement with Japanese Diet members. Cultural exchanges also proliferated with the inauguration of a programme of invitations to intellectuals, cultural and scientific groups. Agreements were also reached on other subjects such as the repatriation of Japanese prisoners of war with the Japanese Red Cross (1954), and the Fishery Agreement with the Japan–China Fishery Association (1955). From the 1950s, all these exchanges had been coordinated by Liao Chengzhi, the deputy director of the State Council's Office of Foreign Affairs.[141] In sum, while the relations between the two countries in the 1950s were non-official, they had nonetheless become quite substantial.

The non-governmental exchanges finally took a semi-official turn in the early 1960s. The Sino-Soviet dispute and the sudden withdrawal of Soviet experts from China in 1960, which had resulted in a reduction of trade between the two countries, created a major hindrance to Chinese technological and industrial development. Under the circumstances, it became necessary to seek out other sources of economic support for which Japan appeared to represent the only alternative at that time. In 1962, Tatsunosuke Takasaki, member of the Liberal Democratic Party and of the Diet and Director of the Economic Planning Agency of the Japanese government, paid a visit to China. He and Liao Chenzhi signed a memorandum for the further development of trade relations on behalf of the two countries and, in 1964, they agreed to establish trade liaison offices in Tokyo and in Beijing.[142]

Only a year later, however, after Eisako Sato became Prime Minister, the Chinese official press suddenly launched a vitriolic campaign against the Japanese government. 'Japan, under Sato', wrote the *People's Daily* in January 1965, 'has gone further than his predecessor in toeing the US line.'[143] Japan was also accused of having formed a 'military bloc' with South Korea and Taiwan, 'masterminded by US imperialism,'[144] and, by 1966, its 'collusion' with the Soviet Union was emphasized.[145] As the Cultural Revolution unfolded, the Chinese press became even more abusive. It extended its attacks to the Japanese ruling elite in general, accusing them of economic aggression and of promoting the revival of Japanese militarism, charges which the Japanese authorities denounced as 'vicious slander' against the Japanese people. As a result of these mutual recriminations, the number of supporters, among Diet members, favouring an amelioration of Sino-Japanese relations dwindled, while the influence of the Taiwan lobby within Japan appeared to grow.[146] The forward momentum in political relations ground to a complete halt.

Relations between the CCP and the Japanese Communist and Socialist Parties also deteriorated considerably. The Cultural Revolution clearly had much to do with it. Domestic radicalization had spilled over on to external affairs leading the Chinese Party and the press to severely criticize the Japanese left in general, but the Japanese Communist Party (JCP) in particular, for having turned revisionist. The attacks on the JCP were all the more surprising since, even before the Cultural Revolution, the Japanese Party had criticized the Soviet Party for being revisionist, for having 'openly split' and for 'recklessly widening disunity' in the international communist movement.[147] In fact, the CCP had published a full text of supportive letters from the Japanese Party. However, if the JCP was criticial of its Soviet counterpart, it had declined openly to side with the CCP in the Sino-Soviet dispute, and this was apparently not acceptable to Beijing – at least not during the Cultural Revolution. But the issue that really angered Beijing was the Japanese position on Vietnam. The JCP considered it necessary for the CCP to seek a united front with the Soviet Union, a suggestion which the Chinese vehemently rejected. In the Chinese view, Moscow was in fact collaborating with the United States, aiming at reaching a 'political deal' in South Vietnam. Since both Japanese parties failed to take a pro-Chinese stance in the Sino-Soviet conflict, increasing numbers of polemical articles began to appear in the Chinese press. The JCP hit back by critically highlighting the 'morbid deification of Mao Zedong', the destruction of 'order and discipline of the party' and of the 'achievements of the Chinese revolution' as well as of the 'state structures of China'.[148] Both parties began to eliminate pro-Beijing elements from their midst and expressed their determination to maintain their 'independence and self-determination'.[149] By the late 1960s, Sino-Japanese relations at all levels – including trade relations – thus had reached a complete impasse.

A real diplomatic breakthrough came only in the early 1970s, in the wake of the new relationship between China and the US. The announcement of the planned visit of President Nixon to China had proved to be a traumatic experience for Japan. It became known as 'the Nixon shock' in Japan. For decades the Japanese authorities had shaped their China policy according to Washington's requirements. Understandably, they were stunned by the unilateral US decision to carry out such a momentous change in its own policy towards China. This was compounded after the UN General Assembly, in October 1971, passed its resolution to expel the Taiwanese representatives from the world organization and transferred membership to the People's Republic.

At the same time, external and internal pressures had built up for the recognition of China by Japan. Externally, the presence of the People's Republic in the UN, the increasing normalization of Sino-American relations, the impending likelihood of relations with Western European countries, all of those factors contributed to the Japanese decision to change its policies towards China. Internally, the retirement of Premier Sato in July 1972 and the arrival of Kakuei Tanaka at the helm paved the way for a change. Discussions about the possibility of restoring diplomatic relations between the two nations concerned had also taken place, in December 1971, at the level of the representatives of the two trade liaison offices. On that occasion the Chinese negotiators tabled three principles as the basis for normalizing relations between the two countries: (a) the government of the People's Republic is the sole representative and legal government of China; (b) Taiwan is an inalienable part of the territory of the People's Republic; and (c) the treaty between Japan and Taiwan is illegal and invalid and should be abrogated.[150] In an answer to an inquiry of the opposition party on 18 July 1972, the Tanaka government expressed its 'full understanding' for the three principles brought forward by China.[151]

Negotiations between the two governments, represented by Tanaka and Zhou Enlai, began on 25 September 1972, in Beijing. They were difficult for several reasons. Japan, after China's admission to the UN and after Nixon's historic visit to Beijing, had little leverage left to negotiate on its own terms with China. But, to Japan, the most important and non-negotiable issue was the continuation of its security arrangements with the United States which China had repeatedly condemned. In his first meeting with Zhou Enlai, Prime Minister Tanaka emphasized the importance of the treaty for Japan's peace and security. He also argued that Sino-Japanese relations should not be normalized at the expense of good relations between the US and Japan, and that China had no reason to regard the treaty as a threat. Zhou, instead of expressing disagreement with the Japanese

views, and much to Tanaka's surprise, articulated his understanding for the Japanese position, emphasizing that the
relations between Japan and the US were a matter entirely
reserved to the two countries. This was indeed the first time
that the Chinese authorities adopted a conciliatory attitude on
this issue.[152]

The second issue of discord – that of past Sino-Japanese
relations – came out into the open on the occasion of a state
banquet in honour of the Japanese Prime Minister. Tanaka
recalled the unfortunate experiences between the two countries
over the past several decades, saying that 'during that time, our
country caused great trouble to the Chinese people for which I
once again make profound self-examination'.[153] The listeners
were mute; there was no applause. Obviously, the Chinese were
dissatisfied with this statement which, in their view, touched
too lightly upon a period which they considered one of the
most dreadful events of their recent history, having cost them
millions of lives and caused incalculable losses of property.[154]
The Chinese also continued to conjure up terrible images of
humiliations and the losses suffered during the Sino-Japanese
War of 1884, culminating in the 1895 Treaty of Shimonoseki
which forced China to cede Taiwan, the Pescadores and the
Liaotung Peninsula to Japan.

The next day a stern-faced Zhou Enlai told Tanaka that his
apology was not acceptable to the Chinese. 'To cause trouble
would have been a suitable apology to a lady whose skirt
had been dirtied. . . . It is too light!' Zhou pointed out.[155] More
differences – mostly related to the Taiwan issue – arose during
the discussions, on 26 September, between the Chinese and the
Japanese Foreign Ministers, Ji Pengfei and Ohira, concerning
the wording of the joint communiqué. The Japanese spokesman,
Takashima, basing himself on a legal approach, contested a
number of points brought forward by the Chinese:

1 According to the Japanese, the 'termination of the state of
war' between the two countries had been proclaimed in the
treaty concluded between Taiwan and Japan in 1952 and was
understood to be valid for all of China. The Chinese authorities, if they so desired, could make a unilateral declaration on
this point.

2 The Chinese contention that the treaty between Japan and

Taiwan was 'illegal and invalid, and should be abrogated' was also rejected by Japan, since the treaty had been signed according to valid principles of international law.[156]

3 Japan was not ready to fully accept the Chinese contention that 'Taiwan is an inalienable part of the territory of the People's Republic of China', since the jurisdiction of the Chinese government had not been extended to the island.

4 The Chinese were prepared to renounce their claim to indemnities from Japan for the losses endured during the Japanese occupation, but the Japanese argued that this problem had also been solved in the Sino-Japanese peace treaty of 1952.[157]

When Zhou Enlai and Tanaka met again in the afternoon of the same day. Zhou asked Tanaka whether Takashima had come to China with the purpose of jeopardizing the Sino-Japanese normalization process. Rejecting Takashima's arguments which, in Zhou's view, were based on a purely legalistic interpretation Zhou argued that normalization between the two countries was not a legal problem but a political one. He also made critical remarks about Tanaka's statement at the banquet in which he had touched so lightly upon the Japanese guilt towards China. Tanaka insisted on defending the Japanese position. Their two-hour talk took place in an extremely tense atmosphere.

The Japanese delegation was in a difficult position since they, too, had a stake in the normalization of relations between the two countries. They began to backtrack, step by step, from their original position. The compromise which was formulated in a joint communiqué on 29 September gives the impression that the Japanese agreed to most of the Chinese demands, most importantly on the Taiwan question. They also accepted the anti-hegemony formulation contained in the Shanghai communiqué on the inclusion of which the Chinese insisted.[158] This was important to the Chinese who, under the banner of anti-hegemonism, tried to establish a kind of 'united front' against the Soviet Union.

As for the Japanese guilt arising out of the war with China, the formulation was that 'the Japanese side is keenly aware of Japan's responsibility for causing enormous damage in the past to the Chinese people through war and deeply reproaches itself'. The joint statement finally adopted the formula that Japan fully understood the three principles of the Chinese government for the restoration of diplomatic relations without making any specific reference to the 1952 treaty with Taiwan.[159]

After Tanaka's historical visit to Beijing, interaction between Japan and the People's Republic developed rapidly in the economic and trade sectors. Within the first year after the signing of the communiqué, 28 Japanese and 30 Chinese economic and trade missions visited their partner country. But in contrast to the take-off in these fields, all other arrangements which were planned to be concluded in connection with the 1972 communiqué encountered serious difficulties. The Taiwan question, although formally solved, overshadowed the development of further relations between the two countries. Problems arose in the areas of civil aviation, where the continuation of air traffic between Japan and Taiwan was at stake, and in the fields of shipping and fishing which China – for military reasons – had unilaterally restricted in certain zones along the coast. That political interaction between the two countries was seriously hampered became evident over the issue of a hegemony clause during the negotiations of a peace treaty which started in April 1975. The Chinese continued to attribute great importance to this clause as a method of containment of the Soviet Union whereas Japan – though it had not objected to the introduction of the clause into the 1972 communiqué – had become extremely cautious about openly offending the Soviet Union, with whom it also had ongoing negotiations on a number of issues. It was only in 1978 that a solution based on mutual compromise was reached on this matter.

5

CONCLUSION

The Cultural Revolution was essentially a domestic phenomenon. Of the ten-year span of this dramatic event, the first few years were full of massive and uncontrollable red guard violence while during the rest of the period, intra-Party factional fights from the highest level downwards formed the domestic backdrop of Chinese policies. Since China was profoundly preoccupied by domestic developments, foreign affairs became peripheral, and the designing of a coherent foreign policy was no longer on the agenda of the country. Interest in the outside world became so marginal that even Chinese diplomatic personnel stationed all over the world had their eyes rivetted on what was happening in China or on the microcosmic Cultural Revolutions that were being staged within the confines of the Chinese missions. Admittedly, there were massive demonstrations against the international 'reactionary' or 'revisionist' forces, but on balance they were less important than what was happening within the country.

Only when China began to perceive a real security threat from the north after the aggravation of the Sino-Soviet dispute, and a possible security threat from the south after the intensification of the Vietnam-US conflict, did the Chinese leadership begin to show an interest in the outside world. While China was still burning and was mired in intra-mural factional strifes, the leadership in Zhongnanhai began to reflect on what it should do in the face of perceived threats from two directions and how it should respond to this dangerous situation.

It is indeed remarkable that in the midst of fractious fights among themselves, the Chinese leaders separated foreign policy issues from domestic irrationalities, opted for the politics of continuing to defy the Russians and of turning to the Americans. Discreet signals were indeed sent out, the most important of which was the well-publicized invitation to Edgar Snow to stand with Mao on the rostrum above Tiananmen Square.

Independently of these subtle signals, the meaning of which the Americans did not catch immediately, the newly installed Nixon administration was striving to do the same – only more boldly and more conspicuously. The classic and rather amusing example of all this was the vain attempt made by the US ambassador in Warsaw to seek out his Chinese counterpart in a party, who literally ran away – obviously ignorant of the fact that the top Chinese leadership, too, was sending out – in fact, too discreetly – its own signals.

American initiatives were in fact a godsend, for, while it made it possible for the Chinese to seize the opportunity – an opportunity they were independently looking for – it made it possible for them to declare that it was the Americans who wanted to seek them out and that it was they who came to China to negotiate. Such an argumentation – publicly aired by Zhou – naturally went down well in turbulent China, for it must have conjured up memories of the good old days when foreigners came to China to pay homage to its court.

But were the innovations introduced in China's foreign policy – catalysed by perceptions of serious threats to its security – basic transmutations in Chinese thinking and Chinese strategic policy? Had China really taken a new road?

During no period of Chinese history since 1949 has it ignored security concerns. They have always been an element of continuity in Chinese foreign policy. In that sense, neither Chinese thinking nor strategic policies underwent any major change. Another element of continuity was the Chinese subscription to the Marxist image of the world and the permanence of Maoist global thinking which still believed in revolution. All the changes of 1971 and 1972 were construed by the Chinese leaders as a victory of its long-standing foreign policy, a victory that had finally pushed the outside world to move towards China. It is therefore not surprising that revolutionary rhetoric continued to be present in China's dealing's with the outside world, and that its new diplomacy towards the Western world did not really take off after the inauguration of the normalization process. While economic relations with the West and with Japan developed, political relations crawled along at a low level and did not really take off for several more years. In the case of both the United States and Japan they reached a stalemate. At the same time, Beijing persisted in vilifying the Soviet Union. Only in the late 1970s, when Deng Xiaoping had been firmly established as the paramount leader of the Chinese government, did relations with most countries reach some level of normalcy.

APPENDIX I: CHRONOLOGY

Late 1965–early 1966

Preliminary stage of the Cultural Revolution with the Beijing literary establishment as its target.

1966

16 May

Publication of the 'May 16th Circular', a Central Committee document inaugurating the Cultural Revolution.

28 May

Establishment of the Central Cultural Revolution Group (CCRG) headed by Chen Boda. Kang Sheng was its adviser. Deputy heads: Jiang Qing, Zhang Chunqiao and others; members: Wang Li, Guan Feng, Qi Benyu, Yao Wenyuan and others.

June

Beginning of 'work teams policy' based on a decision of the Central Committee under the presidency of Liu Shaoqi.

June–end of 1966

In the Foreign Ministry: first stage of the Cultural Revolution, directed by the Foreign Ministry Party committee.

June

Campaign 'to sweep away all demons and eradicate all poisonous weed'.

June–early August

Practice of 'work teams policy'.

28 June

Diplomatic incident at the Chinese embassy in Indonesia.

25 July

Mao Zedong condemns 'work teams policy' as a 'disservice' and as 'obstructive'.

1–12 August 1966

11th Plenum of the Central Committee issuing the '16 points'; from then until end of 1966 criticism of the Liu-Deng line.

18 August

Mao Zedong receives 1 million red guards at Tiananmen Square. Between now and 26 November, Mao reviews red guards eight times. Altogether 11 million of them parade before Mao at Tiananmen Square.

29 August

Agreement between the Chinese and the Vietnamese governments on China's economic and technical assistance to Vietnam.

9–28 October

Central working conference stressing the importance of the campaign against the Liu-Deng line considered as 'reactionary' and 'bourgeois'.

15 November, 3–4 December

Riots of local Maoists opposed by Portuguese authorities in Macao

December

Establishment of the 'liaison station' in the Foreign Ministry.

1967

January–October 1967

The second stage of the Cultural Revolution in the Foreign Ministry.

6 January

Rebel groups seize power in the Party and municipality of the city of Shanghai. This action, approved by Mao, was followed by power seizures in different provinces as well as in central government institutions.

18 January

The liaison station's power seizure in the Foreign Ministry.

24 January

Chen Yi makes self criticism to the representatives of the 'masses' concerning his 'work teams policy' in the Foreign Affairs System.

25 January

Red Square incident in Moscow – Chinese radical students opposed by the Soviet police.

27 January

Chinese students protest in front of the Soviet embassy in Paris against the Soviets' reaction to the activities of the Chinese students at Moscow's Red Square. Their demonstration is suppressed by the police.

11 February

Mass rally at the Beijing Workers' Stadium against the Soviet Union.

11–16 February

In several meetings, Chen Yi and other members of the Politburo raise questions about the Cultural Revolution and denounce Lin Biao and the CCRG for their persecution of veteran cadres. Mao severely condemns this criticism as a 'February Adverse Current'.

25 February–18 March

Meetings at the Central Committee criticizing Chen Yi and the other members of the Politburo involved in the February Adverse Current.

27 February

Signing of a Sino-Japanese people's protocol on friendship and trade.

20 March

Note of the Chinese Foreign Ministry to the Indian embassy in Beijing protesting against India's support of the 'traitor bandits' of Tibet.

24 April

The Chinese Chargé d'Affaires in Indonesia, Yao Dengshan, and the Chinese Consul-General, Xu Ren, are declared *personae non grata*.

27 April

A mass rally of 100,000 people denounces the Indonesian government for their 'anti-Chinese crimes'.

30 April

Yao Dengshan and Xu Ren are received at the airport by members of the Politburo, the CCRG, the PLA and thousands of red guards and acclaimed as 'red diplomats'.

6 May

Start of the Hong Kong riots.

11 May

Mass rally at Tiananmen Square demanding that Chen Yi make self criticism in front of the 'masses'.

11–12 May

Nightly discussion between Zhou Enlai and red guards from the Foreign Affairs System about Chen Yi's self criticism concerning his involvement in the February Adverse Current.

15 May

The Chinese Foreign Ministry lodges the 'strongest protest' against the British authorities in Hong Kong for the suppression of the riots.

15–17 May

Mass demonstrations in Beijing and other cities against the British actions in Hong Kong.

21 May

Incidents involving Chinese diplomatic personnel and red guards in Mongolia.

7–10 June

Demonstrations in Beijing and other cities against US and Soviet policy in the Middle East.

14 June

Accusations of espionage against Indian embassy personnel in Beijing.

16 June

Demonstrations against the Chinese embassy in New Delhi.

26–28 June

Incidents involving the Chinese embassy and Chinese nationals in Burma where about 50 Chinese were killed and several hundred were arrested.

June–August

Continuation of strikes in Hong Kong.

July

Riots and rebellion in Wuhan. Guan Feng and the CCRG call for the elimination of 'capitalist roaders in the army', thus starting a wave of attacks against army institutions throughout the country.

15 July

Red guards from the foreign languages institutes set up camp in front of the Foreign Ministry to force the issue of Chen Yi's self criticism.

7 August

Agreement between China and Vietnam on technical and economic assistance to Vietnam.

Wang Li's talk with rebel representatives in the Foreign Ministry. First 'small' meeting for criticism of Chen Yi in the Foreign Ministry.

12 August

First 'medium-sized' meeting for criticism of Chen Yi in the Great Hall of the People.

14 August

The liaison station takes over the personnel department of the Foreign Ministry.

20 August

Ultimatum delivered by the Foreign Ministry to the British Mission concerning Hong Kong. Demonstrations in front of the office of the British Chargé d'Affaires in Beijing ended on 22 August with the office being set on fire.

26 August

Second small meeting in the Foreign Ministry for criticize of Chen Yi. Red guards and rebels storm the Foreign Ministry in an attempt to abduct Chen Yi.

1 and 5 September

Jiang Qing signals a change of policy by publicly denouncing 'ultra-leftism' in the mass organizations and especially the 'May 16th group'.

October–second half of 1971

Third phase of the Cultural Revolution in the Foreign Ministry under the direction of the 'Committee of great unity'.

1 October

Suspension of diplomatic relations with Indonesia.

4 October

Closing down of the Chinese embassy in Tunisia.

1968

January

Beginning of a campaign against 'ultra-leftism' in the Foreign Ministry of which the rebels become the main target. Parallel to this, a campaign against 'renegades' was carried out.

13 February

A poster signed by 91 leading cadres criticizing 'ultra-leftism' and challenging the accusations against Chen Yi appeared in the Foreign Ministry.

March

Provoked by this poster, beginning of a campaign against the 'rightist deviationist wind' and the purge of three military leaders known as the 'Yang-Yu-Fu event'.

August

Soviet invasion of Czechoslovakia

September

End of the process of establishing revolutionary committees in 29 provinces and municipalities. Full swing of the campaign to purify class ranks with the aim to uncover 'renegades', 'enemy agents', 'illicit relations with foreign countries', 'anti-Party elements'.

October

Issue of instructions to establish May 7th Cadre Schools.

13–31 October

Twelfth Plenary Session of the Eighth Central Committee preparing the Ninth Party Congress of the CPC. Expulsion of Liu Shaoqi from the Party 'forever'.

12 November

Announcement of Brezhnev's 'theory of limited sovereignty'.

1969

1969–71

Acceleration of Third Line construction.

2, 15 March

Border incidents at Zhenbao Island.

1–24 April

Ninth Party Congress praising the 'great achievements' of the Cultural Revolution and electing Lin Biao, Jiang Qing and their followers into the Politburo. The Cultural Revolution enters the phase of 'struggle-criticism-transformation'.

27 August

Establishment of the National Defence Leading Group and similar groups at central, provincial and municipal levels. Start of a mass movement for digging air-raid shelters.

11 September

Zhou Enlai meets the Chairman of the Council of Ministers of the Soviet Union at Beijing airport to discuss the border issue.

30 September

Lin Biao's no. 1 order by which the air force is put under first degree alert. The army is instructed to evacuate their bases.

October

Evacuation of the Chinese leadership to different provinces.

Two-thirds of the Foreign Ministry staff is moved to Cadre Schools in Jiangxi and Hunan provinces.

20 October

Beginning of the Sino-Soviet border talks in Beijing.

1970

15 February–21 March

National Planning Conference of the State Council discusses the Fourth Five-Year Plan, giving priority to 'Third Line construction'.

27 March

'Circular on ferreting out the conspirational May 16 clique'. By the middle of the year, 1,500 people (out of a staff of roughly

2,000) in the Foreign Ministry are accused of being members of that group.

23 August–6 September

Second Plenary Session of the Ninth Central Committee in Lushan. Chen Yi inadvertently supports Chen Boda whom Mao severely criticized for claiming that Mao was a genius.

18 December

Mao talks with Edgar Snow about a possible visit of President Nixon to China.

1971

10–17 April

Visit to China of an American table tennis team.

9–11 July

Talks between Zhou Enlai and Henry Kissinger in Beijing.

16 July

Announcement that President Nixon has been invited to visit China in 1972.

13 September

Lin Biao's death.

Autumn 1971–autumn 1976

Fourth phase of the Cultural Revolution in the Foreign Ministry.

20–26 October

Henry Kissinger's second visit to Beijing for talks with Zhou Enlai.

25 October

The UN General Assembly adopts a resolution in favour of restoring China's seat at the UN.

1972

21–28 February

US President Richard Nixon visits China. Mao receives him in his residence on 21 February.

27 February

A joint Sino-American communiqué is issued in Shanghai.

25–30 September

Japanese Prime Minister Kakuei Tanaka visits China. Establishment of diplomatic relations between China and Japan.

October

Zhou Enlai's campaign against Lin Biao's 'ultra-leftism'. It is cut short by Mao who said, on 17 December, that Lin Biao was 'ultra-right'.

1973

10 March

Reinstatement of Deng Xiaoping in his former position as vice premier.

4 July

Mao's criticizes the Foreign Ministry.

24–28 August

Tenth National Congress confirms the importance of the Cultural Revolution.

October

Beginning of a campaign against right deviation at Beijing and Qinghua Universities and of criticism against Lin Biao and Confucius.

1974

5 January

Trade agreement between China and Japan.

January

Extension of the campaign to criticize Lin Biao and Confucius to include Zhou Enlai, who is attacked under the name of 'the Duke of Zhou'.

22 February

Mao Zedong puts forth his theory of the Three Worlds in a talk with Zambian President Kaunda.

June

Jiang Qing intensifies the campaign against Zhou Enlai.

17 July

Mao criticizes Wang Hongwen, Jiang Qing, Zhang Chunqiao and Yao Wenyuan, warning them about turning into a 'Gang of Four'.

4 October

Deng Xiaoping is appointed first vice premier of the State Council.

1975

8–10 January

Deng Xiaoping is appointed vice chairman of the Central Committee and member of the Standing Committee of the Politburo.

13–17 January

Fourth National People's Congress where Zhou Enlai presents the 'report on the work of the government', mentioning the 'four modernizations'. After the Congress, Zhou is seriously ill. Deng Xiaoping takes charge of the day-to-day work of the Central Committee and the government.

1 March

Beginning of a campaign against 'empiricism' directed against Zhou Enlai, Deng Xiaoping and veteran cadres.

14 August

Another campaign against Zhou Enlai, Deng Xiaoping and other veteran leaders was started under the epithet of 'Water Margin' referring to a classical Chinese novel.

1976

8 January

Zhou Enlai dies.

End of January

Deng Xiaoping is purged. Hua Guofeng is appointed acting premier.

9 September

Mao Zedong dies.

6 October

Hua Guofeng, Ye Jianying and Li Xiannian acting on behalf of the Politburo, arrest the 'Gang of Four'.

APPENDIX II: DOCUMENTS

Document 1: Diagram of the Foreign Affairs System

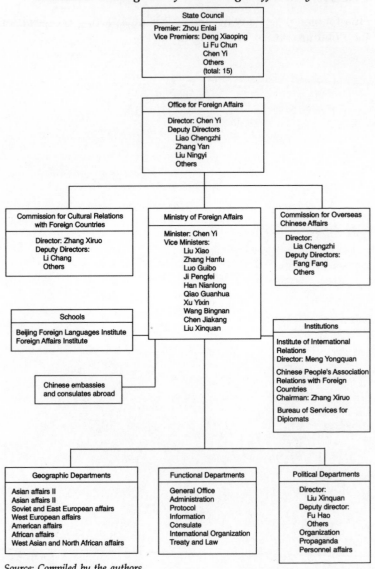

State Council

Premier: Zhou Enlai
Vice Premiers: Deng Xiaoping
　　　　　　 Li Fu Chun
　　　　　　 Chen Yi
　　　　　　 Others
　　　　　　 (total: 15)

Office for Foreign Affairs

Director: Chen Yi
Deputy Directors
　Liao Chengzhi
　Zhang Yan
　Liu Ningyi
　Others

Commission for Cultural Relations with Foreign Countries

Director: Zhang Xiruo
Deputy Directors:
　Li Chang
　Others

Ministry of Foreign Affairs

Minister: Chen Yi
Vice Ministers:
　Liu Xiao
　Zhang Hanfu
　Luo Guibo
　Ji Pengfei
　Han Nianlong
　Qiao Guanhua
　Xu Yixin
　Wang Bingnan
　Chen Jiakang
　Liu Xinquan

Commission for Overseas Chinese Affairs

Director:
　Lia Chengzhi
Deputy Directors:
　Fang Fang
　Others

Schools

Beijing Foreign Languages Institute
Foreign Affairs Institute

Institutions

Institute of International Relations
Director: Meng Yongquan

Chinese People's Association Relations with Foreign Countries
Chairman: Zhang Xiruo

Bureau of Services for Diplomats

Chinese embassies and consulates abroad

Geographic Departments

Asian affairs II
Asian affairs II
Soviet and East European affairs
West European affairs
American affairs
African affairs
West Asian and North African affairs

Functional Departments

General Office
Administration
Protocol
Information
Consulate
International Organization
Treaty and Law

Political Departments

Director:
　Liu Xinquan
Deputy director:
　Fu Hao
　Others
Organization
Propaganda
Personnel affairs

Source: Compiled by the authors.

138

Document 2: 'A preliminary assessment of the possibility of war'

[Excerpts of the report to Mao by a special group headed by Chen Yi, the Foreign Minister, 11 July 1969; edited by Xiong Xianghui, Beijing, *Liaowang*, August 1992]

1. The confrontation between the three big powers: China, the United States and the Soviet Union

The class struggle between the two classes (the proletariat and the bourgeoisie) internationally is demonstrated in a very concise way by the contention between the three big powers. The rivalry between China, the US and the USSR is different from that between the seven powers before the Second World War, or from the confrontation between the US and the USSR in the post-war years. China represents the basic interests of the proletariat throughout the world, while the American imperialists and the Soviet revisionists are representatives of different brands of international capitalism. The two of them, on the one hand, regard China as their enemy but, on the other hand, they regard each other as enemies. As for China, it is still a 'potential threat' in Richard Nixon's view, but not yet a realistic one.

The US imperialists and the Soviet revisionists constitute a real threat to each other. They are a real threat to other countries as well. The US imperialists and the Soviet revisionists collude as well as fight with each other, often under the guise of opposing China. The contradictions between them have not eased on account of their collusion. On the contrary, they have become more acute.

All other countries, either under the influence of the US or of the USSR, do not represent a force to challenge the two big powers. Their attitude to China is based on their own interests. A few of them, following the footsteps of the US imperialists and Soviet revisionists, are hostile to China but most of them act differently from the US and USSR. Some of them have employed dual tactics; some of them have played the role of onlookers; some of them are friendly to China because they are opposed to the dominance and oppression of US imperialism and Soviet revisionism; they are dissatisfied with US imperialists and Soviet revisionists who have divided the world into different spheres of influence. Some of them have even shown their opposition openly. While China becomes increasingly stronger and the US imperialists and Soviet revisionists continuously weaker, more countries will come out into the open to oppose the US and the USSR. It will be increasingly difficult for the US imperialists and the Soviet revisionists to form a united front against China and to find someone to serve them militarily.

2. An assessment of the possibilities of a major war against China

We are of the opinion that there is no great possibility for the US imperialists or the Soviet revisionists to launch a large-scale war against China in the foreseeable future either independently or jointly. For the following reasons, the US imperialists will not readily start a war against China:

(a) The two countries are separated by the vast Pacific Ocean. The US has been defeated twice, namely in the Korean War and in the Vietnam War. As a result, they have been confronted with a lot more difficulties both internally and externally. Since they learned a lesson from the two wars they have made it clear that they would not take part in a similar war. Furthermore, China is neither Korea nor Vietnam and the US wouldn't start a war with China lightly.
(b) The strategic focus of the US lies in the West. Having mired themselves in South Vietnam, the US found its position in the West weakened to a large extent. A war with China would be a protracted one with awful consequences. The US wouldn't fight a war individually against China since this would only benefit the USSR.
(c) It would be ideal for the US imperialists to have the Asians at the forefront against China and especially to use the Japanese as the vanguard. The Japanese have suffered defeat in the war against China which now is far more strong than before. This would stop the Japanese reactionaries from going to war with China easily. Since the Japanese refuse to be the gunpowder in an anti-Chinese war, the US imperialists would not rashly fight a war with China all by themselves.

The Soviet revisionists, who regard China as their chief enemy, constitute a more serious menace to our national security than anybody else. They have been creating tension, massing huge armed forces and launching armed intrusions along the Sino-Soviet borders. They have spared no efforts in making anti-Chinese propaganda internationally and have left nothing undone to draw Asian countries over to their side in their attempt to form an anti-Chinese encirclement. These are indeed the most serious steps taken by the Soviet revisionists in their preparation for an aggressive war against China. But when it comes to a major war in concrete terms against China, the Soviet revisionists have a lot of hesitations and difficulties because:

(a) Both China and the US consider the Soviet revisionists as their enemy. The Soviet revisionists do not dare to fight on two fronts at the same time. The US imperialists deliberately remain aloof from the Sino-Soviet differences, making no comment and claiming non-interference. But, in reality, they are using tactics of relaxation with the Soviet revisionists in the West with the aim of pushing the latter to the forefront of a major anti-Chinese war in the East. The US imperialists will watch with folded arms until both China and the Soviet Union become exhausted, before they take over Eastern Europe, or even push forward deep into the heart of the Soviet Union.

(b) If the Soviet revisionists decided to launch a large-scale attack against China, they would prefer to fight a quick war, or else they would follow the Japanese with their policy of nibbling away at Chinese territory. But, once they start the war, we absolutely shall not let them fight a war of quick decision. We shall give them no breathing space, and we shall allow them no freedom of activities. We are going to fight a protracted war to the very end.

The Soviet revisionists have a lot of difficulties. First, a war against China will be very unpopular. They have cheated their people with the excuse of 'defence'. Their people will oppose them if they start the war. Secondly, the Soviets have their industries in the European part of their territory. Everything they need will have to come from Europe and there is only one railway line for transportation. Already now, the Soviet revisionists are in seriously short supply of daily necessities. A war will make things worse. Third, one has to have a secure rear area if one goes to war. The Soviet revisionists do not have secure rear areas because of class contradictions and contradictions between the different nationalities [living in their territories].

A prolonged war against China can only make the contradictions worse. Moving Soviet armed forces towards the east does not necessarily mean that their strategic focus has also moved to the East. The strategic focus of the Soviet revisionists remains in Europe.

Is there a danger of a sudden nuclear attack on us from the US imperialists or from the Soviet revisionists? We shall be fully prepared for this possibility. But nuclear weapons are not to be used easily; to threaten other countries with the use of nuclear weapons will put one's own country in danger from nuclear weapons too, and will provoke strong opposition from one's own people. Even if nuclear weapons are used, people with indomitable will will not be conquered.

In the final analysis, the outcome of war is decided by the ground forces. Nuclear weapons cannot save the lives of the imperialists or the revisionists.

Judging from the present situation, it can be gauged that it is difficult for the US imperialists or the Soviet revisionists to wage a war against China either individually or together, or by ganging up with Japan and India. They are trumpeting about a war against China. In reality everybody knows that China cannot be bullied easily. Whoever comes into China will have difficulties in getting out. Either the US imperialists or the Soviet revisionists would like the other party to fight it out with China, so that they themselves would benefit from the result. We shall be ready for them to come either individually or jointly. In either case we will thoroughly smash the aggressors.

Document 3: *Our view of the current situation*

[Excerpts of a report by Chen Yi and his group to Mao Zedong, 17 September 1969, edited by Xiong Xianghui, Beijing, *Liaowang*, August 1992]

The central issue of the complicated international class struggle is the struggle between the three big powers: China, the US and the USSR.

A big question now is whether the Soviet revisionists are going to attack our country on a large scale. The Soviet revisionists are brandishing their swords, the American imperialists are adding fuel to the fire, and we are intensifying our efforts in war preparation. It is at this particular moment that Kosygin made a detour to come to China to express hopes for the relaxation of the situation at the border and for the improvement of relations between the two countries.[1]

The real motives of the Soviets should be studied carefully. The Soviet revisionists indeed have the intention of starting a war of aggression against China. Their strategic aim is to partition the world into spheres of influence between themselves and the US imperialists. They are vainly attempting to make China a part of their empire. Quite recently, they have intensified their anti-Chinese war propaganda, voiced nuclear threats against us and plotted a sudden strike on our nuclear installations. All this shows that a group of adventurists among the Soviet revisionist leading clique is planning a quick war against us in an attempt to destroy us by relying on their superiority in missiles and in tanks and by taking advantage of the fact that the Cultural Revolution in our country is still going on, that our nuclear weapons are still in the stage of development, and the war in Vietnam has not yet come to an end.

Although the Soviet revisionists have the intention of waging a war of aggression against China and have made military arrangements accordingly, they have not yet made the decision politically, because a war against China is a matter of life and death and the Soviets are not sure of the outcome. The political decision for Soviet aggression against China depends to a large extent on the United States. Up till now the US imperialists have not made things easier for them. On the contrary, they have handicapped the Soviet revisionists to a large extent. The US imperialists would not like to see a victory of the Soviet revisionists in a Sino-Soviet War resulting in the emergence of a huge empire possessing richer natural resources and more manpower than the United States. The US imperialists have often expressed their willingness to improve their relations with China, this has become particularly clear prior to and after Nixon's visit to Asia.

The Soviet revisionists are very much concerned with the possibility of an alliance [between China] and the US imperialists, against them. The fact that the Soviet revisionists are in a state of panic was demonstrated by the delivery of a statement of the Council of Ministers of the USSR to our government on the 26th of July, the day when Nixon set off to visit Asia.

Their hesitation in attacking China has been greatly enhanced by their concern with a possible alliance between China and the US. It is for this and other reasons that the Soviet revisionists do not dare to launch a war against China.

Document 4: 'Ultra-left ideology interferes with Chinese foreign policy'

[Excerpts of Zhou Enlai's talk with Ne Win, Prime Minister of Burma on 7 August 1971 in Beijing; in: *Zhou Enlai Waijiao Wenxuan*, Beijing, Central Documention Press, 1990]

This morning, Your Excellency mentioned the events in 1967. They are indeed, just as Your Excellency put it, very sad. The border questions had not much to do with these events. Your visit to the United States gave rise to some comments here, but they did not impress me much.

You understand that, in 1967, the Great Proletarian Cultural Revolution was going on in our country. At that time, there existed some ultra-left ideology, your new ambassador might have learned more about that later. The immediate cause of the 1967 incidents was the fact that the Chinese ethnic students (in Burma) wore Chairman Mao's badge. This gave rise to conflicts. Our embassy in Burma got involved. A few dozens of people got killed and many more ethnic Chinese were arrested.

Our government then believed that the best thing to do would be to confine the matter to the scope of government negotiations. We began with a note of protest including a 5-point demand from the Chinese embassy to the Foreign Ministry of your country. This was followed by a Foreign Ministry statement of our country in support of the demands put forward in the protest note. *The People's Daily* published a few articles and news dispatches about the matter. By then the Cultural Revolution was at a peak. In several days more than a million demonstrators passed by the gate of your embassy. In Rangoon the Chinese embassy was broken into and people were injured. We were afraid that similar violence would take place (in Beijing). I telephoned the Foreign Ministry and the Beijing Garrison and succeeded in preventing any further deterioration of the situation. Fortunately what I said still counted so that your embassy was protected. At another time, in early July, masses of people, who were then under the influence of ultra-left ideology and manipulated by bad persons, tried to break into the Foreign Ministry and the Burmese embassy after holding a meeting. Again I stopped them. Other things happened in August. The Foreign Ministry was also influenced by ultra-left ideology and bad persons who got into the Ministry and seized power there. The masses of the people surrounded the office of the British Chargé d'Affaires. I knew nothing beforehand. When we learned about it, it was already too late, the office was on fire. We gave orders to the people to leave, but those bad persons refused to listen. One interesting thing is that the British Chargé d'Affaires had heard our broadcast [the broadcast tried to persuade the red guards not to break into the British Mission]. Believing that it was the Chinese government's view [that the mission should not be attacked], he went to seek protection from the Liberation Army; as a result, he was not injured. There were bad persons behind the two incidents, the one to try to break into the Burmese embassy and the other to burn down the office of the British of Chargé d'Affaires. They intended to disrupt our foreign relations. In addition, things happened to our embassies abroad too, that is, they sent out notes of protest on important political issues without seeking approval from the Foreign Ministry at home. It is unprecedented that our embassy sent notes of protest to your Ministry of Foreign Affairs without the prior approval of the Foreign Ministry.

Our Foreign Ministry was also influenced by ultra-left ideology. We tried to control the situation and to maintain our relations with Burma. Our experts stayed in Burma though they had little to do. In October 1967, you told them to go home. They came back home in early November and the relations between our two countries became very tense. On May Day at the tower gate of the Tiananmen Square last year, Chairman Mao asked your Chargé d'Affaires to transmit his regards to Your Excellency. Your Excellency also took some steps [for the improvement of relations]. Consequently, things changed for the better.

I am talking about all this to say that the policy of our government has been clear. This is the main aspect. There was interference of ultra-left ideology in 1967. In the Cultural Revolution, things could be rectified if it was only a matter of ultra-left ideology among young people. The problem was that there were bad persons who had made use of the opportunities to manipulate the mass movement, to split the mass movement and to disrupt our foreign relations. Only when things were fully exposed, could bad persons be discovered. Once they were discovered, they were no longer able to function.

Luckily the Sino-Burmese relations did not deteriorate further. Our relations with Britain went from bad to worse and these bad relations lasted much longer. . . . More damage was been done to Sino-British relations. Similar problems occurred in our relations with other countries. I am not going into details today. Maybe we can talk more about our Cultural Revolution another time.

Document 5: *Selection of Mao Zedong's statements on foreign affairs (Mao Zedong waijiao wenxuan)*

[Published by the Foreign Ministry of the People's Republic of China and the Central Research Institute for Documentation, Beijing, Central Documentation Publishing House and World Knowledge Publishing House, 1994]

Support Vietnam's policy of war and negotiations

[Main part of Mao Zedong's talk with the Vietnamese Premier of the Democratic Republic, Pham Van Dong, 17 November 1968. Based on the minutes of the original talk.]

Because recently you did not have a war to fight, you are considering negotiations with the US. Negotiations are alright, but you will not get the Americans out just by talks. The US also want to negotiate with you because they are in a considerably difficult situation. They have problems in three areas. One is the area of the Western Hemisphere, another is Europe and the third is Asia. Although, since many years, the Americans have sent large numbers of troops to Asia, the balance has been disrupted. In this respect, the American capitalists investing in Western Europe are not satisfied. At the same time, the US has a history of always letting other countries fight, while they participate only halfway. Since the Second World War, the US first started the Korean War, afterwards they attacked Vietnam. They took the lead while other countries hardly participated.

No matter to what special or local warfare they refer, so far as the US are concerned, they go all for it. At this time they do not take other countries into account. For example their troops stationed in Europe complain that there are too few of them. Experienced soldiers and leading commanders have been removed, and valuable military equipment was also moved (to Vietnam). Have their troops, whether stationed in Japan, Korea or in other Asian countries, not all been withdrawn (to Vietnam)? Is not that their own country has a population of 200 million? But they do not have the guts to fight. They mobilize several hundreds of thousands of soldiers, but their military strength is very limited.

You have been fighting for 10 odd years. So do not simply look at your difficulties, look at those of your enemy. Since Japan's surrender in 1945, already 24 years have past and your country has survived. Three imperialist countries have invaded you, namely Japan, France and America. Nonetheless, your country still exists, now it has to develop.

Imperialism is certainly aggressive. Its aim is first to put down the revolution. You have made revolution, they want to put it down. Secondly, they fight for the interests of those who produce weapons, since in order to put down the revolution it is necessary to manufacture war machinery. The Americans have to spend more than US$ 30 billion on your country every year.

The US have regularly shown their unwillingness to fight a long war. Generally their wars have lasted more or less four years. In your case, it is impossible to eliminate the revolution – on the contrary, it must become even stronger. The capitalists are divided, one group will benefit more than another. The unevenly divided spoils cause internal troubles. Such contradictions can be used to your advantage. Those monopolistic capitalists who make relatively little money are unwilling to really persevere in fighting. This question can be understood from the speeches made by the two American candidates for election. The US have a journalist by the name of Walter Lipman. In his latest article he held the view that a defense must be put up against pitfalls. He wrote that, in Vietnam, there surely must be a pitfall, the present problem is to think of a way to climb out of it. He also fears that the US might fall into other traps. Therefore your cause is very hopeful.

In 1966, I had talks with Chairman Ho Chi Minh in Hang-zhou. At this time, the US had already attacked North Vietnam, but they had not yet resumed bombing. I said, the US will probably have enough of fighting this year, because it is America's election year. Notwithstanding which president will come to office, there will be only one problem: will he continue to fight or will he withdraw? In my view, to continue to fight will considerably increase their problems. No European country has participated in the fighting. This is not the same as in the Korean War. Japan will probably also not participate in the war, but it is possible that they will help economically; to produce war material brings profits. In my view, the Americans by far overestimated their own strength. Today's Americans still use methods of the past, they scattered their armed forces. It is not only we who said this, but Nixon also did. Not only are the military forces scattered in the Western Hemisphere and in Europe, but also in Asia. In the past I did not believe that the US would attack North Vietnam, but then they bombed North Vietnam, so I was wrong. At this time they do not bomb it, so I am right. The US promised that they will resume the bombing, so I might be wrong again. But I think there will be one day when I am right, they have to call off the bombing. Therefore, in my opinion, it is good for you to have made several plans.

In sum, in the past years, American ground forces did not attack North Vietnam, they did not blockade your Haiphong and they also did not bomb the urban district of Hanoi. They have something in reserve. Sometimes they talk about 'hot pursuit', but your airplanes, taking off from our country, fly back and forth. The Americans do not practise 'hot pursuit'. Therefore they speak empty words. Your airplanes come and go from our airfields but the Americans do not say a word. There is another example: they realize that many Chinese are working in your country, but there is not one word about it. It seems that these things do not exist at all. As for those people of ours who are with you but are kept in reserve, they could be withdrawn. Did you discuss this question among yourselves? If the enemy comes again, we just come back. You think it over, who should stay, who should not stay. Those who are useful to you should stay, those who are not useful should withdraw. If they will be useful in the future, they may go back. This is the same principle as your aircraft using Chinese airfields or not; if they need them they use them, if not, they do not use them. Generally speaking, this is how we should proceed.

I support your policy of war and negotiations. We have a few comrades who fear that the US might fool you. I do not see it that way. Are negotiations and war not the same? In the course of war, you gain experience and you obtain an objective pattern. Sometimes it is unavoidable to be fooled. Just as you say, Americans do not mean what they say. Johnson once say publicly, sometimes even treaties do not mean anything. But matters always follow a rule. As for your negotiations, for example, can one say you have to negotiate for 100 years? Our premier said: 'If Nixon talks for two years but does not solve any problems, then, if he becomes president again, there will be difficulties.'

There is still another matter. The South Vietnamese puppet government is very much afraid of the South Vietnamese liberation front. In America, some people say, the really effective and influential force among the South Vietnamese people is not the South Vietnamese government but the National Liberation Front. This is not mentioned in the American Congress, but reported by journalists. The name of whoever said this was not quoted; it was only said that it was a well-known American government official. This statement raises one question, namely which government in South Vietnam really has prestige? Is it the one headed by Nguyen van Thien or the one of Nguyen Hun Tho? In name, the US is praising Nguyen Van Thien to the sky; and said that he does not go to Paris to participate in the negotiations. In fact, this is not true. The Americans know that without the participation of the South Vietnamese liberation front in the negotiations, the question will not be solved.

International matters must be decided through consultation with everybody

[Excerpts of Mao Zedong's talk with a French delegation, 13 July 1970]

In today's world there is no stability. On the one hand you have your love for independence, on the other hand there are people who want to disturb you. In my last talk with you I said that in this world there are a few countries who like to interfere with other countries independence. You might say, there is no

Hitler, Japanese imperialism has also been defeated, France is independent, China is also liberated. But there is still no peace in the world today. Of course, today nobody will invade France, and, with the exception of Taiwan, nobody will invade China. But I must tell you, we have to be prepared for a fight. Not that we will originate it, but once other countries come out to invade us, we have to eliminate them. Now the situation is not the same as it was a few decades ago when anybody could shit and piss on China's head.

With the exception of the type of defence as the Maginot line and the atomic bomb, it is necessary to prepare other methods such as civil defense. You know the changes which have taken place in the world. We are the not chief of staff of some of the big countries [to be able to make decisions for them] You are also bullied by other countries.

In the present situation in Europe, it seems to me that it is difficult for you or England to start a war. The so-called allies are not necessarily allies. They might agree with each other on a certain question, but they might not be able to agree on another issue. For us, discussions have been easier; discussions with the United States and the Soviet Union would be rather difficult. France has never occupied a part of China, and China has never occupied France's Corsica.

World affairs must be discussed. Internal affairs have to be decided by the country's own people, international matters have to be talked over and decided by everybody, they cannot be decided by two big countries.

'Do not seek foreigners' recognition of Chinese thinking.

[These are Mao Zedong's written comments on a memorandum submitted by the Liaison Office of the Party Centre, 6 December 1970]

Concerning certain foreigners, one should not seek their recognition of Chinese thinking. One should only expect their recognition of the combination of the universal truth of Marxism-Leninism with the concrete practice of their own national revolution. This is a fundamental principle. I have said this many times before. As for their thinking, if in addition to Marxism-Leninism, there is some unhealthy ideology, they have to sort it out themselves. We should not consider this as a serious problem and talk with our foreign comrades about it.

We must look at the lessons we learned through the mistakes of line our party has committed in the course of its history, then we progressively reached the right path. Besides, there are still other questions. Internally and externally there is a threat of great power chauvinism which we must overcome, only then can we understand.

'If Nixon is willing to come, I am willing to talk to him.'

[Mao's talk with the American writer Edgar Snow, 18 December 1970]

We are happy that Nixon has come to power. Why? He is deceiving, but less than others. Do you also believe that? He was very tough on you, but sometimes he can also be soft. If he wants to come to Beijing, give him the following message: say, he might come secretly; there is no need for publicity, he might just board a plane and come. If our talks are not successful, that's alright; if they are successful that's alright. There is no need for rigidity. But you Americans are unable to keep secrets; it cannot be kept secret, when a president leaves the country. It would certainly make a great deal noise if he wanted to come to China, it would be said that his objective is to draw closer to China and to repel the Soviet Union. Therefore, he does not yet dare to act like this. To repel the Soviet Union, at this time, does not bring any advantage to the United States, but neither does the rejection of China.

Presently we have a policy which forbids Americans to come to China. Is this a correct policy? The Foreign Ministry should examine this question. Left-, centre-, right-wing people should all come. Why let right-wingers come? As fas as Nixon is concerned, he is the representative of monopoly capitalists. But he should certainly be permitted to come because centrists and left wingers alone cannot solve problems. At this time, it is Nixon who makes the decisions.

Earlier he sent letters everywhere saying that he wants to send a delegation. We did not publicize it, we kept the secret. He is not interested in the Warsaw talks, he wants to take up matters personally. Therefore I say, if Nixon is willing to come, I am willing to talk with him whatever the results may be. If we quarrel, it is alright, if we don't, it is also alright. It is alright to regard him as a traveller who comes to talk or as a president who comes to talk. In short, everything goes. As I see it, I will not quarrel with him, but I will criticize what needs to be criticized. We have to make our own self criticism and talk about our mistakes and shortcomings, for example, our level of production is lower than the one in the US. Otherwise we do not make self criticism.

Nixon suggested himself that he wants to send a delegation to hold talks in China, there is a document to prove this. He is willing to talk face to face in Beijing or in Washington. Our Foreign Ministry does not need to know about it, neither does the American State Department need to be informed. This is very mysterious, not only should there be no publicity, but also should the news be kept completely secret.

In 1972, elections will take place in America. As I see it, in the first half of that year, Nixon might be sending people to China, he himself would not be able to come. If ever someone comes, it will be at that time. He hates to part with Taiwan, Chiang Kai-shek is not yet dead. What does the Taiwan problem have to do with him [Nixon]? It was created by Truman, Acheson and afterwards by another president with whom Nixon was involved. Afterwards there was also Kennedy. When Nixon was vice president, he ran to Taiwan. He said that Taiwan had a population of more than 10 million. I say, Asia has several 100 million people, Africa has hundred million, they are all there in revolt.

China and America have to establish relations. It cannot be possible that China and America do not establish relations in hundred years? Anyway, we still have not occupied this great island of yours.

'About the division of the world into three parts.'

[Excerpts from Mao Zedong's talks with Zambia's President Kaunda, 22 February 1974. This is Mao's first public exposition of his Three Worlds Theory]

Mao: I hope that the Third World will unite. The population of the Third World is very large.

Kaunda: This is correct.

Mao: Who represents the First World?

Kaunda: I think it should be the world of the exploiters and imperialists.

Mao: And the Second World?

Kaunda: They are those people who have already changed into revisionists.

Mao: In my view, the United States and the Soviet Union are the First World. Those in the middle of the road like Japan, Europe, Australia and Canada, are the Second World. We are the Third World.

Kaunda: I agree with the Chairman's analysis.

Mao: The United States and the Soviet Union have many atomic bombs and are also relatively rich. Europe, Japan, Australia, Canada do not have so many atomic bombs and are also not so wealthy, but still richer than the Third World. Do you think this is a good explanation?

Kaunda: Mr Chairman, your analysis is very true, extremely precise.

Mao: Study this a bit.

Kaunda: I think it is not necessary to study this further. We have identical views, because as I see it, this analysis is certainly very correct.

Mao: The population of the Third World is very large.

Kaunda: This is really so.

Mao: Asia with the exception of Japan belongs to the Third World, The entire continent of Africa belongs to the Third World, so does Latin America.

'No Sino-American war'

[Excerpts from Mao Zedong's talk with Richard Nixon, 21 February, 1972]

The possibility of aggression from the United States, or from China, is comparatively small. Or it can be said that it is not a big question, because there are no problems which might lead our two countries into a war against each other. You are ready to move some of your troops back home, we are not going to send our troops out of the country. It is indeed strange that our two countries did not get along in the past 22 years. It is only 10 months since we have had contacts with each other, we started with playing ping-pong. It's two years and more if we count from the time when you made the suggestion in Warsaw. On our side, we have the problem of bureaucracy. So we were deadly opposed to your suggestions to have personnel exchanges or to do some small business. For more than ten years, we, myself included, insisted that we were not going to deal with any small problems if major issues remained unresolved. Then it was found that it was you who were right, therefore we began to play ping-pong.

We began to know each other through the introduction of the former President of Pakistan. At that time, our Ambassador to Pakistan was firmly opposed to any contacts with you. He suggested a comparison between the former Democratic President L. B. Johnson, and yourself, to see who is better. We, on our side, were not so happy with President Johnson. From Truman to Johnson, we were not so happy, although for eight years in between there was a Republican President. But at that time you were not ready either.

'Make a feint to the East but attack in the West'

[Excerpts from Mao's talk with French Foreign Minister M. Schuman, 10 July 1972]

It is chaotic in Europe, isn't it? When I say 'chaotic', I mean there are US$ 60 billion running amuck in Europe which are inconvertible. Alas, I think things are pretty hard. The United States represent hegemonism, but there is the Atlantic Ocean between it and Europe. Big powers are bound to be at odds with one another. We don't want you Europeans in a chaos. But you must take care. The policy of the Soviet Union is to make a feint to the East but to attack in the West. They talk profusely about attacking China, but in reality they want to swallow Europe. It is dangerous.

'Sino-Japanese diplomatic relations'

[Excerpts from Mao's talk with Japanese Prime Minister Tanaka, 27 September 1972]

You came to Beijing and the whole world seemed to be panic-stricken. In particular, the two big powers, the USSR and the USA, are not at ease. What plot are you up to there!?

It is not that much to the US, but still, they do not feel quite comfortable. They came here in February this year without establishing diplomatic relationship [with China]. You went beyond them, therefore they are not quite happy.

Sometimes questions remain unresolved for decades or hundred years, and then can be settled in a matter of days.

Now we have the mutual need to solve questions, this is what President Nixon told me. He asked me, whether there was such a need. I said, there was. I said, I had the bad reputation of ganging up with the rightists. [I told him] there are two parties in your country. It was said that the Democrats are much more liberal, and that the Republicans are oriented towards the right. I said the Democrats are just so so, I don't like them, I am not interested in them. I told Nixon that I voted for him when he was campaigning, but he didn't know that.

This time we voted for you. Just as you said, if you the boss of the Free Democratic Party had not come to China, how could we resolve the problem of resumption of Sino-Japanese diplomatic relations?

Therefore somebody accused us to collude with the rightists. I said, your opposition in Japan cannot resolve problems, to resolve the problem of resumption of Sino-Japanese diplomatic relations, we have to deal with the Free Democratic Government.

Document 6: Wang Li's talk with a delegation representing the liaison station of the Foreign Ministry.

[*Waishi, Feuglei* (Events in Foreign Relations) 7 August 1967 Beijing, August 1967]

After some preliminaries concerning the Wuhan Event and Chen Yi, Wang Li talks about the Cultural Revolution movement in the Foreign Ministry, saying that it is generally assumed that foreign affairs are very complicated and have to be handled by experts in the field of which there are only a few. In his view, internal matters of the red guards are even more complicated. So why should red guards not be able to handle foreign affairs? He then inquires about two other rebel organizations in the Foreign Ministry, named 'Climbing the Dangerous Peak' and the 'Revolutionary Headquarters' and their political tendencies. From the explanations he receives it is clear that there are two opposing tendencies in the Foreign Ministry. The first is represented by the two above-mentioned organizations and the second by the liaison station. They disagree on some key issues which are then under debate, namely the assessment of Chen Yi's policies and the extent and efficiency of the power seizure in the Foreign Ministry.

Wang Li: In January you seized power, but how much power did you seize? How large is your supervisory capacity? Can you supervise? The office of the Party committee has not moved? The revolution did not remove it? What kind of great revolution is this if it is alright to leave it in place? Why can you not remove it? . . . Did the Premier not talk about the 'cooperation between the three age groups the old, middle aged and the young'? Why then can the Foreign Ministry not practice this principle?

The representative of the liaison station explains that some department heads, after reading certain documents, draw a circle on the paper. In one case, the person just noted 'what to do?' on the document and passed it on to vice ministers who also drew circles. The document went around with only 'What to do?' written on it.

Wang Li: These are the bureaucrats . . .

Why did you retreat? Before, you moved forward, now you have stopped and do not move. You did not think seriously about what you want to do in the next period?!

Liaison Station: During the rectification campaign [June–July 1967], some people criticized our seizure of power for having gone too far. They said that foreign affairs are the domain of the centre.

Wang Li: This is not true. General principles governing foreign policy are concentrated in the hands of the centre, in the hands of the Chairman. One cannot separate revolution and professional activity. If your seizure of power modifies general policy principles, then it is not correct. According to central policy principles it is a different question, how such principles are implemented and how they are used. If you say that the power in the personnel department cannot be changed, this implies the restoration of the Central Organization Department which held the largest personnel department in its hands.

You have to fully use your supervisory power. The personnel department also has to be supervised, the line of the cadres has to be the guarantee of the political line. To choose cadres will then mean one chooses revolutionaries, not conservatives. To avoid unreasonable choice of cadres, you have to use your supervisory power even more. To choose cadres to go outside the country and to function properly, the first condition is to establish whether they are revolutionaries or not, whether they support Chairman Mao's revolutionary line or not. If this condition is not fulfilled completely, if it is not considered, if you think only about rank, experience and position, this approach has to be completely rejected.

A person in his 20s can serve as the head of a central department; Chairman Mao said, why should that not be possible? A person of that age can go out to do the work of a leader. Our comrades of the small group [the Central Cultural Revolution Group, CCRG], Qi Benyu and Yao Wenyuan are in their 30s. If a person does not fulfil this most important condition, then no matter what position, what grade he has, who to represent outside? Will he represent Chairman Mao or Liu Shaoqi and Deng Xiaoping? In my view, you have not seized power well, if you have some power, then you also have prestige. To go abroad, they [the conservatives] consider only position and grade but not whether they support Chairman Mao or Liu Shaoqi. This is not possible. This shows the discrepancy between the principle and its application. If it is like this, we do not need the revolution. The revolutionary must choose and verify the persons who go abroad. Our revolutionaries must first see where a person stands. If you do not participate in the revolution, even if you have a certain position or a long experience, you do not qualify. Of course, we must also be responsible for all aspects of examination and guarantee that there will be no mistakes. In my view, in the Foreign Ministry the old staff still predominates. The rebels are not against old people. But in order to implement the policy principles decided by the centre and the Chairman, it is better to combine the three groups of old, middle-aged and young people in which the revolutionary rebels should play the major role, and where everybody contributes his ideas. In foreign affairs, we need to choose some 'heads', but this does not mean that they have to be the same as before, they should be those who are active revolutionaries. The new staff has to firmly criticize the 'three capitulations and one elimination' (*san xiang yi mie*)[1] and implement Chairman Mao's line. You have to remember a fundamental demarcation line which is whether Chairman Mao's revolutionary line is supported or opposed. Whatever is not in accordance with this principle has to be criticized' ...

Wang Li: Why are you so civilized? This is a revolution. Why can people who are not working, read documents? Why should rebels not be able to read documents? If their work requires it, they should read them. Why can only those who oppose Mao read documents? That is a joke ...

Talking about a complaint the conservatives of the Foreign Ministry had made Wang Li say:

Actually some people transmitted their disagreement to the Premier and to the 'small group'. This proves that after one year of Cultural Revolution there still are people in the Foreign Ministry who think that this is not normal ... I am clearly against the actions of the 'Revolutionary Headquarters' [a conservative organization] ...

Concerning the Foreign Minister Chen Yi, Wang Li says:

Chen Yi has to come to the masses to be criticized, this is the Premier's and the CCRG's common suggestion. They do not want to find a pretext to create a split. I am talking like that because I do not want to believe just your side. We did not know the Headquarters (*Zhong bu*) very well. Now they introduced themselves in their letter. We often discovered problems because of complaints. We do not approve of this letter ... This kind of action is wrong, this kind of view is wrong ...

Talking about the oppression felt by the rebels during the rectification campaign in June–July 1967, Wang Li says: 'The rectification campaign must increase the self confidence of the rebels; it must eliminate the defects, but not their self confidence.'

The Liaison Station: Our station has existed only for a little more than half a year, the rectification campaign used up almost three months, we made self criticism three times.

Wang Li: Why did you need to make self criticism? They [the conservatives] have so many serious problems, but they never made self criticism. In the future, if you gather some material about them, please send it to us. I have said for a long time that I want to talk to you, but problems in other provinces were more urgent. Chairman Mao and the premier said that I should intervene in the Foreign Ministry, this was said in the Chairman's place. But I did not have the time, I could not follow this up, the problems in other provinces had to be solved before. Every day I also have to handle the media. The CCRG always supported the revolutionary faction. Did you really go too far? I cannot see it. I did not ask you to go too far, to 'attack, break, rob' (*da, za, qiang*). We firmly oppose '*da za qiang*' . We support a thorough revolution, the thorough carrying out of Chairman Mao's line, and the elimination of *san xiang yi mie*. The supervisory group cannot be a vase and a decoration. You must really supervise and have your own opinion on important issues. Your opinion could be right or not. All important issues related to principles you have to submit to the party centre ...

When the Headquarters sent its complaint, we realized that their problem is serious. We can give you our position: we do not approve of the Headquarters, their views are not correct ... As for us, we firmly support you.

Document 7: Irresistible Historical Trends

Statement of the Government of the People's Republic of China (October 29, 1971)

At its 26th Session, the General Assembly of the United Nations adopted on October 25, 1971 by an overwhelming majority the resolution put forward by Albania, Algeria and 21 other countries demanding the restoration of all the lawful rights of China in the United Nations and the immediate expulsion of the representatives of the Chiang Kai-shek clique from the United Nations and all the organizations related to it. This represents the bankruptcy of the policy of depriving China of her legitimate rights in the United Nations obdurately pursued by US imperialism over the past 20 years and more and of the US imperialist scheme to create 'two Chinas' in the United Nations. This is a victory of Chairman Mao Tsetung's proletarian revolutionary line in foreign affairs and a victory for the people of the whole world and all the countries upholding justice.

The Governments of Albania, Algeria and the other sponsor countries have made outstanding contributions in this struggle. Many friendly countries, especially the Royal Government of Cambodia under the leadership of Samdech Norodom Sihanouk, have over a long period of time made unremitting efforts for and played an important role in the restoration of the legitimate rights of our country in the United Nations. The Chinese Government and people express their hearty thanks to the governments and people of all the friendly countries which uphold principle and justice.

The outcome of the voting at the present session of the UN General Assembly reflects the general trend of the peoples of the world *desiring friendship with the Chinese people*. At the same time, it indicates that the one or two superpowers are *losing ground daily in engaging in truculent* acts of imposing their own will on other countries and manipulating the United Nations and international affairs. All countries, big or small, should be equal; the affairs of a country must be handled by its own people; the affairs of the world must be handled by all the countries of the world; the affairs of the United Nations must be handled jointly by all its member states – this is the irresistible trend of history in the world today. The restoration of the legitimate rights of the People's Republic of China in the United Nations is a manifestation of this trend.

However, *not reconciled to their defeat*, the US and Japanese reactionaries are continuing to spread the *fallacy* that 'the status of Taiwan remains to be determined' and are *frenziedly* pushing their scheme of creating 'an independent Taiwan' in a wild attempt to continue to create 'one China, one Taiwan' which is in effect *tantamount* to 'two Chinas'. While instigating the representatives of the Chiang Kai-shek clique to hang on in some specialized agencies of the United Nations, they are even vainly attempting to let the Chiang Kai-shek clique *worm its way back* into the United Nations under the name of a so-called 'independent Taiwan'. This is a desperate struggle put up by them, and their scheme must never be allowed to succeed. The just resolution adopted by the UN General Assembly must be speedily implemented *in its entirety*. All the representatives of the Chiang Kai-shek clique must be expelled from the United Nations Organization and all its bodies and related agencies.

Aggression and interference in other's internal affairs are *incompatible with* the UN Charter. The Government of the People's Republic of China and the Chinese people have consistently opposed the imperialist policies of aggression and war and supported the oppressed nations and peoples in their just struggles to win national liberation, oppose foreign interference and become masters of their own destinies. The Chinese people have suffered enough from imperialist oppression. China will never be a superpower bullying other countries. The Government of the People's Republic of China will soon send its representatives to take part in the work of the United Nations. The People's Republic of China will stand together with all the countries and peoples that love peace and justice and, together with them, struggle for the defence of the national independence and state sovereignty of various countries and the cause of safeguarding international peace and promoting human progress.

Speech by Chiao Kuan-Hua, chairman of the delegation of the People's Republic of China, at the plenary meeting of the 26th session of the UN General Assembly (November 15, 1971)

Mr President,

Fellow Representatives,

First of all, allow me, in the name of the Delegation of the People's Republic of China, to thank Mr President and the representatives of many countries for the welcome they have given us.

Many friends have made very enthusiastic speeches expressing their trust in as well as encouragement and fraternal sentiments for the Chinese people. We are deeply moved by this, and we shall convey all this to the entire Chinese people.

It is a pleasure for the Delegation of the People's Republic of China to be here today to attend the 26th Session of the General Assembly of the United Nations and take part together with you in the work of the United Nations.

As is known to all, China is one of the founding members of the United Nations. In 1949, the Chinese people overthrew the reactionary rule of the Chiang Kai-shek clique and founded the People's Republic of China. Since then, the legitimate rights of China in the United Nations should have gone to the People's Republic of China *as a matter of course*. It was only because of the obstruction by the United States Government that the People's Republic of China was deprived of its legitimate rights in the United Nations for a long time and that the Chiang Kai-shek clique long repudiated by the Chinese people was able to usurp China's lawful seat in the United Nations. This was a *gross interference in* China's internal affairs as well as a *wilful trampling on* the Charter of the United Nations. Now such an unjustifiable state of affairs has finally been *put right*.

On October 25, 1971, the current session of the General Assembly of the United Nations adopted by an overwhelming majority the resolution restoring to the People's Republic of China all its lawful rights in the United Nations and expelling *forthwith* the representatives of the Chiang Kai-shek clique from the United Nations and all the organizations related to it. This proves the bankruptcy of the policies of hostility towards the

Chinese people and of isolating and imposing a blockade on them. This is a defeat of the plan of the US Government in collusion with the *Sato government* of Japan to create 'two Chinas' in the United Nations. This is a victory for Chairman Mao Tsetung's revolutionary line in foreign affairs. This is a common victory for the people all over the world.

Upholding principle and justice, the 23 sponsor countries of the resolution, Albania, Algeria, Burma, Ceylon, Cuba, *Equatorial Guinea*, Guinea, Iraq, Mali, Mauritania, Nepal, Pakistan, the People's Democratic Republic of Yemen, the People's Republic of the Congo, Romania, *Sierra Leone*, Somalia, the Sudan, Syria, the United Republic of Tanzania, the Arab Republic of Yemen, Yugoslavia and Zambia have made unremitting and fruitful efforts to restore China's legitimate rights in the United Nations; many friendly countries which supported this resolution have also made contributions to this end. Some other countries have expressed their sympathy for China in various ways. On behalf of the Chinese Government and people, I express heartfelt thanks to the governments and people of all these countries.

Twenty-six years have elapsed since the founding of the United Nations. Twenty-six years *are but a brief span in human history,* yet during this period profound changes have taken place in the world situation. When the United Nations was first founded, there were only 51 member states and now the membership has grown to 131. Of the 80 members that joined later, the overwhelming majority are countries which achieved independence after World War II. In the past 20 years and more, the peoples of Asia, Africa and Latin America have waged *unflinching* struggles to win and safeguard national independence and oppose foreign aggression and oppression. In Europe, North America and Oceania, too, mass movements and social tides for the change of the present state of affairs are rising. An increasing number of medium and small countries are uniting to oppose the hegemony and *power politics* practised by the one or two superpowers and to fight for the right to settle their own affairs as independent and sovereign states and for equal status in international relations. Countries want independence, nations want liberation and the people want revolution, this has become an irresistible trend of history.

Human society invariably makes constant progress, and such progress is always achieved through innumerable revolutions and transformations. Take the United States, where the United Nations headquarters is situated. It was owing to the victory of the revolutionary war of 1776 led by Washington that the American people won independence. And it was owing to the great revolution of 1789 that the French people rid themselves of the yoke of feudalism. After mankind entered the 20th century, the victory of the 1917 Russian October Socialist Revolution led by the great Lenin opened up a broad path to freedom and liberation for the oppressed nations and peoples of the world. The advance of history and social progress gladden the hearts of and inspire the peoples of the world and throw into panic a handful of decadent reactionary forces who do their utmost to put up desperate struggles. They commit armed aggression against other countries, subvert the legal governments of other countries, interfere in other countries' internal affairs, subject other countries to their political, military and economic control and bully other countries at will. Since World War II, no new world war has occurred, yet local wars have never ceased. At present, the danger of a new world war still exists, but revolution is the main trend in the world today. Although there are twists and turns and reverses in the people's struggles, *adverse currents* against the people and against progress, in the final analysis, cannot hold back the main current of the continuous development of human society. The world will surely move towards progress and light, and definitely not towards reaction and darkness.

Mr President and fellow representatives,

The Chinese people have experienced untold sufferings under imperialist oppression. For one century and more, imperialism repeatedly launched wars of aggression against China and forced her to sign many unequal treaties. They divided China into their spheres of influence, plundered China's resources and exploited the Chinese people. The degree of poverty and lack of freedom suffered by the Chinese people in the past are known to all. In order to win national independence, freedom and liberation, the Chinese people, advancing wave upon wave in a dauntless spirit, waged protracted heroic struggles against imperialism and its lackeys and finally won the revolution under the leadership of their great leader Chairman Mao Tsetung and the Chinese Communist Party. Since the founding of the People's Republic of China, we, the Chinese people, *defying* the tight imperialist blockades and *withstanding* the terrific pressure *from without*, have built our country into a socialist state with *initial prosperity* by maintaining independence and keeping the initiative in our own hands and through self-reliance. It has been proved by facts that we the Chinese nation are fully capable of standing on our own feet in the family of nations.

Taiwan is a province of China and the 14 million people who live in Taiwan are our fellow-countrymen by flesh and blood. Taiwan was already returned to the motherland after World War II in accordance with the Cairo Declaration and the Potsdam Proclamation, and our compatriots in Taiwan already returned to the embrace of their motherland. The US Government officially confirmed this fact on more than one occasion in 1949 and 1950, and publicly stated that the Taiwan question was China's internal affair and that the US Government had no intention to interfere in it. It was only because of the outbreak of the Korean war that the US Government *went back on its own words* and sent armed forces to invade and occupy China's Taiwan and the Taiwan Straits, and *to date* they are still there. The spreading in certain places of the *fallacy* that 'the status of Taiwan remains to be determined' is a conspiracy to plot 'an independent Taiwan' and continue to create 'one China, one Taiwan', which is in effect to create 'two Chinas'. On behalf of the Government of the People's Republic of China, I hereby *reiterate* that Taiwan is an inalienable part of China's territory and the US armed invasion and occupation of China's Taiwan and the Taiwan Straits cannot in the least *alter* the sovereignty of the People's Republic of China over Taiwan, that all the armed forces of the United States definitely should be withdrawn from Taiwan and the Taiwan Straits and that we are firmly opposed to any *design* to separate Taiwan from the motherland. The Chinese people are determined to liberate Taiwan and no force on earth can stop us from doing so.

Mr President and fellow representatives,

The Chinese people who suffered for a long time from imperialist aggression and oppression have consistently opposed the imperialist policies of aggression and war and supported all the oppressed peoples and nations in their just struggles to win freedom and liberation, oppose foreign interference and become masters of their own destiny. This position of the Chinese Government and people is in the fundamental interests of the peoples of the world and is also in accord with the spirit of the United Nations Charter.

The US Government's armed aggression against Vietnam, Cambodia and Laos and its encroachment upon the territorial integrity and sovereignty of these three countries have aggravated tension in the Far East, and met with strong opposition of the people of the world, including the American people. The Chinese Government and people firmly support the peoples of the three countries of Indochina in their war against US aggression and for national salvation and firmly support the Joint Declaration of the Summit Conference of the Indochinese Peoples and the 7–point peace proposal put forward by the Provisional Revolutionary Government of the Republic of South Vietnam. The US Government should withdraw immediately and unconditionally all its armed forces and the armed forces of its followers from the three countries of Indochina so that the peoples of the three countries may solve their own problems independently and free from foreign interference; this is the key to the relaxation of tension in the Far East.

To date, Korea still remains divided. The Chinese People's Volunteers have long since withdrawn from Korea but up to now the US troops still remain in South Korea. The peaceful unification of their fatherland is the common aspiration of the entire Korean people. The Chinese Government and people firmly support the 8–point programme for the peaceful unification of the fatherland put forward by the Democratic People's Republic of Korea in April this year and firmly support its just demand that all the illegal resolutions adopted by the United Nations on the Korean question be *annulled* and the 'United Nations Commission for the Unification and *Rehabilitation* of Korea' be dissolved.

The essence of the Middle East question is aggression against the Palestinian and other Arab peoples by Israeli *Zionism* with the support and *connivance* of the superpowers. The Chinese Government and people resolutely support the Palestinian and other Arab peoples in their just struggle against aggression and believe that persevering in struggle and upholding unity the heroic Palestinian and other Arab peoples will surely be able to recover the lost territories of the Arab countries and restore to the Palestinian people their national rights. The Chinese Government maintains that all countries and peoples that love peace and uphold justice have the obligation to support the struggle of the Palestinian and other Arab peoples, and no one has the right to engage in political deals behind their backs bartering away their right to existence and their national interests.

The continued existence of colonialism in all its manifestations is a provocation against the peoples of the world. The Chinese Government and people resolutely support the people of Mozambique, Angola and Guinea (Bissau) in their struggle for national liberation, and resolutely support the people of Azania, Zimbabwe and Namibia in their struggle against the white colonialist rule and racial discrimination. Their struggle is a just one, and a just cause will surely triumph.

The independence of a country is *incomplete* without economic independence. The economic backwardness of the Asian, African and Latin American countries is the result of imperialist plunder. Opposition to economic plunder and protection of national resources are the inalienable sovereign rights of an independent state. China is still an economically backward country as well as a developing country. Like the overwhelming majority of the Asian, African and Latin American countries, China belongs to the Third World. The Chinese Government and people resolutely support the struggles initiated by Latin American countries and peoples to defend their rights over *200-nautical-mile territorial sea* and to protect the resources of their respective countries. The Chinese Government and people resolutely support the struggles unfolded by the petroleum-exporting countries in Asia, Africa and Latin America as well as various regional and specialized organizations to protect their national rights and interests and oppose economic plunder.

We have consistently maintained that all countries, big or small, should be equal and that the Five Principles of Peaceful Coexistence should be taken as the principles guiding the relations between countries. The people of each country have the right to choose the social system of their own country according to their own will and to protect the independence, sovereignty and territorial integrity of their own country. No country has the right to subject another country to its aggression, subversion, control, interference or bullying. We are opposed to the imperialist and colonialist theory that big nations are superior to the small nations and small nations are subordinate to the big nations. We are opposed to the power politics and hegemony of big nations bullying small ones or strong nations bullying weak ones. We hold that the affairs of a given country must be handled by its own people, that the affairs of the world must be handled by all the countries of the world, and that the affairs of the United Nations must be handled jointly by all its member states, and the superpowers should not be allowed to manipulate and monopolize them. The superpowers want to be superior to others and lord it over others. At no time, neither today nor ever in the future, will China be a superpower subjecting others to its aggression, subversion, control, interference or bullying.

The one or two superpowers are *stepping up* their arms expansion and war preparations and vigorously developing nuclear weapons, thus seriously threatening international peace. It is understandable that the people of the world *long for* disarmament and particularly for nuclear disarmament. Their demand for the dissolution of military blocs, withdrawal of foreign troops and *dismantling* of foreign military bases is a just one. However, the superpowers, while talking about disarmament every day, are actually engaged in arms expansion daily. The so-called nuclear disarmament which they are supposed to seek is entirely for the purpose of monopolizing nuclear weapons in order to carry out nuclear threats and blackmail. China will never participate in the so-called nuclear disarmament talks between the nuclear powers behind the backs of the non-nuclear countries. China's nuclear weapons are still in the experimental stage. China develops nuclear weapons solely for the purpose of defence and for breaking the nuclear monopoly and ultimately eliminating nuclear weapons and nuclear war. The Chinese Government has consistently stood for the complete prohibition and thorough destruction of nuclear weapons and proposed to convene a summit conference of all countries of the world to discuss this question and, as the first step, to reach an agreement on the non-use of nuclear weapons. The Chinese Government has on many occasions declared, and now on behalf of the Chinese Government, I once again solemnly declare that at no time and under no circumstances will China be the first to use nuclear weapons. If the United States and the Soviet Union really and truly want disarmament, they should *commit themselves not to be the first* to use nuclear weapons. This is not something difficult to do. Whether this is done or not will be a severe test as to whether they have the genuine desire for disarmament.

We have always held that the just struggles of the people of all countries support each other. China has always had the sympathy and support of the people of various countries in her socialist revolution and socialist construction. It is our bounden duty to support the just struggles of the people of various countries. For this purpose, we have provided aid to some friendly countries to help them develop their national economy independently. In providing aid, we always strictly respect the sovereignty of the *recipient countries*, and never attach any conditions or ask for any privileges. We provide free military aid to countries and peoples who are fighting against aggression. We will never become *munition merchants*. We firmly oppose certain countries trying to control and plunder the recipient countries by means of 'aid'. However, as China's economy is still comparatively backward, the material aid we have provided is very limited, and what we provide is mainly political and moral support. With a population of 700 million, China ought to make a greater contribution to human progress. And we hope that this situation of our *ability falling short of this wish of ours* will be gradually changed.

Mr President and fellow representatives,

In accordance with the purposes of the United Nations Charter, the United Nations should play its due role in maintaining international peace, opposing aggression and interference and developing friendly relations and cooperation among nations. However, for a long period the one or two superpowers have utilized the United Nations and have done many things *in contravention of the* United Nations Charter against the will of the people of various countries. This situation should not continue. We hope that the spirit of the United Nations Charter will be really and truly followed out. We will stand together with all the countries and peoples that love peace and uphold justice and work together with them for the defence of the national independence and state sovereignty of various countries and for the cause of safeguarding international peace and promoting human progress.

Telegram from Chi Peng-Fei, Acting Minister of Foreign Affairs of the People's Republic of China, To U Thant, Secretary-General of the United Nations

His Excellency Secretary-General U Thant

United Nations Headquarters
New York

I have received your telegram of October 26 informing me that at its 26th Session the General Assembly of the United Nations adopted on the 25th of October the resolution restoring to the People's Republic of China all its rights in the United Nations and expelling forthwith the representatives of Chiang Kai-shek from the place which they unlawfully occupy at the United Nations and in all the organizations related to it.

I have also noted that you have notified all the bodies and related agencies of the United Nations of this resolution adopted by the UN General Assembly and believe that the above-mentioned resolution will be speedily implemented in its entirety.

I now inform you that the Government of the People's Republic of China will send a delegation in the near future to attend the 26th Session of the General Assembly of the United Nations. The name list of the delegation will be sent to you later.

Please accept the assurances of my highest consideration.

Chi Peng-fei

Acting Minister of Foreign Affairs of the People's Republic of China

Peking, October 29, 1971

Telegram from Chi Peng-Fei, Acting Minister of Foreign Affairs of the People's Republic of China, to U Thant, Secretary-General of the United Nations

His Excellency Secretary-General U Thant

United Nations Headquarters

New York

I have the honour to inform you that the composition of the delegation of the People's Republic of China to the 26th

Session of the General Assembly of the United Nations is as follows:

Chairman of the delegation: Chiao Kuan-hua, Vice-Minister of Foreign Affairs of the People's Republic of China;

Vice-Chairman of the delegation: Huang Hua;

Representatives: Fu Hao, Hsiung Hsiang-hui, Chen Chu;

Alternate representatives: Tang Ming-chao, An Chih-yuan, Wang Hai-jung (f), Hsing Sung-yi, Chang Yung-kuan.

I will inform you later of the date of departure of the delegation of the People's Republic of China.

Highest consideration.

Chi Peng-fei

Acting Minister of Foreign Affairs of the People's Republic of China

Peking, November 2, 1971

Telegram from Chi Peng-Fei, Acting Minister of Foreign Affairs of the People's Republic of China, to U Thant, Secretary-General of the United Nations

His Excellency Secretary-General U Thant

United Nations Headquarters
New York

I have the honour to inform you that the Government of the People's Republic of China has appointed Huang Hua as the permanent representative (ambassadorial rank) and Chen Chu as the deputy representative (ambassadorial rank) of China on the Security Council of the United Nations.

Please accept the assurances of my highest consideration.

Chi Peng-fei

Acting Minister of Foreign Affairs of the People's Republic of China

Peking, November 2, 1971

171

Statement of Chiao Kuan-Hua, Chairman of the delegation of the People's Republic of China, at New York airport (November 11, 1971)

It is a pleasure today for the delegation of the Government of the People's Republic of China to come to New York to attend the 26th Session of the General Assembly of the United Nations. We express deep thanks to the representatives of the United Nations Headquarters, the representatives of various countries and all friends who have come to meet us.

The Chinese people and the peoples of the world have always been friendly. The Chinese Government has consistently stood for the establishment and development of normal relations with other countries on the basis of the Five Principles of Peaceful Coexistence and has all along supported the oppressed peoples and nations in their just struggles to win freedom and liberation, oppose foreign interference and become masters of their own destiny. Following the established policies of the Chinese Government, our delegation will work jointly in the United Nations with the representatives of all the countries that love peace and uphold justice for the cause of safeguarding international peace and promoting human progress.

The people of the United States are a great people and there exists a profound friendship between the peoples of China and the United States. We would like to take this opportunity to convey our good wishes to the people of all walks of life of New York City and the American people.

Irresistible historical trend

[*Renmin Ribao (People's Daily)* Editorial, October 28, 1971]
The so-called 'important question' draft resolution of the United States was defeated on October 25 at the 26th Session of the UN General Assembly, and the draft resolution put forward by Albania, Algeria and 21 other countries demanding the restoration of all the lawful rights of the People's Republic of China in the United Nations and the *immediate expulsion* of the Chiang Kai-shek clique from that body was adopted by an overwhelming majority. This proclaimed the utter bankruptcy of the US imperialist policy of permanently depriving China of her legitimate rights in the United Nations and of the US imperialist

scheme to create 'two Chinas' in that organization. It is a victory for all countries upholding justice in the United Nations and for the people of the whole world.

Many friendly countries have made unremitting efforts for years to restore to China her legitimate rights in the United Nations. At the current UN General Assembly Session, the 23 *co-sponsors* – Albania, Algeria, Burma, Ceylon, Cuba, Equatorial Guinea, Guinea, Iraq, Mali, Mauritania, Nepal, Pakistan, the People's Democratic Republic of Yemen, the People's Republic of the Congo, Romania, Sierra Leone, Somalia, the Sudan, Syria, the United Republic of Tanzania, the Arab Republic of Yemen, Yugoslavia and Zambia – and many other friendly countries spoke out of a sense of justice and upheld principles, rendering our country valuable support. We extend our heartfelt thanks to all the governments and people who have upheld justice in this struggle.

The UN General Assembly vote shows that calling for friendship with the Chinese people is the general trend and popular feeling among the world's people. *This is a historical trend no force on earth can hold back.*

The vote also reflects the resistance and opposition of ever more countries to the *truculent* acts of US imperialism in imposing its will on others in the United Nations. It is becoming more and more difficult for one or two superpowers to manipulate and monopolize this organization.

China is one of the founding members of the United Nations. After the Chinese people overthrew the reactionary rule of the Chiang Kai-shek clique and founded the People's Republic of China in 1949, it was both natural and right for the Government of the People's Republic of China, the sole legal representative of China, to have its legitimate seat in the United Nations. However, in the last twenty-*odd* years, China was deprived of her legitimate rights only because of the unreasonable obstruction by US imperialism. This year, the United States again *ganged up with* Japan and fabricated two absurd draft resolutions in a vain effort to create a situation of 'two Chinas' in the United Nations. To carry out this scheme, it resorted to various tricks to retain the Chiang Kai-shek clique in the United Nations. But all US efforts were *of no avail*: only a pitiably few countries followed at its heels. One resolution was defeated and the other annulled following the passing of the draft resolution of

Albania, Algeria and 21 other countries. The United States thus suffered a big defeat. One US news agency even said 'It was considered the worst US defeat in UN history.'

The reactionary Sato government of Japan has been busy exerting itself to serve the US plot of creating 'two Chinas' in the United Nations. Disregarding the strong opposition of the Japanese people of all strata, it not only made Japan a co-sponsor of the US draft resolution but also did its utmost to *canvass* votes. However, all the Sato government's efforts were fruitless, except for more clearly revealing its ugly features in remaining stubbornly hostile towards the Chinese people.

It has been announced that the representatives of the Chiang Kai-shek clique were expelled from the United Nations. But US imperialism is still forcibly occupying China's Taiwan Province and the US–Japanese reactionaries continue to spread the fallacy that 'the status of Taiwan remains to be determined'. With their *connivance* and support, a handful of plotters for 'an independent Taiwan' have been carrying out *unbridled* activities. There are indications that the US–Japanese reactionaries are stepping up their scheme of a so-called 'Taiwan independence movement', vainly trying to *sever* Taiwan Province from China. So long as the US–Japanese reactionaries carry on with their plot, the Chinese people will not for a single day cease their struggle against the 'two Chinas' or 'one China, one Taiwan' schemes. The Chinese people are determined to liberate their sacred territory Taiwan! Taiwan will certainly return to the embrace of the motherland!

Draft resolution of Albania, Algeria and other countries calling for the restoration of China's lawful rights in the UN and the expulsion of the Chiang gang adopted by an overwhelming majority at the UN General Assembly

The UN General Assembly concluded its debate and voted on the question of 'restoration of the lawful rights of the People's Republic of China in the United Nations' on the evening of October 25. By an overwhelming majority of 76 votes to 35, with 17 *abstentions*, the General Assembly adopted the draft resolution of Albania, Algeria and 21 other countries demanding the restoration of all the lawful rights of the People's Republic of China in the United Nations and the immediate expulsion of the representatives of the Chiang Kai-shek clique from all UN organs. Before voting on this draft resolution, the United States and the reactionary Sato government of Japan had put up a desperate struggle, demanding that the UN General Assembly should first vote on the so-called 'important question' resolution they had manufactured, i.e. the expulsion of the Chiang Kai-shek clique from the UN is 'an important question' requiring adoption by a two-thirds majority vote. The General Assembly rejected this so-called 'important question' resolution 59 votes to 55, with 15 abstentions. As a result of the voting on the two resolutions, the 'dual representation' resolution, also concocted by the United States and Japan, became useless.

Prolonged warm applause burst out when the resolution of Albania, Algeria and 21 other countries was adopted and the US–Japanese resolution defeated. This is a victory for the world's people and the complete bankruptcy of the US imperialist plot to use the UN to push its power politics and stubbornly prevent the restoration to the People's Republic of China of its legitimate rights in the UN, thus dealing a heavy blow to the US imperialist scheme to create 'two Chinas' in the UN and carve out China's sacred territory Taiwan. It reflected the feelings of the people of the world and the current of the times. It bore out the fact that most of the countries, with the exception of a handful of US–Japanctionaries, recognize that the Government of the People's Republic of China is the sole legitimate government of China and that Taiwan is an inalienable part of China's territory.

Debate on the restoration to the People's Republic of China of its legitimate rights in the UN began on October 18. During a week's debate, representatives of about 80 member states spoke at the General Assembly. Their speeches clearly show that the US–Japanese plot to create 'two Chinas' has become more and more unpopular and the world's people and all countries upholding international justice are *vehemently* opposed to any tricks of the United States and a handful of its followers to continue to prevent the restoration of all legitimate rights of the People's Republic of China in the UN, and demand an immediate return of China's seats in the UN to the Government of the People's Republic of China – the lawful representative of the 700 million Chinese people – and the expulsion from all UN organs of the Chiang Kai-shek clique's representatives who have illegally usurped the seats.

In their speeches, the US and Japanese representatives tried their utmost to *plug* and defend the two draft resolutions they had *devised*, aimed at creating 'two Chinas'. But their *deceptive* propaganda and absurd arguments were forcefully unmasked and refuted by the majority of the representatives. These representatives pointed out that the essence of the two draft resolutions jointly concocted by the United States and Japan is to create 'two Chinas' *de facto* in the United Nations so as to permanently separate China's territory and occupy China's territory Taiwan Province by force. Therefore, these resolutions were unacceptable. They sternly pointed out that there is only one China in the world, the People's Republic of China, and that Taiwan is an inalienable part of the territory of the People's Republic of China, and all arguments such as 'two Chinas', 'one China, one Taiwan', 'the status of Taiwan remains to be determined' and similar arguments are illegal, absurd and entirely *untenable*.

Confronted by this unfavourable situation, the US and Japanese representatives were *tearing around, like ants on a hot pan*, to put pressure on other countries and to deceive and win them over. Just a few minutes before the formal vote, the United States still instigated some countries to ask for a postponement of the vote, 'in the hope that it *might prevail upon* a few still wavering members to support the American resolution' (according to Reuter). But this manoeuvre of the US–Japanese reactionaries was rejected 56 votes to 53, with 19 abstentions, at the General Assembly. Then, the so-called 'important question' resolution was voted down 59 votes to 55, with 15 abstentions. Western news agencies reported that '*bedlam* broke out when the result of the vote appeared on *the electronic tabulating board* showing that the American proposal had been defeated', that 'the announcement of the vote was greeted by prolonged applause from the packed assembly hall' and was 'applauded for two minutes', and that representatives of various countries friendly to China were 'cheering, singing, shouting', 'and some dancing in the *aisles*'.

At this moment, the gloomy-faced US representative George Bush rushed to the *rostrum*, trying to make a last-ditch struggle. He moved that the provision for the immediate expulsion from the UN of the representatives of the Chiang gang be *deleted* from the resolution sponsored by Albania, Algeria and 21 other countries before being put to a vote. But this attempt of the US representative was also *foiled* when his motion was *blocked* by the opposition of other representatives and *ruled out of order* by UN General Assembly President Adam Malik. Seeing that the situation was hopeless and it was impossible for the Chiang gang *to hang on* any longer, Chou Shu-kai, the Chiang gang's 'foreign minister', had to announce his retreat from the UNO and soon headed his *underlings* in their *dismal* departure from the assembly hall.

The resolution sponsored by Albania, Algeria and 21 other countries then was put to a vote and adopted by an over-whelming majority, 76 votes to 35, with 17 abstentions. Resounding loud applause and cheers again burst forth in the assembly hall.

According to reports from US news agencies, US adminis-tration sources 'were caught by surprise' and 'expressed strong disappointment' in the face of the 'worst US defeat in UN history'. In a statement after the vote, Bush said he 'couldn't help but be *affected*' by the result of the vote. He said *despondently* that this is a 'moment of *infamy*' and that 'I am tremendously disappointed'. But he had to admit that 'no one can escape the fact, unpleasant though it may be, that the votes which have just been *cast* do, in fact, represent the views of the majority of UN members'.

For more than 20 years, the United States used every trick to obdurately obstruct the restoration to the People's Republic of China of all its legitimate rights in the United Nations. However, it has *lifted a rock only to drop it on its own feet*, and has suffered repeated defeats and increasing isolation. In the 1950s, by putting its voting machine into action, the United States *arbi-trarily brushed aside* the question of restoring to China its legitimate rights in the United Nations. Since 1961, when more and more countries expressed opposition to its tactics of 'delaying the discussion', the United States again manipulated the voting machine and wilfully asserted that the restoration of China's legitimate rights in the United Nations was a so-called 'important question' requiring a two-thirds majority vote to carry it. However, at the 25th Session of the UN General Assembly last year, a majority was in favour of the draft resol-ution of Albania, Algeria and 16 other countries calling for the restoration of the legitimate rights of the People's Republic of

China in the UN and the expulsion of the Chiang gang. The US scheme faced *imminent* total bankruptcy. Under such circumstances, the United States concocted an 'important question' resolution and a 'dual representation' resolution in collaboration with Japan at the current 26th Session of the UN General Assembly, thus openly coming out with their long-time plot of creating 'two Chinas' or 'one China, one Taiwan'.

According to Western press reports, in order to push the 'two Chinas' scheme at the current UN General Assembly Session, US President Nixon personally wrote to the heads of state of many countries; 'the United States is *applying the full weight of its diplomacy* in scores of foreign capitals'; William Rogers and George Bush *scurried* around and held more than 200 talks with representatives of more than 100 countries inside and outside the United Nations; 'promises of US favours, or hints of withdrawal of US aid' were made as *bribery* or thinly *disguised* threats; some US senators even threatened that the United States would reduce its funds to the United Nations if the resolution of Albania, Algeria and other countries was adopted. Japan also sent important personages to join its UN delegation and coordinated with the United States in the latter's vote-seeking efforts. However, although the United States and Japan had resorted to various tricks and *racked their brains*, their scheme to create 'two Chinas' or 'one China, one Taiwan' aimed at separating China's sacred territory was seen through by more and more countries and suffered a serious defeat.

This significant victory in foiling the US–Japanese reactionaries' plot to create 'two Chinas' in the United Nations was won by the Chinese people and the people of the world and friendly countries upholding international justice through a protracted joint struggle. But the US–Japanese reactionaries will never be reconciled to their defeat; they continue to step up their criminal schemes of 'two Chinas', 'one China, one Taiwan', 'the status of Taiwan remaining to be determined' and 'an independent Taiwan'. The Chinese people will continue to maintain high vigilance and fight together with the people of various countries to completely *frustrate* these schemes of the US–Japanese reactionaries.

(Hsinhua, October 26 and 27, 1971)

Text of the resolution of Albania, Algeria and 21 other countries and the UN General Assembly voting results

The 26th Session of the United Nations General Assembly voted on the question of 'restoration of the lawful rights of the People's Republic of China in the United Nations' at a meeting on the evening of October 25. The draft resolution jointly submitted by Albania, Algeria and 21 other countries to the General Assembly was adopted 76 votes to 35, with 17 abstentions.

The text of the draft resolution of Albania, Algeria and other countries reads as follows:

'The General Assembly,

Recalling the principles of the Charter of the United Nations,

Considering that the restoration of the lawful rights of the People's Republic of China is essential both for the protection of the Charter of the United Nations and for the cause that the United Nations must serve under the Charter,

Recognizing that the representatives of the Government of the People's Republic of China are the only lawful representatives of China to the United Nations and that the People's Republic of China is one of the five permanent members of the Security Council,

Decides to restore all its rights to the People's Republic of China and to recognize the representatives of its government as the only legitimate representatives of China to the United Nations, and to expel forthwith the representatives of Chiang Kai-shek from the place which they unlawfully occupy at the United Nations and in all the organizations affiliated to it.'

In accordance with the stipulations of the UN Charter and the Rules of Procedure of the UN General Assembly, the draft resolution has become a formal resolution of the UN General Assembly immediately after its adoption.

The 76 member states voting for the draft resolution of Albania, Algeria and 21 other countries were Afghanistan, Albania, Algeria, Austria, Belgium, Bhutan, Botswana, Bulgaria, Burma, Burundi, Byelorussia, Cameroon, Canada, Ceylon, Chile, Cuba, Czechoslovakia, Denmark, Ecuador, the Arab Republic of Egypt, Equatorial Guinea, Ethiopia, Finland, France, Ghana, Guinea, Guyana, Hungary, Iceland, India, Iran, Iraq, Ireland, Israel, Italy, Kenya, Kuwait, Laos, Libya, Malaysia, Mali, Mauritania, Mexico, Mongolia, Morocco, Nepal, the Netherlands,

Nigeria, Norway, Pakistan, the People's Democratic Republic of Yemen, the People's Republic of the Congo, Peru, Poland, Portugal, Romania, Rwanda, Senegal, Sierra Leone, Singapore, Somalia, the Sudan, Sweden, Syria, Togo, Trinidad and Tobago, Tunisia, Turkey, Uganda, Ukraine, the Soviet Union, the United Kingdom, the United Republic of Tanzania, the Arab Republic of Yemen, Yugoslavia and Zambia.

The United States and Japan were among those which voted against the draft resolution of Albania, Algeria and other countries.

Prior to this, the General Assembly voted down the 'important question' draft resolution concocted by the United States in collusion with the Sato government of Japan by 59 votes to 55 with 15 abstentions. The 59 member states voting against the US–Japanese draft resolution were Afghanistan, Albania, Algeria, Bhutan, Bulgaria, Burma, Burundi, Byelorussia, Cameroon, Canada, Ceylon, Chile, Cuba, Czechoslovakia, Denmark, Ecuador, the Arab Republic of Egypt, Equatorial Guinea, Ethiopia, Finland, France, Guinea, Guyana, Hungary, Iceland, India, Iraq, Ireland, Kenya, Kuwait, Libya, Malaysia, Mali, Mauritania, Mongolia, Nepal, Nigeria, Norway, Pakistan, the People's Democratic Republic of Yemen, the People's Republic of the Congo, Peru, Poland, Romania, Sierra Leone, Singapore, Somalia, the Sudan, Sweden, Syria, Trinidad and Tobago, Uganda, Ukraine, the Soviet Union, the United Kingdom, the United Republic of Tanzania, the Arab Republic of Yemen, Yugoslavia and Zambia.

After the draft resolution of Albania, Algeria and other countries was adopted and the aforementioned US–Japanese draft resolution defeated at the General Assembly another US–Japanese draft resolution, the so-called 'dual representation' draft resolution, which calls for admitting the People's Republic of China into the United Nations and according it the seat of a permanent member of the Security Council, while at the same time retaining the representation of the Chiang Kai-shek clique, was automatically killed at the General Assembly.

(Hsinhua, October 26 and 27, 1971)

Taiwan has been China's sacred territory since ancient times

Lying off China's southeastern coast, Taiwan is its largest island. The close cultural and economic ties between Taiwan and the mainland date back to ancient times. In AD 230, during the period of the Three Kingdoms, the Kingdom of Wu dispatched Generals Wei Wen and Chukeh Chih, in command of over 10,000 troops, to 'Yichou', China's Taiwan Province today. The Penghu Islands came under the jurisdiction of Chinchiang County in Fukien Province during the Southern Sung Dynasty in the 12th century, and became one of China's administrative districts. By the mid-13th century, a magistracy was set up in Penghu by the government of the Yuan Dynasty to exercise jurisdiction over Taiwan and other islands. This office was under the administration of Tungan County in Chuanchou Prefecture. From that time, Taiwan has formally been part of the *dominion* of China.

Since the Ming Dynasty, Taiwan and Penghu have been important strategic regions in China's coastal defence. During the 16th century, the Western colonialists began to scramble for possessions in the seas of the Orient. Japan joined in. In 1557, Portugal seized the possession of China's Macao and using it as a base, proclaimed Taiwan to be Macao's dependency in an attempt to invade and occupy the island. In the 17th century, naval supremacy passed to the Dutch and British colonialists and Portugal's aggressive designs on Taiwan failed to materialize. The European colonial powers Holland and Spain invaded and occupied Tainan and Keelung in China's Taiwan Province in 1624 and 1626 respectively. With these two places as centres, they expanded their aggressive activities. China was thus robbed of its territory Taiwan for the first time. Thereafter, these two aggressors engaged in a bitter war of *contention* in northern Taiwan. In 1642 the Spaniards were defeated and withdrew from the island. Cheng Cheng-kung, a national hero who lived during the closing years of the Ming Dynasty, entered Taiwan in command of a big army in 1661. With the close cooperation of the local people, he rapidly drove out the Dutch aggressors and recovered Taiwan. In 1684, the government of the Ching Dynasty set up Taiwan *Prefecture* and placed it under the jurisdiction of the Taiwan-Amoy *Tao* of Fukien Province. In 1885, Taiwan formally became one of China's provinces.

For more than a thousand years, Taiwan Province has been

developed principally by settlers from the coastal provinces of Fukien and Kwangtung together with the fraternal people of the Kaoshan nationality of Taiwan Province. To this day the over-whelming majority of the compatriots in Taiwan Province speak the south Fukien dialect or the Hakka dialect of Kwangtung Province. The foregoing historical facts show that Taiwan has long been China's dominion and an inalienable part of China's sacred territory, the Kaoshan nationality in the province is one of the nationalities of China and the compatriots there are a component part of the great Chinese people.

After the Opium War in the mid-19th century, the imperialist powers, US and Japanese imperialism in particular, *covetous* of China's rich and fertile province of Taiwan, *incessantly* intensi-fied their activities of aggression to seize Taiwan and make it a stepping-stone for aggression against the Chinese mainland. After the Sino-Japanese War in 1894, the corrupt government of the Ching Dynasty signed the unequal Treaty of Shimonoseki with Japan, and Taiwan Province was forcibly occupied by Japanese imperialism. During the 50 years of ruthless colonial rule by Japanese imperialism, the struggle of the compatriots in Taiwan to return to the embrace of the motherland never ceased. Courageous and unyielding, and advancing wave upon wave, they waged a protracted struggle against the Japanese imperialist occupationists, a struggle that moved people to songs and tears. There were more than 20 uprisings of considerable *magnitude*, including the heroic uprising of the people of Kaoshan nationality in Taichung, and hundreds of thousands of people gave their lives in the struggle. The US State Depart-ment's White Paper, *United States Relations with China*, had to admit this. It said, 'The native population for 50 years had been under the rule of a foreign invader and therefore welcomed the Chinese forces as liberators. During the Japanese occupation the principal hope of the people had been reunion with the mainland.'

It is precisely because Taiwan has been China's territory since ancient times that the Cairo Declaration signed by China, the United States and Britain on December 1, 1943, provided in *explicit* terms that all the territories Japan had stolen from the Chinese, such as Manchuria, Taiwan and the Penghu Islands, shall be restored to China. The 8th item of the Potsdam Procla-mation defining terms for Japanese unconditional surrender issued by China, the United States and Britain on July 26, 1945 and subsequently *acceded* to by the Soviet Union, *reiterated*: 'The terms of the Cairo Declaration shall be carried out and Japanese sovereignty shall be limited to the islands of Honshu, Hokkaido, Kyushu, Shikoku and such minor islands as we determine.' On August 14, 1945, Japan was defeated and surrendered unconditionally. On October 25 of the same year, in accordance with the Cairo Declaration and the Potsdam Proclamation, the then Chinese Government held a ceremony in Taipei to accept the surrender of the Japanese forces in Taiwan. Thus Taiwan. Province finally returned to the embrace of the motherland.

Since then, China has recovered its sovereign rights over Taiwan Province.

Former US President Harry Truman admitted in his statement on Taiwan on January 5, 1950, that the purpose of the Cairo Declaration was that the territories Japan had stolen from China, such as Taiwan, should be restored to China. 'The provisions of the Declaration were accepted by Japan at the time of its surrender. ... for the past 4 years the United States and the other Allied Powers have accepted the exercise of Chinese authority over the Island.' On February 9 of the same year, commenting on the question of Taiwan raised by the Foreign Affairs Committee of the US House of Representatives, the US Department of State said that Taiwan had been administered by China since Japanese forces on the island surrendered to China; 'It was incorporated into China as a province. ... The Allied Powers associated in the war against Japan have not questioned these steps. The United States Government has not questioned these steps because they were clearly in line with its commitments made at Cairo and reaffirmed at Potsdam. In other words, the Allied Powers including the United States have for the past 4 years treated Formosa [meaning Taiwan Province of China – Ed.] as a part of China.'

All the facts mentioned above testify that Taiwan is an inalienable part of China's territory both historically and from a point of view of the present situation. Taiwan was completely returned to China after the defeat and surrender of Japanese imperialism in World War II. The Government of the People's Republic of China has full sovereign rights over it. The fact that the Chiang Kai-shek clique, long repudiated by the Chinese people, can still hang on in Taiwan is wholly the creation of US imperialism which, in order to achieve its criminal aim of aggression, has gone back on its own word and trampled upon the international agreements it had signed in total disregard of international faith. On June 25, 1950, the United States launched the war of aggression against Korea. Two days later, on June 27, US President Harry Truman flagrantly ordered the 7th Fleet into the area of the Taiwan Straits to occupy China's Taiwan Province, placing the Chiang Kai-shek clique under the protection of US bayonets. At the same time, Truman *perfidiously* and truculently claimed that determination of the future status of Taiwan 'must await the restoration of security in the Pacific'. Since then, US imperialism, in collusion with the forces of Japanese militarism, has created and disseminated such absurdities as 'the status of Taiwan remains to be determined' and sovereignty over Taiwan is 'unsettled', and instigated and controlled a handful of plotters for 'an independent Taiwan' to push the schemes of the so-called 'Taiwan independence movement', in a vain attempt to *sever* Taiwan from China, occupy it permanently and make it a military base for the invasion of the mainland of China and other Asian countries. This will never be tolerated by the Chinese people, nor by those who uphold justice and respect international agreements.

As early as June 28, 1950, premier Chou En-lai issued a statement on behalf of the Chinese Government, pointing out that Truman's statement and the actions of the US navy 'constitute armed aggression against the territory of China, and total violation of the United Nations Charter'. The statement solemnly declared: 'No matter what obstructive action the US imperialists may take the fact that Taiwan is part of China will remain unchanged for ever.... All the people of our country will certainly fight to the end single-mindedly to liberate Taiwan from the grasp of the American aggressors.' Any US scheme will finally meet with thorough bankruptcy. The just cause of the Chinese people will certainly win.

> (Background material by Hsinhua, published by *Renmin Ribao*, October 23, 1971)

US Imperialist 'Independent Taiwan' Plot is doomed to failure

Following adoption of the draft resolution of Albania, Algeria and 21 other countries at the 26th Session of the UN General Assembly and the bankruptcy of the US imperialist scheme of creating 'two Chinas' in the United Nations, some US personages in power, while *wailing* over their dismal defeat, refuse to accept it and, bent on pushing their scheme to create 'one China, one Taiwan' or 'an independent Taiwan', they are putting up a desperate struggle.

The day after the resolution was adopted on the night of October 25, US Secretary of State Rogers hurriedly held a press conference in Washington. He shouted that US policy towards the Chiang Kai-shek clique will not be affected by the UN vote and insisted that the *outsted* Chiang Kai-shek clique 'continues to be a respected and valued member of the international community, and the ties between us [the US and the Chiang gang] remain, unaffected by the action of the United Nations'. Speaking at the Senate Foreign Relations Committee on October 27, Rogers again clamoured that the UN decision would 'not in any way change the policy of the United States *vis-à-vis* China [meaning the Chiang gang]', and asserted that US 'defence arrangements' with the Chiang gang would continue.

On October 27, Senator Javits ridiculously called for a 'plebiscite' in Taiwan so that one day there can be 'self-determination' in Taiwan which will be admitted to the UN as an 'independent country'. This rabid nonsense fully demonstrates that even after its defeat in the General Assembly, US imperialism is still pushing the scheme to create 'one China, one Taiwan', which is in effect tantamount to 'two Chinas', and stepping up the plot to create 'an independent Taiwan'.

Meanwhile, the US Senate openly decided on October 28 not to *repeal* the so-called 1955 emergency resolution in which the US Senate and House of Representatives authorized the US president to use US armed forces in the Taiwan Straits. The repeal of the resolution was proposed by the Senate Foreign Relations Committee last July. The resolution was adopted by the US Congress after the United States and the Chiang Kai-shek clique signed the so-called 'mutual defence treaty' in 1954, with the aim of strengthening the military occupation of Taiwan and further interfering in China's internal affairs. It was reported that in discussing the decision, one senator even *howled* that 'we should not indicate to anybody anywhere in the world we are in the mind to abandon the protection to those in Taiwan'. This is *a voluntary confession* that US imperialism harbours the wild ambition of insisting on occupying Taiwan and carving out China's sacred territory.

Some US bourgeois journals have insolently been spreading the fallacy about 'the status of Taiwan remains to be determined' and 'an independent Taiwan', alleging that 'the regime on Taiwan can continue to exist and be available outside the United Nations' and that the Government of the People's Republic of China does not speak for the people of Taiwan, and so forth.

It should be pointed out in particular that a handful of plotters for 'an independent Taiwan', dancing to the tune of US imperialism, are feverishly active in the United States. According to an AP report, Chen Lungchu, one of the chieftains of the so-called 'Taiwan independence league', held a press conference in New York on October 26, calling for a so-called 'free and honest election' 'under international supervision' in Taiwan so as to make Taiwan 'an independent state'. Clear-sighted people can see at a glance that this is a farce stage-managed exclusively by US imperialism.

The intensified US imperialist scheme to create 'an independent Taiwan' is the continuation of its policy of insisting on antagonizing China and creating 'two Chinas'.

However, just as its scheme of creating 'two Chinas' in the United Nations ended in utter defeat, 'one China, one Taiwan', 'an independent Taiwan' and other tricks which the United States is continuing with are bound to fail more dismally, like lifting a rock only to drop it on its own feet.

(Hsinhua, October 31, 1971)

Japanese reactionaries' plot to create 'an independent Taiwan' will never succeed

Headed by Eisaku Sato, the Japanese reactionaries are not reconciled to their crushing defeat at the 26th Session of the UN General Assembly. They are continuing with redoubled efforts their scheme to create 'an independent Taiwan' in a wild attempt to re-occupy China's territory Taiwan Province.

Japanese Prime Minister Sato carried on with the 'two Chinas' plot while answering questions in the Japanese Diet on October 26, the day after the defeat in the General Assembly of the joint resolution worked out by the United States and Japan to create 'two Chinas', and the adoption by an overwhelming majority of the resolution by Albania, Algeria and 21 other countries demanding the restoration of all the lawful rights of the People's Republic of China in the United Nations and the immediate expulsion of the Chiang Kai-shek gang. He asserted that 'two governments exist in China' and the illegal 'Japan–Chiang treaty' between the Japanese reactionaries and the Chiang Kai-shek clique 'should not be *abrogated* in a simple way'. On the same day, the television station of the government-controlled Japanese Broadcasting Association promptly *rounded up* a number of reactionary, *scibblers* for a televised forum to create reactionary opinion for the Sato government's 'one China, one Taiwan' scheme by agitating for a 'Taiwan state'.

The Japanese reactionaries have been very active of late in their scheme to create 'an independent Taiwan'. *Ringleaders* of the 'Taiwan independence movement', living in Japan were allowed to go back to Taiwan to influence the Chiang gang from within. At the same time, Japanese reactionary *bigwigs* were sent to Taiwan for direct collusion with pro-Japanese elements in the Chiang gang. According to Kyodo reports, at the heels of *archwar* criminal Kishi, brother of Sato who went to Taipei in early October to plot with pro-Japanese elements in the Chiang gang, another Japanese ultra-Rightist, Ryoichi Sasakawa who 'has an intimate friendship' with 'secretary-general' Chang Chun of the Chiang gang, sneaked into China's Taiwan Province on October 19 and stayed there till October 23. Apart from conferring with Chang Chun, he 'had long talks with Ho Ying-chin, Ku Cheng-kang and others'. After returning to Japan, he clamoured wildly that Taiwan 'should be separated from the Chinese mainland and become independent'.

Meanwhile, under the instigation and with the participation of the Japanese reactionaries, the plotters for 'an independent Taiwan' in Japan have been more *unbridled* in their manoeuvres. They have openly held meetings and 'demonstrations' and screamed out reactionary slogans such as 'an independent

Taiwan' and 'one Taiwan, one China'. According to an October 28 Kyodo report, Japanese quarters concerned held that 'former Japanese Prime Minister Kishi and other Japanese reactionaries must be manoeuvring' behind these moves for 'an independent Taiwan'.

The obstinate hostility to the Chinese people of the Japanese reactionaries who are scheming to create 'an independent Taiwan' is absolutely contrary to the desires of the Japanese masses. Their vicious manoeuvring is bound to arouse deeper indignation among the Japanese people and land them in greater isolation. Their scheme will never come off.

(Hsinhua, October 31, 1971)

Document 8a: Zhou En-lai's internal report to the Party on the international situation, December 1971 (Excerpts)[1]

Chinese Law and Government Spring 1977/Vol. X, No. 1.

A. Characteristics of the current international situation

1. The characteristics of the current international situation can be summarized into four phrases: 'one trend,' 'two possibilities,' 'three parts,' and 'four contradictions.'

'One trend' reflects what Chairman Mao said in this statement of May 20: 'The main trend in the world today is revolution.'

The 'two possibilities' are the possibility of circumventing war by revolution and the possibility of revolution triggered by a war. The possibility of a war still exists; we must maintain vigilance.

The 'three parts' refer to the two superpowers, the United States and the Soviet Union, and to the Third World. We are resolutely on the side of the Third World.

'Four contradictions' are the basic contradictions of the contemporary world manifested by the contradiction between the two superpowers, the US and USSR, and the people throughout the world; the contradiction between the US and USSR for gaining world hegemony; the contradiction among the imperialist countries shifting [the causes] for the economic crisis on each other; and the contradiction of the medium-sized and small countries struggling together against the US and USSR.

2. The present global strategy of the US is contained in five phrases mentioned by Kissinger: 'the Americas as the base,' 'Western Europe as the pivotal point,' 'Asia as the flank,' 'the Middle East as the throat,' and 'the oceans being the centre of the world struggle in the future.' The strategy of the USSR is to step up the contention for hegemony with the US, with their arms stretching out ever further and their ambition ever increasing. The US and USSR are both contending and compromising. They compromise when their contention is without result and contend again when compromise is fruitless. The Soviet revisionists compromised with Western countries on the Berlin issue with an eye to consolidating their foothold in Western Europe in preparation for contention. The key points for which the USSR is contending with the US are: (a) Europe, (b) Middle East.

3. The general strategy of our nation for the present is: to push forward [preparations against] war and promote revolution.

(a) In Asia: Korea is our No. 1 comrade-in-arms. We are closely united with her and we support each other, seeking common ground while maintaining our differences and resisting enemies jointly. With respect to 'differences,' there were two of them recently: The first is that while we say there is no longer a socialist camp presently, Korea still adheres firmly to a proposition that there is; the second is that while we say that 'anti-imperialism' is not to be mentioned in the Afro-Asian ping-pong game, Korea is determined to mention it, saying that it is revisionist not to.

The relations between Vietnam, Laos, Cambodia and us are like those between the front line and the rear. But, for the present, it is not appropriate to praise Vietnam excessively; we should treat her as we do the other two nations. The contradictions among them should be solved by themselves. *Vietnam shows anxiety over Nixon's visit to China. We have provided explanations*. If she cannot figure it out for the moment, just let her watch the development of the truth.

Burma has restored normal relations with our country. Ne Win has visited our country this year and made three major points: (1) He was sorry for the events of 1967 in which the Chinese Embassy in Burma was assaulted; (2) He was appreciative of [our] permitting him to visit China; (3) He wondered what he should do about the losses of the overseas Chinese [in Burma] incurred by the 1967 events. To the third point, we answered that he should compensate for the losses. After he returned to Burma, a special committee was immediately organized by a vice foreign minister to handle the matter of reparations for losses suffered by overseas Chinese [in Burma].

India and Pakistan. While the Soviet revisionists back India, we support Pakistan. In supporting Pakistan, we support her resistance to Indian aggression. But there are mistakes in the domestic policy of Pakistan, [such as] the massacre in East Pakistan and the lack of a policy toward nationalities. India is the head of the reactionaries among the imperialists, revisionists and reactionaries. In spite of this, we still want to restore normal diplomatic relations with her at an opportune moment, for the purpose of furthering the people's revolution in India.

Singapore and Malaysia. Lee Kuan Yew said that, with respect to the problem of improving relations with China, Singapore will move one step when Malaysia moves two. In short, he follows others and is not eager to improve relations with China. He is very much interested in the investments of the US, Japan, and the USSR. The potential influence of Britain in Singapore is still strong. Although overseas Chinese comprise seventy per cent of the population of Singapore, we cannot count Singapore as Chinese territory. This demarcation must be clear.

If Singapore [proposes to] establish diplomatic relations with us, we can take it into consideration. But, presently, it would be better [just to maintain] commercial relations.

Malaysia upholds neutralism and wants to improve relations with us. We have complied with her demands, and relations will also develop step by step from now on. There is also the possibility of establishing diplomatic relations [with us] in the future. The Soviet revisionists take great interest in this area, but Britain, the US, and Japan will not relinquish the area.

The Philippines already has commercial relations with our country and relations will continue to develop. Yet it remains to be seen how things will develop in the future.

Japan. Sato is increasingly unstable. But, for the time being, it is the Japanese Communist revisionists and the Komeito that are best able to appeal to the masses. There are only one thousand-odd people who are real leftists. Wang Kuo-ch'üan did a good job when he was sent to Japan for a couple of days. He helped to revive the cooperation between the two factions of Hisao Kuroda and Seimin Miyazaki and a celebration was held on that occasion. It will take time for the Japanese revolution to create unity out of division.

b) It is necessary to do a good job of dealing with the people of the US Chairman Mao said: 'Place great hope in the people of the United States.' As the people's revolution in the US gradually gains momentum, we have to do more work.

c) In the areas of Africa and Latin America, generally speaking, we support national revolution, chiefly with moral support. Lately the Soviet revisionists have been engaged in sabotage. Recently the situation in Zambia became unstable mainly because the Soviet revisionists are playing tricks.

d) In the Middle East, we [aim] mainly to uncover the intrigues of deception and division of the US and USSR. The Soviet revisionists are not faring well in the Middle East, Egypt toppled Ali Sabri and Sudan crushed the *coup d'état* machinated by the Soviet revisionists. But the Soviet revisionists have increased their influence in Syria, Iraq, Yemen, and South Yemen. The current situation in Palestine is not very good, with a decrease to 20,000 people from 50,000. Struggle is complicated.

e) Europe: The ten countries of the European Economic Community will deal a heavy blow to the USSR and US Health said that 'The era of the control of the two superpowers over the world has already come to an end.' This is indeed the truth. However, Britain, France, and West Germany all have their own plans; contradictions do exist. That the rise of European power has broken down the power division between the US and USSR is one of the signs of global upheaval. The linchpin of the diplomatic relationship between China and Britain lies in the Taiwan issue. The British said that 'The uncertain status of Taiwan, as Churchill called it, has become law. It is now inappropriate to change our position.' We must persist in this matter. As long as this problem remains unsolved, the Chiang gang Taiwan will reapply for admission to the United Nations at any time. We cannot give way.

f) The Balkan Peninsula: Brezhnev asked Tito: 'Who is the hypothetical enemy when you practice military manoeuvers?' Tito answered: 'Whoever attacks us is the enemy.' The petty revisionists of Eastern Europe are now also beginning to fall away from the USSR. Moreover, with regard to the matter of invectives unleashed against us by the newspapers and radios of the petty revisionists of Eastern Europe, Chairman Mao said: 'They are ordered to call [us] names and cannot do otherwise.'

B. Why will Nixon come to our country for negotiations?

1. The visit of **the head of US imperialism to China is a victory for the people of the entire world and renders bankrupt the China policy of the US.**

2. It is the outcome of the development of the four basic contradictions in the world.

3. [It is due to] **the immense internal pressure of the people in the US demanding improvement in US–China relations.**

4 When the US got stuck in Vietnam, the Soviet revisionists used the opportunity to extend vigorously their sphere of influence in Europe and the Middle East. **The US imperialists have no choice but to improve their relations with China in order to counter the Soviet revisionists.**

5. **Improving relations with China is great capital in the coming presidential election.** Therefore, **Nixon is 'dressing up elaborately and presenting himself at our door.'**

C. Why did our country accede to Nixon's request for a visit?

1. Chairman Mao made it clear in his talk with Snow. It will not do to discuss the problems of the world only with leftist or middle-of-the-road or ordinary rightist opponents. Problems cannot be solved. Until the people hold power, only by negotiating directly with the head of the rightists will what has been said count.

2. At this stage, it is necessary to take full advantage of the contradiction between the US and USSR and to magnify it.

3. After improving US–China relations, it will be easier to do a good job in dealing with the people of the US. The strength of the US people's revolution is growing little by little; this problem must be handled seriously. As long as relations between countries [the US and us] remain unimproved, our work will be difficult to carry out.

4. **Because Nixon has encountered difficulties both domestically and internationally, he has requested eagerly to visit China. When he comes, he has to bring along something in**

his pocket; otherwise, he will find it hard to give explanations when he returns to the US. It is to our advantage if the negotiation succeeds but it constitutes no detriment to us if the negotiation fails. We will never give up our principles and sell out our people and revolution. If Vietnam does not comprehend this, we can persuade her gradually. **That US–China relations are a betrayal of principle, of revolution, of Vietnam, as Lin Piao said, is nonsense and an insult to the Party**. Furthermore, some say that we are helping Nixon to run for president. How should this be viewed? The Republicans and Democrats are of the same ilk. How can it be said that it is right to help the Democrats? Any question should be studied from the viewpoint of class analysis.

D. The current situation of Soviet revisionism

1. The development of new internal power struggles and Brezhnev's reckless power grabbing are exemplified by the postponement of the Soviet revisionist Communist Party's twenty-fourth congress. Their domestic economy is in a mess, their five-year plan is unfulfillable. Their agricultural production targets have fallen through, the supply of commodities in cities is under stress, their social morality is decadent, and their society is tending to polarize into the two extremes of rich and poor.

2. The petty revisionists of Eastern Europe are unstable and discontented with the USSR. The USSR sold out East Germany to win over West Germany. But both the stick and carrot used on Yugoslavia and Rumania have been ineffective. A new phase will appear in Eastern Europe, namely, one of turning against [the Soviet Union] by all and desertion by their kin.

3. In the Middle East, the Soviet revisionists have expanded their military bases in Iraq, Syria, Yemen and South Yemen. Although they have intensified their control over Egypt, they have also increased the contradictions. Sudan's Nimieri implacably hates the Soviet revisionist tyrant. In Asia, Afghanistan is leaning toward the Soviet revisionists. Nepal has received much aid [from the Soviet revisionists], but her basic policy is to balance the power among the USSR, China, the US, and India. For the present, Burma is not buying [the Soviet] line. Kosygin passed through Burma twice and Ne Win met with him only the second time. The collusion between the Soviet revisionists

and Japan is developing somewhat, but, when the Soviet revisionists want the Japanese to exploit Siberia, the Japanese answer: What we really want to exploit is Sakhalin. The contradiction between the two countries is irreconcilable. In Asia only India is comparatively receptive to the Soviet revisionists and the Soviet revisionists have supported Indian moves against Pakistan. Yet, India is a heavy burden; to have the Soviet revisionists bear it is a good thing.

The struggle between the US and USSR for hegemony over the Mediterranean Sea is a heated one. Previously the Mediterranean Sea was part of the world of the US. Now the Soviet fleet has increased from six or seven ships to fifty or sixty (and more than seventy, at times). Their ambition is ever increasing.

E. The problem of the expansion of the international united front

1. Our strategy is: *The US and USSR are our main enemies.* The first intermediate zone comprises Asia, Africa, and Latin America; the second includes Western Europe, Japan, Canada, and Oceania.

2. The Japanese people belong to the sphere of the Asian, African, and Latin American revolutionary forces while Japan's rulers belong to the category of the second intermediate zone.

3. When de Gaulle assumed the reins of French government, Chairman Mao said: 'It is a good thing and, at the same time, a bad thing for de Gaulle to come to power. It is a bad thing because he is anti-Communist and a good thing because he is a man with backbone.'

Toward Britain, France, and West Germany, we must use abusive language less frequently and must apply strategy.

4. The work of dealing with high-level people in the capitalist countries must be furthered vigorously. They are transitional figures; the power will in the end fall into the hands of the people. Nevertheless, doing a good job of dealing with these people will spare us an enemy and give us one more indirect ally.

F. Correctly understanding the five principles of peaceful coexistence

1. The five principles are applicable to the two intermediate zones and the two superpowers, the US and USSR. But [the superpowers], in reality, do not want these principles.

2. Correctly utilize these principles to win over the two intermediate zones.

3. The normalization of a country's relations [with us] makes it easier for us to bolster the people's revolution of that country. That Lenin established relations with China's northern warlords while simultaneously helping China's revolution in a big way is an example of this.

4. The 'peaceful coexistence' of the Soviet revisionists is capitulationism; our 'peaceful coexistence' is for the purpose of revolution.

G. The problem of fully taking advantage of the contradictions and weaknesses of the enemy

1. Lenin taught us that we must discreetly and extremely cautiously exploit all the contradictions and weaknesses of the enemy camp. This is both a strategy and a matter of revolutionary principle.

2. It is necessary to adhere to principle while strategy can be changed considerably and manipulated flexibly. The contradictions between the US and USSR, the contradictions between the US and Japan, and the contradictions between the US and Europe must all be exploited.

H. Appropriate use of dual revolutionary tactics to oppose dual counter-revolutionary tactics

1. Chairman Mao's 'Chungking negotiations' were a typical precedent.

2. The USSR and US are now dealing with us by means of dual tactics. The US invades Taiwan and Indochina and negotiates with our country at the same time. The Soviet revisionists deploy millions of soldiers along the Sino-Soviet border and simultaneously engage in negotiations on the border issue with

us. These are dual tactics and we [should] respond to them with dual revolutionary tactics.

3. Properly employ dual revolutionary tactics to win the sympathy and support of the people.

I. Push forward [preparations against] war and promote revolution. But it is still necessary to be ready for a surprise attack by the enemy at any time and we must continue to do a good job of preparing for war.

J. Oppose great power chauvinism

1. Great power chauvinism is the mortal wound of the US and USSR. This is the point that creates the most antipathy in the Third World. The Third World admires China primarily because China opposes great power chauvinism.

2. The better the situation is and the more help we give to other countries, the more we should pay attention to opposing great power chauvinism.

3. We must oppose the 'favour-granting viewpoint.' The help given to other countries is not a favour but mutual aid.

Document 8b: Zhou En-lai's internal report to the Party on the problem of the current international situation, March 1973[1] (Excerpts)

Chinese Law and Government, Spring 1977, Vol. X, No.1

A. The situation concerning the two superpowers

The global struggle between the two superpowers, the US and USSR, continues to be heated. Western Europe is a juicy piece of meat and Japan is a juicy piece of meat; they [the US and USSR] are both striving for them. China is a piece of meat which is both large and juicy which they are attempting to acquire. However, this piece of meat is too large for them to swallow.

In Europe, the USSR intends to keep the current border line (Eastern Europe); it is 'hammering in a nail' among Western

European countries (the nail is France); and it is 'neutralizing' Western Europe after expelling US influence. Soviet power has expanded to the point where they can do whatever they want. Japan relies on the US, is luring China toward herself and is also improving her relations with the USSR. The emphasis of our policy toward Japan lies in the broad masses of the Japanese people while the USSR and US maintain relations with her for the sake of their own strategic and economic advantage.

Is the strategic deployment of the USSR now directed eastward or westward? Chairman Mao has developed the following assessment of the current military deployment of the Soviet revisionists: for the time being, *the Soviet revisionists have deployed 111 divisions in the west, 20 divisions in Central Asia, and 40 divisions in the vicinity of China's frontier.* As viewed from the dispersal of troops, the primary strategic deployment of the Soviet revisionists is directed westward – toward Europe.

At present, the Soviet revisionists are chiefly contending with the US for Europe. To 'concentrate troops on the frontier' of China is just fanfare and intimidation. We must not fall for their ploy. It seems likely that, for a comparatively long period, the Soviet revisionists will not dare have a big fight with us except for provoking a few skirmishes along the frontier. They all have the figures on their minds, since they understand that we are prepared to fight a big battle.

The European countries all take different views on the wild ambitions of the Soviet revisionists. Chairman Mao holds that the Conservative government of Britain is relatively sober-minded because it perceives more clearly the ambition of the USSR. When Chairman Mao met the Foreign Minister of France, Maurice Schumann, he said to him: 'We are very clear on the fact that the USSR is trying to lure you over and that you will be taken in. For is it possible for France to stand by the side of the USSR in case a world war arises? No, you French will still side with the US'. According to what we know, Schumann immediately conveyed his remark to Minister of National Defence Michel Debré after his return to France.

In the areas of Asia, Africa, and Latin America as a whole, the two superpowers, the US and USSR are intensifying their struggle. Once the Vietnam War is concluded, the problem of the Middle East will be given priority. The two tyrants are still engaged in both collusion and contention, dividing the spheres of influence and obstructing each other. There is a place of news that has not been announced publicly; When Nixon paid a visit to Moscow in 1972, he reached a secret agreement with the Soviet revisionists; the US agreed that the USSR would allow 35,000 Jews to go to Israel annually in exchange for a US–Soviet agreement which would favour the trading and economy of the USSR. Now Israel is supplied with military equipment by the US. The latest news is that the US will furnish Israel with forty Phantom Fighters and eighty Eagle Fighters while the USSR will provide her manpower to carry on war with the Arab countries. In the midst of competition between the US and USSR, the Arab countries are disintegrating and are incapable of uniting, this being the most disadvantageous thing in their combat against Israel. Recently, Sudan's relations with Egypt have further deteriorated while there are other dangerous enemies ahead such as Algeria, Syria, Iraq, Libya, Jordan, Lebanon. They are fighting each other and creating contradictions among themselves day in and day out.

In the Middle East, the US intends to take hold of two 'bridgeheads'; one is Iran and the other is Saudi Arabia.

The struggle of the Palestinian guerrillas is beset by pressures and difficulties. This is induced by the disunity of the Arab countries. In an attempt to broaden their influence in the Middle East, the Soviet revisionists have made some changes in their attitude toward the Palestinian guerrillas by publishing a few statements of support.

Since the deterioration of relations between the USSR and Egypt, the Middle East policy of the Soviet revisionists has shifted from the management of key points to diversified management. Lately they have vigorously aided Syria and Iraq and offered to extract a rather large quantity of natural gas for Algeria after which a contract was signed. Egypt has two facets. On the one hand, she cannot completely get out of the control of the Soviet revisionists, exemplified by their driving away the Soviet specialists in July and requesting them to return in October; she still cannot do without the USSR. On the other hand, that she dared oust the Soviet specialists is an outgrowth of the deep development of the struggle against the two superpowers by the people of the Middle East.

Our attitude toward the Middle East has always been clear. We oppose the practice of both struggle and collusion by the two superpowers in the Middle East and the betrayal of the Arabian people by the Soviet revisionists. We support the struggle of the Palestinian guerrillas against Israel.

B. Questions concerning the Vietnam peace agreement

1. After years of hard-fought battles, the Vietnamese people have finally won a basic victory. The ultimate goal of the Vietnamese people's struggle was **to expel US troops**. Now that the US troops have withdrawn, the victory is extremely clear. Nevertheless, the struggle is still very complicated. We have told the Vietnamese comrades: we must be practical and realistic. The US herself knows that to continue fighting means to drag things out without knowing how long. Therefore, she will make an 'honourable withdrawal' following negotiation. Besides, having fought for so many years, the Vietnamese people have suffered great losses. **To continue fighting would not produce instant results [for them] either. But to compel the Americans to withdraw through negotiation will leave you yourselves** [the Vietnamese] **a half to one year for rest and consolidation. You can consider the problem of liberating South Vietnam later. The Vietnamese comrades have received our suggestion.**

2. Upon the signing of the Paris Agreement, **we differed from the Vietnamese comrades on a couple of issues**: (a) On the matter of the US military bases in South Vietnam, the US said that she had dismantled her military bases in South Vietnam in the wake of each successive troop withdrawal. This is not true. But the Vietnamese comrades did not resolutely refute this. (b) On the question of holding democratic elections among 'three political forces' in Vietnam in the future, there are no concrete provisions but only empty talk. This is disadvantageous to the leftist forces in South Vietnam. (c) We exhorted the Vietnamese comrades to persist in preventing the United Nations from taking a hand in the Paris Conference. [We felt that] the chairmanship of the Conference should be assumed by the US and Vietnam representatives in rotation, and not by the Secretary-General of the UN because, once the UN stepped in, all problems concerning Vietnam afterwards would have to be handled through the UN and things would become complex. Later the problem was handled through a compromise with the UN Secretary-General being 'seated as an observer' and not as the Conference chairman. (d) [We felt that] in the Paris Agreements,

only the Vietnam issue should be discussed; the problems of Cambodia and Laos should not be dragged in. Yet, the problems of the two countries [Cambodia and Laos] were still mentioned in the Agreements. This was not good because we cannot impose the Vietnam issue on these two countries.

3. The Soviet revisionists will intensify economic aid to the Vietnamese people after the Vietnam war comes to an end to balance out our influence in Vietnam. The struggle from now on will become complicated and acute.

C. The world situation after Vietnam signed the peace agreement and our assessment of the strategic position of countries concerned

1. The Indochina region

With the truce in Vietnam, the people of North Vietnam will acquire rest and consolidation and achieve economic reconstruction within a short period. Their chief means will be self-reliance, but, without international support, there will be difficulties. The US planes bombarded Vietnam too extensively and destroyed too much. Reconstruction will require some international support. The Chinese people will provide the Vietnamese comrades with necessary aid. The Soviet revisionists will also offer them rather considerable economic assistance. **They contend with us on this point, mainly vying with us to exert influence over Vietnam.**

The Vietnamese comrades will continue **to work out a 'Sino-Soviet balance.'** This depends on how good a job we do. Of course, our aid is devoid of any conditions and is sincere and selfless.

At the Paris Conference, the Vietnamese comrades did not take our advice regarding the question of inviting the UN Secretary-General to the Conference. The reason is that the Vietnamese comrades maintained **an illusion about the UN**, hoping to obtain economic aid from the UN and gain an opportunity to join the UN faster.

We advise the Vietnamese comrades to heighten their vigilance a hundred-fold during the period of rest and consolidation because the US left 10,000 armed military personnel dressed in civilian clothes and appearing in the form of technical specialists and because US military equipment was handed over to Nguyen

Van Thieu in large quantities. Nguyen Van Thieu now maintains 800,000 troops. The Paris Cease-fire Agreement contains only a few empty phrases on the problem of holding democratic free elections among the three political powers in South Vietnam. These empty phrases are useless.

If war breaks out again in Vietnam, would the US Army send hundreds of thousands of men to Vietnam as they did before? It seems unlikely. The Americans oppose this war and the US government does not want to get deeper into an awkward situation because there are many problems facing the US in Europe, the Middle East, and all areas where the Soviet revisionists are expanding their influence. The Vietnamese people can crush Nguyen Van Thieu politically and militarily, but they need a period of time as well as correct political [analysis] and high sensitivity to the 'false support and real betrayal' of the Soviet revisionists.

The political status of Laos is favourable to her people and the signing of the Laotian armistice agreement is advantageous to the leftist forces. Future changes are dependent on a correct political line. The current situation in Cambodia is also good. The Lon Nol regime now controls only a small piece of land, and moreover, it seems that the Americans do not respect this president very much. Lately the attitude of Prince Sihanouk has been tough and resolute. Men are always subject to change and a change in the direction of progress is good. The peace in Indochina is temporary; no one is sleeping. Our basic policy is to support all revolutionary progressive forces in overthrowing all reactionary forces and to support the struggles of the Vietnamese, Cambodian, and Laotian people just as we have always been doing.

2. Assessment of the strategic deployment of the Soviet revisionists: Since the cease-fire in Vietnam, the key strategic points of **the Soviet revisionists have become, first, Europe and, second, the Middle East**. Of course, sometimes it is very hard to discriminate between the first and the second.

As I have said before, their European policy is primarily a policy of polarization, a policy of compelling Western Europe to 'neutralize,' and a policy of going a step further to control the whole Europe. In the Middle East, they both struggle and collude with the US, dividing equally the spheres of influence. Their contention with the US will get more intense, but they avoid face-to-face military clashes with the US. Lifting high the signboard of the October Revolution and the homeland of Lenin, the Soviet revisionists still maintain their global deceptiveness. Many countries become aware of this only after they have suffered bad losses.

In Asia as a whole, the Soviet revisionists are intensifying the adoption of a policy of subversion and ingratiation and will take advantage of **the US withdrawal of troops from Asia by** attempting **to 'fill the vacuum'**. Will the US give up Asia? Impossible! The US will not relinquish its advantage in Asia. The US has simply placed herself on the second line, but in some other places she is still on the first line. It will not be as easy as the Soviet revisionists figured to turn a profit in the future Asia, for there stands China!

On the South Asian subcontinent, the Soviet revisionists will **foster '*détente*' among 'India, Pakistan and Bangladesh' and** improve and mend their relations **with Pakistan** in order to **place India, Pakistan and Bangladesh within their 'Asian Collective Security Treaty' sphere of influence**.

Toward Japan, the Soviet revisionists use the exploitation of the Tyumen oilfields as a lure to improve relations with her. However, Japan will not abandon its demand for the return of the four islands north of Japan. Under Japan's strategy of 'separation of politics and economics', it is impossible for relations between Japan and the USSR to make any progress. The Soviet revisionists are also attempting to lure the US into opening up the Tyumen oilfields, but the US capitalists have not shown great interest. First, the USSR uses US capital to promote construction and her own capital to amplify her armaments. Second, it will require five years after the initial in investment to produce petroleum products and who knows what will happen in the world in those five years.

In the future, the entire strategic deployment of the Soviet revisionists is global, confronting not only the US but also us. While **they simultaneously struggle against and collude with the US, they maintain completely antagonistic relations with us. This is the essence of the problem.**

Our opposing the two superpowers is a slogan. Its essence lies principally in opposition against this most realistic enemy, Soviet revisionist social-imperialism, and the main thing is to

combat this social-imperialism. We have a clear understanding of this problem and so does the US.

Last year we made comparatively good progress in our diplomatic work in Southeast Asian countries. Several countries will probably establish relations with us this year and those who do not entertain relations with us will develop closer contacts [with us]. The situation in the South Asian subcontinent is, in contrast, relatively complicated; the Soviet revisionists have a tight grip on it. Nevertheless, India's attitude toward us has changed.

We support the European Common Market because it is a kind of force which resists the USSR and the US. Among the three principal countries in Europe, Britain, France and West Germany, Britain has maintained rather positive relations with us over the past year or more, for the British have accurately sensed the trend.

The Middle East is still in a phase of neither war nor peace; neither the US nor the USSR desire a face-to-face conflict.

However, the possibility of a partial solution also exists. We have always backed the Arab countries and the struggle of the Palestinian guerrillas but have never actually meddled.

It is all right to uphold people's struggles but not adventurist actions. The foreign minister of the Malagasy Republic told me: 'There are also "ultraleftist" elements in the Malagasy Republic who hope to drive away all the French.' I told him: 'That isn't strange, for China has those kinds of people and so do the Soviet revisionists; they pressure us to recapture Hong Kong and Macao.' We said that Macao cannot be recovered, not to mention Hong Kong. **To take it back would shock the British in Hong Kong and cause Britain and the US to unite together;** we cannot do that. There is still the Taiwan [problem]. The work [of solving it] will also require some time. It will not do to be impetuous. We must take all sides of the issue into account. Hong Kong and Macao and Taiwan are two different matters and must be handled in different ways.

We are now promoting criticism of Lin Piao and rectification with emphasis placed on the criticism of Lin on the one hand, and are driving all kinds of construction and all kinds of [other] work by criticizing Lin on the other. The most important kind of strategic deployment is to have a great leap forward in all areas, such as industry, agriculture, and technology, by adopting the advanced techniques of other countries.

3. Assessment of the strategic deployment of the US:
With the truce in Vietnam, US military forces will be deployed as follows:

a) The key strategic focus point will shift to Europe and Middle East;
b) Japan will be placed on the first line in Asia;
c) Construction of military bases on the Mariana Islands will be stepped up as a defensive measure on the second line against the USSR;
d) Building up the navy in the Pacific Ocean and the two wings of the West, South, and North Indian Ocean will be stepped up to block the expansion of Soviet maritime strength.

4. Evaluation of Japan's future orientation:
Japan is now standing at a crossroads.

There are two reasons which account for Japan's becoming an aggressive country since the nineteenth century: first, Japan has neither [internal] resources nor markets; second, the national economic budget of Japan is small, [thus] she has to expand outward when her domestic economic development reaches the saturation point.

The strategy of Japan after the Vietnam war has been discussed before. Of course, the pivotal point rests will her attitude toward the USSR. Ostensibly, she applies a strategy of '*détente*,' but in essence she has adopted, politically and militarily, a policy of 'resisting the USSR.'

Japan has expressed some apprehension about the military threat of the USSR. Previously she relied on the protection of the US nuclear umbrella, but what will she do now? Japan understands clearly that if she depends entirely on US military protection, the US will squeeze her neck economically. Therefore, Japan cannot help but develop her own military power. Yet would the development of military power lead her back on the old road of militarism? This is what troubles her.

Japan's Nakasone drew a 'picture of displaying the armies' on his visit to China. He told us of the current military deployment of Japan, saying that Japan has only nine land divisions concentrated mostly in Hokkaido to guard against the USSR. Japan's navy is now also very small, a fleet of small vessels. What Nakasone meant is that (a) the important thing is for Japan to take military precautions against the USSR in the future, but her military strength is small and needs development; (b) as Japan's military strength is now so small, it is wrong to call her 'militarist.' The situation described by Nakasone is basically true.

Japan plans to expand economically to a larger area of Asia; one is Southeast Asia and the other is postwar Vietnam. She now shows deep interest, engaging in positive activities. Is Japan's future in the direction of 'democracy, neutralization, independence and peace'? Or is it a return to the old road of militarism? We must carry out our work as we wait to see.

5. Our basic strategy:

It is to oppose the two superpowers, chiefly the most direct, the most perilous and the most real enemy, Soviet revisionist social-imperialism. **This strategy was laid down by Chairman Mao. Chairman Mao said: 'We must not fight on two fronts; it is better to fight on one front.'**

Should we now declare war on the Soviet revisionists? Not necessarily. The current strategy of the USSR is directed at the West, Europe and the Middle East. Toward us, she makes a lot of noise but also knows that we have been prepared for a long time. So, for a time, the situation will remain a 'cold war', a diplomatic 'bull fight', a 'baring of teeth'. But it is still necessary to guard against her taking a great risk.

We must still condemn the US for whatever is reprehensible. When she oppresses the small and medium-sized countries, we must reprimand her. **Of the two world superpowers, one is the most direct enemy. Now the US retires to the second position. We cannot propose 'uniting with the US to oppose the USSR' though we have points in common with the US on certain issues.** Furthermore, there is the Pentagon, a den of war-mongering elements, supported by the great arms manufac-turers. **We must maintain our vigilance against the US all the same;** we cannot lose it.

We are in the midst of working on Japan, sending many delegations, including political, economic and cultural ones as well as people-to-people friendship groups. **The problem of Japan is a serious one. She is now standing at a crossroads and still has ambitions.**

Document 9: Unite to win still greater victories

[1972 New Year's Day Editorial by *Renmin Ribao (People's Daily)*, *Hongqi (Red Flag)* and *Jiefangjun Bao (Liberation Army Daily)* *Foreign Languages Press, Peking*, 1972]

Nineteen seventy-one was a year of victory. Marching forward courageously along Chairman Mao's proletarian revolutionary line, the people of all nationalities in China confidently step into 1972, a year of militancy.

When the world entered the 1970s, Chairman Mao pointed out in his statement of May 20, 1970: 'The danger of a new world war still exists, and the people of all countries must get prepared. But revolution is the main trend in the world today.' Developments in the international situation in the past year have further confirmed this scientific thesis.

The world has been in a state of great upheaval in the past year. The basic contradictions in the contemporary world have sharpened. In particular, the contradictions between US imperialism and Soviet revisionism on the one hand and the people of the world including the American and Soviet people on the other, and the contradictions between the two superpowers in their *scramble* for *world hegemony* and *spheres of influence* have become even more acute and widespread. Aggression, subversion, control, interference and bullying by imperialism and social-imperialism have aroused the people of Asia, Africa, Latin America and the rest of the world to rise against them. Local wars between aggression and resistance to aggression and between revolution and counter-revolution have never ceased. **The imperialist camp is split**. The revisionist bloc is falling apart. The reactionaries of various countries are *sitting on thorns*. Various political forces are in the process of further division and reorganization. The characteristic feature of the world situation today can be summed up in one word, 'upheaval', or *'global upheaval'*. In this situation, the political consciousness of the proletariat and people of various countries has rapidly risen, Marxist-Leninist Parties and organizations have been tempered in the course of struggle, and the revolutionary movements of the oppressed nations and people have deepened. From the strategic rear areas of imperialism to the 'heartland' of capitalism, revolutionary struggles are surging forward. *Countries want independence, nations want liberation and the people want*

206

revolution – this great historical tide is pounding the decadent rule of imperialism and all reaction.

Never before did US imperialism find itself in such a *plight*. Its counter-revolutionary global strategy has suffered one defeat after another. Its powers of aggression have been enormously weakened by the magnificent victories of the people of Vietnam, Laos and Cambodia in their war against US aggression and for national salvation, by the growth of the struggle of the Palestinian and other Arab peoples against US–Israeli aggression, by the rise of the revolutionary mass movement of the American people and by the upsurge of the world people's struggle against US imperialism. *The profound change in the balance of forces between the United States on the one hand and Japan and the West European and other capitalist countries on the other has intensified their fight to shift their crises on to each other and their scramble for markets and sources of raw material.* And the United States is faced with its toughest challenge in the 26 post-war years. All this has aggravated the political, economic and social crisis in the United States.

Following in the footsteps of US imperialism, Soviet revisionist social-imperialism is *grabbing* out everywhere under all sorts of covers. While oppressing the people of different nationalities in the Soviet Union itself, the Brezhnev renegade clique is doing its utmost to control and exploit the people of the other countries in its 'community' and working *feverishly* to expand its spheres of influence all over the world. Thus it is putting more and more nooses round its own neck. In the past year, Soviet revisionism has *colluded* with US imperialism in *nuclear deals*, signed the agreement on West Berlin selling out the sovereignty of the German Democratic Republic, conducted subversion in many countries, threatened the Balkans, undermined the armed struggle of the Palestinian and other Arab peoples against the US–Israeli aggressors and, above all, shamelessly and flagrantly supported the Indian reactionaries' armed aggression against Pakistan. All this has further exposed its social-imperialist features before the people of the world, subjected it to their fierce *denunciation* and landed it in a more and more isolated position.

Chairman Mao points out: 'Affairs in the world require consultations. The internal affairs of a country must be settled by the people of that country, and international affairs must be settled by all concerned through consultation. They must not be decided by the two big powers.' Gone are the days when representatives of the two superpowers could decide the destinies of other countries at will by sitting down together and making deals behind their backs. More and more medium and small countries are joining forces to oppose the hegemony and power politics of the two superpowers; countries of the Third World are increasingly playing a positive role in international affairs; and all the countries and people suffering from aggression, subversion, control, interference and bullying by the two superpowers are forming a broad united front. This is an important trend in international relations today. At the 26th Session of the UN General Assembly, US Government obstruction was broken through and the resolution was adopted by an overwhelming majority restoring China's lawful rights in the United Nations and immediately expelling the representatives of the Chiang Kai-shek clique from that world body and all its related organizations; and, against the will of Soviet social-imperialism, the resolution calling upon India and Pakistan to cease fire and withdraw their armed forces was adopted with an overwhelming majority of 104 votes. Never before had there been a situation in which medium and small countries were able to play such an inspiring role in the United Nations through their joint efforts, the voice of justice was able to prevail to such an extent, and the two superpowers, the United States and the Soviet Union, were so isolated. The changes in the United Nations are a vivid reflection of the excellent international situation.

But imperialism, social-imperialism and the reactionaries of various countries are not reconciled to their defeat; they are bound to struggle desperately and continue to make trouble. The events of the past year have again vividly proved that the harder things go for them, the more frenziedly do they want to carry out aggression, interference and subversion, and even unscrupulously to provoke new wars of aggression. Therefore, the people of various countries must maintain high vigilance, constantly sum up their experience, reinforce their unity, build up their strength and persist in struggle so as to win new victories.

Implementing Chairman Mao's revolutionary line and policies in foreign affairs, the Chinese people have achieved important successes in the past year. Together with the people of other countries, we have carried out resolute struggles against imperialism, expansionism, colonialism and neo-colonialism, and against the hegemony and power politics of the two superpowers. Our revolutionary friendship with fraternal socialist countries has continued to grow, and we have marched shoulder to shoulder with the Albanian Party of Labour and all genuine Marxist-Leninist Parties and organizations in the world in the struggle against modern revisionism with the Soviet revisionist renegade clique at its centre. Our militant unity with the people of Vietnam, Laos and Cambodia in the struggle against US imperialist aggression has grown stronger; we have acted in close coordination with the people of Korea, Japan and other Asian countries in the struggle against US imperialism and Japanese militarism; and we and the Arab, African and Latin American peoples have supported one another in the anti-imperialist struggle. In the past year, our friendly contacts with the people of various countries have developed continually, our cooperation with many friendly countries has advanced, we have established diplomatic relations with 15 more countries, and, in particular, our lawful rights in the United Nations have been restored; the growing influence of our socialist motherland in the world has thus been fully demonstrated. All this inspires us with immense confidence to work hard and continue to implement Chairman Mao's revolutionary line and policies in foreign affairs.

The past year has been a year of great victory in carrying out education in ideology and political line throughout the Party and among the people of the whole country. Adhering to Chairman Mao's teachings, the whole Party, through reading and studying, opposing arrogance and doing away with complacency, and criticizing revisionism and rectifying the style of work, has carried forward the struggle between the two classes, the two roads and the two lines in a deep-going way and consolidated and developed the gains of the Great Proletarian Cultural Revolution. The masses of cadres and Party members, and senior Party cadres in particular, have engaged in a serious study of the works of Marx, Engels, Lenin and Stalin and Chairman Mao's works, and this has gradually become a common practice. They have raised their ability to distinguish genuine from sham Marxism and further exposed and criticized the conspiracies of Liu Shao-chi and other *swindlers* who had *illicit* relations with foreign countries and attempted to change the line and policies of the Party and the socialist system. The whole Party, the whole army and the people of the whole country have rallied still more closely around the Party Central Committee headed by Chairman Mao. This is of profound, far-reaching significance for consolidating the dictatorship of the proletariat and preventing capitalist restoration in China, and is a very heavy blow to social-imperialism and to imperialism, revisionism and *reaction* throughout the world. It is a great victory for the proletariat and people of China, for Marxism-Leninism-Mao Tsetung Thought, and for Chairman Mao's proletarian revolutionary line.

The victorious progress of the Great Proletarian Cultural Revolution and the ever-deepening process of education in ideology and political line have enhanced the enthusiasm for socialism of the masses of workers, peasants, soldiers and revolutionary intellectuals and promoted the steady advance of industry, agriculture, commerce, science and technology, culture and education and work in other fields; our socialist construction is thriving. In 1971 we successfully fulfilled the fighting tasks of the first year of the Fourth Five-Year Plan for the development of the national economy. Total value of industrial and agricultural output increased by about 10 per cent over 1970. In agriculture, a good harvest was reaped for the tenth year in succession. In spite of relatively serious natural calamities, China's 1971 grain output surpassed that of the rich harvest year of 1970, reaching 246 million tons. Change the situation in which grain has to be transported north from the south, a task laid down by Chairman Mao, began to become a reality. Industrial production continued to rise, and the quality of products improved and their variety increased. Steel output reached 21 million tons, or 18 per cent above 1970. This marked the rise of China's industry to a new level. Capital construction went ahead fairly fast. Prices remained stable and the market *brisk* throughout the country. The material reserves of the state and the people increased further. There was some improvement in the living standards of the people. There were a number of new developments and creations in the revolution on the cultural and educational fronts. Scientific and technological standards improved to some extent. The People's Liberation

Army has become stronger and our national defence is more consolidated than ever.

Chairman Mao points out: 'The line is the key link; once it is grasped, everything falls into place.' Our work in the past year has fully testified to the correctness of this thesis. In the new year the whole Party, the whole army and the people throughout the country should continue to carry out deep-going education in ideology and political line, strengthen Party leadership and deepen struggle-criticism-transformation on all fronts, bring about greater progress in socialist revolution and socialist construction, further consolidate the dictatorship of the proletariat and firmly pursue the line put forward by the Ninth Party Congress, Unite to win still greater victories.

In carrying out education in ideology and political line and unfolding the movement to criticize revisionism and rectify the style of work, it is essential, in line with Chairman Mao's teaching, to take the following as the important content: Practise Marxism, and not revisionism; unite, and don't split; be open and aboveboard, and don't intrigue and conspire. Whether to practise Marxism or to practise revisionism has always been the *crux* of the struggle between the two lines. It is essential to continue the deepening of the mass movement for studying Marxism-Leninism-Mao Tsetung Thought, to read and study seriously and have a good grasp of Marxism and do a good job of revolutionary mass criticism to eliminate the *virus* of the revisionist line. It is necessary to integrate theory with practice, and link past struggles with current ones so that we can make a still clearer distinction between Chairman Mao's Marxist-Leninist line and policies and the anti-Marxist-Leninist line and policies of Liu Shao-chi and other swindlers, between the materialist theory of reflection and idealist apriorism, between the socialist road and the capitalist road and between what helps strengthen Party leadership and what weakens or rejects it. Chairman Mao has always advocated being open and aboveboard. Liu Shao-chi and other swindlers, engaged in counter-revolutionary activities for the purpose of restoring capitalism, are extremely isolated in the whole Party and the whole army and among the people throughout the country, and they cannot *bear the light of day*; they can therefore only resort to intrigue and conspiracy, and rumour-mongering and mud-slinging. By insisting on being open and aboveboard we will be able to detect and resist the anti-Party and anti-popular *evil wind* and constantly strengthen the unity of the Party. Chairman Mao points out: **'What do we mean by unity? Of course we mean unity on the basis of Marxism-Leninism, and not unprincipled unity.' 'Both inside and outside the Party it is necessary to unite with the vast majority. Only thus can things be done well.'** We must follow this teaching of Chairman Mao's and unite with the vast majority of the people, including those who have wrongly opposed us but are sincerely correcting their mistakes. Deepening education in ideology and political line is sure to raise the consciousness of the whole Party and people throughout the country in continuing the revolution under the dictatorship of the proletariat and is sure to give a tremendous impetus to all kinds of work.

Education in ideology and political line should go hand in hand with the tasks of struggle-criticism-transformation. The aim of the movement of struggle-criticism-transformation in the Great Proletarian Cultural Revolution is, in accordance with Chairman Mao's revolutionary line, to transform all those parts of the superstructure that are not *in conformity with* the socialist economic base and to ensure that the task of consolidating the dictatorship of the proletariat is fulfilled in every basic unit. Only by grasping education in ideology and political line can the movement of struggle-criticism-transformation on all fronts have a correct orientation and go really deep. Struggle-criticism-transformation develops unevenly, much work remains to be completed, weak links and units still exist, and some new problems have cropped up and need to be solved. We must analyse the situation, sum up experience, study policies and make overall plans so that our work will conform still more with objective reality.

It is essential to continue to strengthen *the Party's centralized leadership* and the ideological and organizational building of Party committees and branches, to do a good job of getting rid of the stale and taking in the fresh according to Party principle and do mass work well among the workers, peasants, youth, women, intellectuals and other people. Party organizations should adhere to the mass line, be good at concentrating the collective wisdom, intensify investigation and study, grasp typical examples well and pay constant attention to Chairman Mao's teaching 'Be concerned with the well-being of the masses, pay attention to methods of work.' We must adhere to the system of cadre participation in collective productive labour and combat the corrosive influence of the bourgeoisie. Communists should stand up for principle and dare to struggle against all erroneous tendencies running counter to Marxism-Leninism-Mao Tsetung Thought. Chairman Mao says: 'Our Party's consistent principle in dealing with comrades who have committed mistakes is to lay the main stress on education, namely, learning from past mistakes to avoid future ones and curing the sickness to save the patient.' We must continue to apply this principle and, under the leadership of the proletariat, unite all the forces that can be united.

Chairman Mao has issued the call: **In industry, learn from Taching; in agriculture, learn from Tachai; the whole nation should learn from the People's Liberation Army; the Liberation Army should learn from the people of the whole country.** We should follow this teaching and promote the vigorous progress of the revolutionary mass movement on all fronts. The revolutionary masses in industry, agriculture, commerce, science and technology, culture and education and other fields should continue to carry forward the spirit of hard struggle and self-reliance, carry out in an all-round way the principle of grasping revolution, promoting production and other work and preparedness against war and go all out, aim high and fulfil or overfulfil the state plan with greater, faster, better and more economical results to greet the *convocation of the Fourth National People's Congress*. In accordance with Chairman Mao's line on army building, the Chinese People's Liberation Army should strengthen army building and energetically grasp military and political training so as to raise its political and military qualities higher. It is necessary to strengthen militia building. It is necessary to **support the army and cherish the people, support the government and cherish the people,** and thus *strengthen army–government and army–civilian unity.* It is necessary to deal resolute blows at the *disruptive* activities of the counter-revolutionaries. The army men and the people throughout the country should conscientiously study the international situation and the Party's line and policies in foreign affairs, heighten our vigilance, defend the motherland, be well prepared against wars of aggression and firmly smash all imperialist and social-imperialist plots of aggression and subversion.

As we greet the new year, we express our deep concern for our *compatriots* in Taiwan. Taiwan Province is an inalienable part of China's territory. Our compatriots there are our brothers by flesh and blood. The liberation of Taiwan is China's internal affair which *brooks* no interference by any outsider. We firmly oppose such *concoctions* as 'one China, one Taiwan', 'one China, two governments', 'the status of Taiwan remains to be determined' or 'an independent Taiwan', and any similar intrigues. All US armed forces must be withdrawn from Taiwan and the Taiwan Straits. The Chinese people are determined to liberate Taiwan! We are convinced that the day is bound to come.

We have *scored* great achievements. But China is still a developing country, its economy is relatively backward and it is confronted with immense tasks in revolution and construction. Our achievements are inseparable from the support of the proletariat and revolutionary people the world over. We must continue to fulfil our internationalist duty and firmly support the just struggle of the oppressed people and oppressed nations throughout the world. In the face of the new fighting tasks at home and abroad, we should remain modest and prudent, guard against arrogance and impetuosity, study and work harder and strive to make a greater contribution to humanity by winning new victories.

Long live the victory of Chairman Mao's proletarian revolutionary line!

Long live Chairman Mao, the great leader of the people of all the nationalities of China! A long, long life to Chairman Mao!

Document 10 Speech by chairman of the delegation of the People's Republic of China, Teng Hsiao-ping, at the Special Session of the UN General Assembly (April 10, 1974)

[Foreign Languages Press, Peking, 1974]

Mr President,

The special session of the United Nations General Assembly on the problems of raw materials and development is successfully convened on the proposals of President Houari

Boumédienne of the Council of Revolution of the Democratic People's Republic of Algeria and with the support of the great majority of the countries of the world. This is the first time in the 29 years since the founding of the United Nations that a session is held specially to discuss the important question of opposing imperialist exploitation and plunder and effecting a change in international economic relations. This reflects that profound changes have taken place in the international situation. The Chinese Government extends its warm congratulations on the convocation of this session and hopes that it will make a positive contribution to strengthening the unity of the developing countries, safeguarding their national economic rights and interests and promoting the struggle of all peoples against imperialism, and particularly against hegemonism.

At present, the international situation is most favourable to the developing countries and the peoples of the world. More and more, the old order based on colonialism, imperialism and hegemonism is being undermined and shaken to its foundations. International relations are changing drastically. The whole world is in turbulence and unrest. The situation is one of 'great disorder under heaven', as we Chinese put it. This 'disorder' is a manifestation of the sharpening of all the basic contradictions in the contemporary world. It is accelerating the disintegration and decline of the decadent reactionary forces and stimulating the awakening and growth of the new emerging forces of the people.

In this situation of 'great disorder under heaven', all the political forces in the world have undergone drastic division and realignment through prolonged trials of strength and struggle. A large number of Asian, African and Latin American countries have achieved independence one after another and they are playing an ever greater role in international affairs. As a result of the emergence of social-imperialism, the socialist camp which existed for a time after World War II is no longer in existence. Owing to the law of the uneven development of capitalism, the Western imperialist bloc, too, is disintegrating. Judging from the changes in international relations, the world today actually consists of three parts, or three worlds, that are both interconnected and in contradiction to one another. *The United States and the Soviet Union make up the First World. The developing countries in Asia, Africa, Latin America and other regions make up the Third World. The developed countries between the two make up the Second World.*

The two superpowers, the United States and the Soviet Union, are vainly seeking world hegemony. Each in its own way attempts to bring the developing countries of Asia, Africa and Latin America under its control and, at the same time, to bully the developed countries that are not their match in strength.

The two superpowers are the biggest international exploiters and oppressors of today. They are the source of a new world war. They both possess large numbers of nuclear weapons. They carry on a keenly contested arms race, station massive forces abroad and set up military bases everywhere, threatening the independence and security of all nations. They both keep subjecting other countries to their control, subversion, interference or aggression. They both exploit other countries economically, plundering their wealth and grabbing their resources. In bullying others, the superpower which flaunts the label of socialism is especially vicious. It has dispatched its armed forces to occupy its 'ally' Czechoslovakia and investigated the war to dismember Pakistan. It does not honour its words and is perfidious; it is self-seeking and unscrupulous.

The case of the developed countries in between the superpowers and the developing countries is a complicated one. Some of them still retain colonialist relations of one form or another with Third World Countries, and a country like Portugal even continues with its barbarous colonial rule. An end must be put to this state of affairs. At the same time, all these developed countries are in varying degrees controlled, threatened or bullied by the one superpower or the other. Some of them have in fact been reduced by a superpower to the position of dependencies under the signboard of its so-called 'family'. In varying degrees, all these countries have the desire of shaking off superpower enslavement or control and safeguarding their national independence and the integrity of their sovereignty.

The numerous developing countries have long suffered from colonialist and imperialist oppression, and exploitation. They have won political independence, yet all of them still face the historic task of clearing out the remnant forces of colonialism, developing the national economy and consolidating national independence. These countries cover vast territories, encompass a large population and abound in natural resources. Having suffered the heaviest oppression, they have the strongest desire to oppose oppression and seek liberation and development. In the struggle for national liberation and independence, they have demonstrated immense power and continually won splendid victories. They constitute a revolutionary motive force propelling the wheel of world history and are the main force combating colonialism, imperialism, and particularly the superpowers.

Since the two superpowers are contending for world hegemony, the contradiction between them is irreconcilable; one either overpowers the other, or is overpowered. Their compromise and collusion can only be partial, temporary and relative, while their contention is all-embracing, permanent and absolute. In the final analysis, the so-called 'balanced reduction of forces' and 'strategic arms limitation' are nothing but empty talk, for in fact there is no 'balance', nor can there possibly be 'limitation'. They may reach certain agreements, but their agreements are only a façade and a deception. At bottom, they are aiming at greater and fiercer contention. The contention between the superpowers extends over the entire globe. Strategically, Europe is the focus of their contention, where they are in constant tense confrontation. They are intensifying their rivalry in the Middle East, the Mediterranean, the Persian Gulf, the Indian Ocean and the Pacific. Every day, they talk about disarmament but are actually engaged in arms expansion. Every day, they talk about *'detente'* but are actually creating tension. Wherever they contend, turbulence occurs. So long as imperialism and social-imperialism exist, there definitely will be no tranquillity in the world, nor will there be 'lasting peace'. Either they will fight each other, or the people will rise in revolution. It is as Chairman Mao Tsetung has said: The danger of a new world war still exists, and the people of all countries must get prepared. But revolution is the main trend in the world today.

The two superpowers have created their own antithesis. Acting in the way of the big bullying the small, the strong domineering over the weak and the rich oppressing the poor, they have aroused strong resistance among the Third World and the people of the whole world. The people of Asia, Africa and Latin America have been winning new victories in their struggles against colonialism, imperialism, and particularly hegemonism. The Indochinese peoples are continuing to press forward in their struggles against US imperialist aggression and for national liberation. In the 4th Middle East war, the people of the Arab countries and Palestine broke through the control of the two superpowers and the state of 'no war, no peace' and won a tremendous victory over the Israeli aggressors. The African people's struggles against imperialism, colonialism and racial discrimination are developing in depth. The Republic of Guinea-Bissau was born in glory amidst the flames of armed struggle. The armed struggles and mass movements carried out by the peoples of Mozambique, Angola, Zimbabwe, Namibia and Azania against Portuguese colonial rule and white racism in South Africa and Southern Rhodesia are surging ahead vigorously. The struggle to defend sea rights initiated by Latin American countries has grown into a worldwide struggle against the maritime hegemony of the two superpowers. The 10th Assembly of the Heads of State and Government of the Organization of African Unity, the 4th Summit Conference of the Non-Aligned Countries, the Arab Summit Conference and the Islamic Summit Conference successively voiced strong condemnation against imperialism, colonialism, neo-colonialism, hegemonism, Zionism and racism, demonstrating the developing countries' firm will and determination to strengthen their unity and support one another in their common struggle against the hated enemies. The struggles of the Asian, African and Latin American countries and people, advancing wave upon wave, have exposed the essential weakness of imperialism, and particularly the superpowers, which are outwardly strong but inwardly feeble, and dealt heavy blows at their wild ambitions to dominate the world.

The hegemonism and power politics of the two superpowers have also aroused strong dissatisfaction *among the developed countries of the Second World. The struggles of these countries against superpower control, interference, intimidation, exploitation and shifting of economic crises are growing day by day. Their struggles also have a significant impact on the development of the international situation.*

Innumerable facts show that all views that overestimate the strength of the two hegemonic powers and underestimate the strength of the people are groundless. It is not the one or two superpowers that are really powerful; the really powerful are the Third World and the people of all countries uniting together and daring to fight and daring to win. Since numerous Third World countries and people were able to achieve political independence through protracted struggle, certainly they will also be able, on this basis, to bring about through sustained struggle a thorough change in the international economic relations which are based on inequality, control and exploitation and thus create essential conditions for the independent development of their national economy by strengthening their unity and allying themselves with other countries subjected to superpower bullying as well as with the people of the whole world, including the people of the United States and the Soviet Union.

Mr President,

The essence of the problems of raw materials and development is the struggle of the developing countries to defend their state sovereignty, develop their national economy and combat imperialist, and particularly superpower, plunder and control. This is a very important aspect of the current struggle of the Third World countries and people against colonialism, imperialism and hegemonism.

As we all know, in the last few centuries colonialism and imperialism unscrupulously enslaved and plundered the people of Asia, Africa and Latin America. Exploiting the cheap labour power of the local people and their rich natural resources and imposing a lopsided and single-product economy, they extorted superprofits by grabbing low-priced farm and mineral products, dumping their industrial goods, strangling national industries and carrying on an exchange of unequal values. The richness of the developed countries and the poverty of the developing countries are the result of the colonialist and imperialist policy of plunder.

In many Asian, African and Latin American countries that have won political independence, the economic lifelines are still controlled by colonialism and imperialism in varying degrees, and the old economic structure has not changed fundamentally. The imperialists, and particularly the superpowers, have adopted neo-colonialist methods to continue and intensify their exploitation and plunder of the developing countries. They export capital to the developing countries and build there a 'state within a state' by means of such international monopoly organizations as 'trans-national corporations' to carry out eco-

219

nomic plunder and political interference. Taking advantage of their monopoly position in international markets, they reap fabulous profits by raising the export prices of their own products and forcing down those of raw materials from the developing countries. Moreover, with the deepening of the political and economic crises of capitalism and the sharpening of their mutual competition, they are further intensifying their plunder of the developing countries by shifting the economic and monetary crises on to the latter.

It must be pointed out that the superpower which styles itself a socialist country is by no means less proficient at neo-colonialist economic plunder. Under the name of so-called 'economic cooperation' and 'international division of labour', it uses high-handed measures to extort superprofits in its 'family'. In profiting at others' expense, it has gone to lengths rarely seen even in the case of other imperialist countries. The 'joint enterprises' it runs in some countries under the signboard of 'aid' and 'support' are in essence copies of 'trans-national corporations.' Its usual practice is to tag a high price on outmoded equipment and sub-standard weapons and exchange them for strategic raw materials and farm produce of the developing countries. Selling arms and ammunition in a big way, it has become an international merchant of death. It often takes advantage of others' difficulties to press for the repayment of debts. In the recent Middle East war, it bought Arab oil at a low price with the large amount of foreign exchange it had earned by peddling munitions, and then sold it at a high price, making staggering profits in the twinkling of an eye. Moreover, it preaches the theory of 'limited sovereignty', alleges that the resources of developing countries are international property, and even asserts that 'the sovereignty over the natural resources is depending to a great extent upon the capability of utilizing these resources by the industry of the developing countries.' These are out-and-out imperialist fallacies. They are even more undisguised than the so-called 'inter-dependence' advertised by the other superpower, which actually means retaining the exploitative relationship. A socialist country that is true to its name ought to follow the principle of internationalism, sincerely render support and assistance to oppressed countries and nations and help them develop their national economy. But this superpower is doing exactly the opposite. This is additional proof that it is socialism in words and imperialism in deeds.

Plunder and exploitation by colonialism, imperialism, and particularly by the superpowers, are making the poor countries poorer and the rich countries richer, further widening the gap between the two. Imperialism is the greatest obstacle to the liberation of the developing countries and to their progress. It is entirely right and proper for the developing countries to terminate imperialist economic monopoly and plunder, sweep away these obstacles and take all necessary measures to protect their economic resources and other rights and interests.

The doings of imperialism, and particularly the superpowers, can in no way check the triumphant advance of the developing countries along the road of economic liberation. In the recent Middle East war, the Arab countries, united as one, used oil as a weapon with which they dealt a telling blow at Zionism and its supporters. They did well, and rightly too. This was a pioneering action taken by developing countries in their struggle against imperialism. It greatly heightened the fighting spirit of the people of the Third World and deflated the arrogance of imperialism. It broke through the international economic monopoly long maintained by imperialism and fully demonstrated the might of a united struggle waged by developing countries. If imperialist monopolies can gang up to manipulate the markets at will, to the great detriment of the vital interests of the developing countries, why can't developing countries unite to break imperialist monopoly and defend their own economic rights and interests? The oil battle has broadened people's vision. What was done in the oil battle should and can be done in the case of other raw materials.

It must be pointed out further that the significance of the developing countries' struggle to defend their natural resources is by no means confined to the economic field. In order to carry out arms expansion and war preparations and to contend for world hegemony, the superpowers are bound to plunder rapaciously the resources of the Third World. Control and protection of their own resources by the developing countries are essential, not only for the consolidation of their political independence and the development of their national economy, but also for combating superpower arms expansion and war preparations and stopping the superpowers from launching wars of aggression.

Mr President,

We maintain that the safeguarding of political independence is the first prerequisite for a Third World country to develop its economy. In achieving political independence, the people of a country have only taken the first step, and they must proceed to consolidate this independence, for there still exist remnant forces of colonialism at home and there is still the danger of subversion and aggression by imperialism and hegemonism. The consolidation of political independence is necessarily a process of repeated struggles. In the final analysis, political independence and economic independence are inseparable. Without political independence, it is impossible to achieve economic independence; without economic independence, a country's independence is incomplete and insecure.

The developing countries have great potentials for developing their economy independently. As long as a country makes unremitting efforts in the light of its own specific features and conditions and advances along the road of independence and self-reliance, it is fully possible for it to attain gradually a high level of development never reached by previous generations in the modernization of its industry and agriculture. The ideas of pessimism and helplessness spread by imperialism in connection with the question of the development of developing countries are all unfounded and are being disseminated with ulterior motives.

By self-reliance we mean that a country should mainly rely on the strength and wisdom of its own people, control its own economic lifelines, make full use of its own resources, strive hard to increase food production and develop its national economy step by step and in a planned way. The policy of independence and self-reliance in no way means that it should be divorced from the actual conditions of a country; instead, it requires that distinction must be made between different circumstances, and that each country should work out its own way of practising self-reliance in the light of its specific conditions. At the present stage, a developing country that wants to develop its national economy must first of all keep its natural resources in its own hands and gradually shake off the control of foreign capital. In many developing countries, the production of raw materials accounts for a considerable proportion of the national economy. If they can take in their own hands the production, use, sale, storage and transport of raw materials and sell them at reasonable prices on the basis of equitable trade relations in exchange for a greater amount of goods needed for the growth of their industrial and agricultural production, they will then be able to resolve step by step the difficulties they are facing and pave the way for an early emergence from poverty and backwardness.

Self-reliance in no way means 'self-seclusion' and rejection of foreign aid. We have always considered it beneficial and necessary for the development of the national economy that countries should carry on economic and technical exchanges on the basis of respect for state sovereignty, equality and mutual benefit, and the exchange of needed goods to make up for each other's deficiencies.

Here we wish to emphasize the special importance of economic cooperation among the developing countries. The Third World countries shared a common lot in the past and now face the common tasks of opposing colonialism, neo-colonialism and great-power hegemonism, developing the national economy and building their respective countries. We have every reason to unite more closely, and no reason to become estranged from one another. The imperialists, and particularly the superpowers, are taking advantage of temporary differences among us developing countries to sow dissension and disrupt unity so as to continue their manipulation, control and plunder. We must maintain full vigilance. Differences among us developing countries can very well be resolved, and should be resolved, through consultations among the parties concerned. We are glad that, on the question of oil, the developing countries concerned are making active efforts and seeking appropriate ways to find a reasonable solution. We, the developing countries, should not only support one another politically but also help each other economically. Our cooperation is a cooperation based on true equality and has broad prospects.

Mr President,

The Third World countries strongly demand that the present extremely unequal international economic relations be changed, and they have made many rational proposals of reform. The

223

Chinese Government and people warmly endorse and firmly support all just propositions made by Third World countries.

We hold that in both political and economic relations, countries should base themselves on the Five Principles of mutual respect for sovereignty and territorial integrity, mutual non-aggression, non-interference in each other's internal affairs, equality and mutual benefit, and peaceful coexistence. We are opposed to the establishment of hegemony and spheres of influence by any country in any part of the world in violation of these principles.

We hold that the affairs of each country should be managed by its own people. The people of the developing countries have the right to choose and decide on their own social and economic systems. We support the permanent sovereignty of the developing countries over their own natural resources as well as their exercise of it. We support the actions of the developing countries to bring all foreign capital, and particularly 'transnational corporations', under their control and management, up to and including nationalization. We support the position of the developing countries for the development of their national economy through 'individual and collective self-reliance'.

We hold that all countries, big or small, rich or poor, should be equal, and that international economic affairs should be jointly managed by all the countries of the world instead of being monopolized by the one or two superpowers. We support the full right of the developing countries, which comprise the great majority of the world's population, to take part in all decision-making on international trade, monetary, shipping and other matters.

We hold that international trade should be based on the principles of equality, mutual benefit and the exchange of needed goods. We support the urgent demand of the developing countries to improve trade terms for their raw materials, primary products and semi-manufactured and manufactured goods, to expand their market and to fix equitable and favourable prices. We support the developing countries in establishing various organizations of raw material exporting countries for a united struggle against colonialism, imperialism and hegemonism.

We hold that economic aid to the developing countries must strictly respect the sovereignty of the recipient countries and must not be accompanied by any political or military conditions and the extortion of any special privileges or excessive profits. Loans to the developing countries should be interest-free or low-interest and allow for delayed repayment of capital and interest, or even reduction and cancellation of debts in case of necessity. We are opposed to the exploitation of developing countries by usury or blackmail in the name of aid.

We hold that technology transferred to the developing countries must be practical, efficient, economical and convenient for use. The experts and other personnel dispatched to the recipient countries have the obligation to pass on conscientiously technical know-how to the people there and to respect the laws and national customs of the countries concerned. They must not make special demands or ask for special amenities, let alone engage in illegal activities.

Mr President,

China is a socialist country, and a developing country as well. China belongs to the Third World. Consistently following Chairman Mao's teachings, the Chinese Government and people *firmly support all oppressed peoples and oppressed nations in their struggle to win or defend national independence, develop the national economy and oppose colonialism, imperialism and hegemonism.* This is our bounden internationalist duty. China is not a superpower, nor will she ever seek to be one. What is a superpower? A superpower is an imperialist country which everywhere subjects other countries to its aggression, interference, control, subversion or plunder and strives for world hegemony. If capitalism is restored in a big socialist country, it will inevitably become a superpower. The Great Proletarian Cultural Revolution, which has been carried out in China in recent years, and the campaign of criticizing Lin Piao and Confucius now under way throughout China, are both aimed at preventing capitalist restoration and ensuring that socialist China will never change her colour and will always stand by the oppressed peoples and oppressed nations. If one day China should change her colour and turn into a superpower, if she too should play the tyrant in the world, and everywhere subject others to her bullying, aggression and exploitation, the people of the world should identify her as social-imperialist, expose it, oppose it and work together with the Chinese people to overthrow it.

Mr President,

History develops in struggle, and the world advances amidst

turbulence. The imperialists, and the superpowers in particular, are beset with troubles and are on the decline. Countries want independence, nations want liberation and the people want revolution – this is the irresistible trend of history. We are convinced that, so long as the Third World countries and people strengthen their unity, ally themselves with all forces that can be allied with and persist in a protracted struggle, they are sure to win continuous new victories.

NOTES

Introduction

1 For detailed description and analysis of the internal events during the Cultural Revolution, see: Barnouin, Barbara and Yu Changgen *Ten Years of Turbulence: The Chinese Cultural Revolution*, London and New York, Kegan Paul International, 1993.

2 Frankel, Joseph, *The Making of Foreign Policy: An Analysis of Decision-Making*, London, Oxford University Press, 1963, 15.

3 Clarke, Michael and White, Brian (eds), *Understanding Foreign Policy: The Foreign Policy Systems Approach*, Aldershot, Edgar Elgar, 1989, 136.

4 Frankel, 15.

5 Xiong Xianghui, a former diplomat, was in charge of foreign relations at the headquarters of the People's Liberation Army General Chief of Staff.

1 The Ministry of Foreign Affairs

1 Very little has been published on the Cultural Revolution in the Foreign Ministry. The best attempt to grasp the issue is Melvin Gurtov's work 'The Foreign Ministry and foreign affairs during the Cultural Revolution', *China Quarterly*, October–December 1969, which covers the period between 1966 and 1968, drawing on red guard and other material which was then available. This material contains a number of inexact and misleading statements and covers only partial aspects of the events in the Foreign Ministry at that time. Although, since the publication of Gurtov's article, material on the subject still remains scarce, it was possible to close a number of informational and analytical gaps though interviews with former and/or present officials of the Foreign Ministry and other persons directly or indirectly involved in the events. Moreover, we are dealing with a longer time span – 1966 to the mid-1970s – than was previously the case.

2 Personal Notes; see also Barnouin and Yu, 51–63.

3 Personal Notes.
4 The *People's Daily* of 4 May 1966 issued instructions 'to criticize and repudiate the reactionary bourgeois academic authorities and the ideology of the bourgeois and all other exploiting classes'.
5 Circular of the Central Committee of the CCP, 16 May 1966, in James T. Myers, Jürgen Domes and Erik Von Groeling, *Chinese Politics, Documents and Analysis*, Columbia, South Carolina, University of South Carolina Press, 1968, vol. 1, 220–5.
6 Personal Notes.
7 Ibid.
8 It should be noted that this was the only occasion when a work team was allowed to operate within the Ministry itself. From early June 1966 when, following a decision by the Politburo under the chairmanship of Liu Shaoqi, work teams were established for the purpose of carrying out the Cultural Revolution, until late July 1966 when Mao decided to abolish them, the Ministry's Party committee did not permit any work teams to operate on its premises. On the contrary, it dispatched work teams composed of Foreign Ministry personnel to the different institutions of the Foreign Affairs System and especially to the foreign languages institutes. For a definition of the term 'Foreign Affairs System', see note 13 in this chapter.
9 On 29 July 1966, Liu Shaoqi and Deng Xiaoping were compelled to make public self-criticism at a mass gathering of 10,000 Beijing high school and university students. The two leaders declared that the establishment of the work teams had been a grave error and that they would be withdrawn without delay.
10 *People's Daily*, 26 August 1966.
11 *The Cambridge History of China*, vol. 14, Cambridge, Cambridge University Press, 1987, 462.
12 Wang Nianyi, 'Guanyu Eryue Niliu Yixie Ziliao' (Some facts about the February Adverse Current), in: *Dangshi Yanjiu Ziliao* (Material for the Study of Party History) no. 1, 1990.
13 Under the State Council, there were 37 ministries and commissions as well as some 30 special offices and agencies. They were divided into administrative systems headed by a vice premier. Chen Yi was in charge of the foreign affairs system which incorporated all ministries, special offices and agencies dealing with political and trade relations with foreign countries and with overseas Chinese. It also incorporated the foreign languages institutes. See: Kaplan, Frederic M., Sobin, Julian M. and Andors, Stephan, *Encyclopedia of China Today*, New York, Eurasia Press, 1979, 71–7; see also Appendix II, Document 1.
14 'Zhonggong Wenhua Dageming Wenjian Huibian' (A collection of major CCP documents on the Cultural Revolution), *Studies on the CCP*, Taipei, 1973, 407.
15 Zhou Ming, *Lishi Zai Zheli Chensi* (Reflections about History), vol. 1, Beijing, Huaxia Press, 1986, 216, 219. According to the practice at that time, Chen's self-criticism had to be delivered in written form

to be submitted to Mao for his approval before it could be read to the 'masses'. Once it had obtained Mao's approval, its acceptance by the 'masses' was a mere formality.

16 Interviews with former officials of the Foreign Ministry and with one of the rebel leaders, Beijing, March 1993.

17 An Jianshe, *Zhou Enlai de Zuihou Suiyue* (The Last Years of Zhou Enlai), Beijing, Central Documentation Press, 1995, 216.

18 Tie Zhuwei, *Chen Yi Yuanshuai Zai Wenhua Dageming Zhong* (Marshal Chen Yi during the Cultural Revolution), Beijing, Historical Material Press, 1986, 163.

19 Personal Notes.

20 Ibid.

21 Ibid.

22 Ibid.

23 Ibid.

24 On the basis of interviews in Beijing it can be concluded that the degree of radicalism within the embassies appeared to be more developed than was the case in the Foreign Ministry itself. More violent tactics were used during the confrontations with the target persons. People to be criticized were asked to kneel down or to stand on a stool; they were forced to lower their heads and sometimes decorated with a dunce's cap or even forced to stand in a 'jet position' with their upper body bending down and their hands stretched up behind their back. Such methods were rarely used by Foreign Ministry rebels in their repudiation of Party bureaucrats. Generally, within the Ministry, the tactics employed during criticism meetings remained relatively civilized despite the fact that the surrounding circumstances were charged with excesses and violence.

25 An Jianshe, 209; see also Quan Yanchi, *Mao Zedong, Man, Not God*, Beijing, Foreign Languages Press 1992, 154–6.

26 An Jianshe, 209.

27 'Zhonggong Wenhua Dageming Wenjian Huibian', 1973, 407–10.

28 Personal Notes.

29 See Chapter 4.

30 *Waishi Fenglei* (Events in Foreign Relations), a tabloid published by red guards, Beijing 12 August 1967.

31 Huairentang is a meeting hall in Zhongnanhai.

32 Barnouin and Yu, 115–18.

33 Wang Nianyi, 'Guanyu Eryue Niliu Yixie Ziliao', 7.

34 An Jianshe, 222.

35 In terms of the popular revolutionary language of that time, the degree of condemnation was expressed by either 'criticize and repudiate' (*pi pan*) and 'bombard' (*pao hong*) – which implied no consequences for the person's professional life – or 'down with' and 'smash' (*da dao*) – which was to be followed by removal from office. It was this latter fate that Zhou wanted to avoid for Chen Yi.

36 An Jianshe, 223–4.

37 Personal Notes.

38 An Jianshe, 219, 222.

39 Ibid., 223.
40 The sequence of these events was established through a series of interviews conducted in Beijing between 1991 and 1993, both with rebel leaders and former embassy staff.
41 Gao Gao and Yan Jiaqi, *Wenhua Dageming Shinian Shi* (A Ten-Year History of the Cultural Revolution), Tianjin, Tianjin People's Publishing House, 1986, 144–5.
42 Personal Notes.
43 For a detailed account of the Wuhan event, see: Barnouin and Yu, 143–50.
44 *Waishi Fenglei.*
45 Interview with former rebel leader, Zhang Dianqing, Beijing, March 1991.
46 In the language of the Cultural Revolution, he was left 'to stand aside' (*kao bian zhan*).
47 See Chapter 4.
48 See Chapter 4.
49 For detailed description of the issue, see Barnouin and Yu, 217–21.
50 Ibid., see also Tie Zhuwei, 257.
51 See Barnouin and Yu, 143–50.
52 Interview with Yao Dengshan, Beijing, March 1991.
53 See excerpts of Wang Li's talk in Appendix II, Document 6; interview with Yao Dengshan, Beijing, March 1991; see also Wang Li's interview in *Herald Tribune*, 12 April 1996.
54 Interview with Zhang Dianqing.
55 Ibid.
56 Ibid. Contrary to the information obtained through this and other interviews with former officials of the Foreign Ministry, reports published in Western literature suggest that the red guards forced their way into an office containing documents and files which they were able to take away. See, for example, Melvin Gurtov, 'Foreign Affairs during the Cultural Revolution', in Thomas Robinson (ed.), *The Cultural Revolution in China*, Berkeley, University of California Press, 1971, 331.
57 Interview with Zhang Dianqing.
58 Interview with Yao Dengshan in Beijing, March 1991.
59 Barnouin and Yu, 153–4.
60 Ibid., 154.
61 Personal Notes.
62 Barnouin and Yu, 192.
63 See Chapter 3.
64 Wang Hairong's grandfather was Mao's cousin.
65 Personal Notes.
66 Tie Zhuwei, 16; see also Gurtov, *China Quarterly*, 94.
67 Barnouin and Yu, 165.
68 The military leaders charged with these 'crimes' – charges which were not substantiated – were Yang Chengwu, acting chief of general staff, Yu Lijin, political commissar of the air force, and Fu Chongbi, commander of the Beijing garrison. Their arrest on 23

March became known as the 'Yang-Yu-Fu event'. It served, especially, Lin Biao's purposes to eliminate 'uncooperative' subordinates. See: Barnouin and Yu, 165–71.

69 Zheng Derong, *Xinzhongguo Jishi, 1949–84,* (Records of New China) Changchun, North-East Normal University Press, 1986, 403.
70 Gurtov, 'The Foreign Ministry and Foreign affairs . . .', *China Quarterly,* 95.
71 Barnouin and Yu, 171–4.
72 Ibid., 176.
73 The May 7th Cadre Schools were organized in paramilitary camps. Roughly one hundred persons from several ministerial departments were grouped into a company. Three companies formed a battalion. Within each company, a Party branch committee comprising three to five members was established. Party committees began to resume their activities in late 1969.
74 Personal Notes.
75 Liu Shaoqi's foreign policy was denounced as capitulating to the imperialists, to the Soviet revisionists and to foreign reactionaries and eliminating the anti-imperialist struggle of the suppressed people of the world.
76 A major exception was the one in Jiangxi Province where a few hundred people considered to have political problems continued to be held. (Personal Notes.)
77 Personal Notes.
78 Barnouin and Yu, 250–2.
79 Ibid., 254.
80 Barnouin and Yu, 263.
81 Peng Cheng, *Zhongguo Zhengju Beiwanglu* (A Memorandum on the Chinese Political Situation), Beijing, The PLA Publishing House, 1989, 36–8.
82 *History of the Chinese Communist Party: A Chronology of Events, 1919–1990,* Compiled by the Central Committee of the Chinese Communist Party, Beijing, Foreign Languages Press, 1991, 360.
83 Peng Cheng, 39.
84 This is defined as 'the course of moderate action between extremes in the development of the virtues of temperance and prudence' (*Webster's Dictionary*).
85 Lin Qingshan, 'Sirenbang Zuguo Meng De Pomie' (The failure of the Gang of Four to seize power) *Mao Zedong Sixiang Yanjiu* (The Study of Mao Zedong Thought), Sichuan Academy of Social Sciences, no. 3, 1988, 105.
86 Zhou Gong was a reference to the Duke of Zhou of the Western Dynasty – eleventh century to 770 BC. It was also a respectful address used to designate Zhou Enlai during his underground work in the 1920s.
87 Barnouin and Yu, 263.
88 Zhang Yufeng, 'Mao Zedong Zhou Enlai Wannian Ersan Shi' (A few things about Mao Zedong and Zhou Enlai's last years) *Yanhuang Zisun* (The offspring of emperors Yan and Huang), no. 1, 1989, 6.

89 Personal Notes.
90 Ibid.
91 Ibid. The group of persons remaining loyal to Zhou Enlai and receiving continuing support from Ji Pengfei, became known as the 'Ji Faction'.
92 Interviews with Foreign Ministry staff members, March 1991.
93 Interview with Zhang Hanzi, Beijing, March 1991.
94 'Report concerning the problem of Qiao Guanhua', submitted by the Party Leading Group of the Ministry of Foreign Affairs to the Party Central Committee and the State Council, *Chinese Law and Government* vol. 10, no. 1, 1977, 106–8; interview with Zhang Hanzhi, Beijing, March 1991.
95 Personal Notes.

2 Perceptions, ideology and decision-making

1 *Selected Works of Mao Zedong*, vol. 4, Beijing, Foreign Languages Press, 1975, 99.
2 'On the People's Democratic Dictatorship', in: *People's Daily*, 1 July 1949. See also: *Cambridge History of China*, vol. 14, Cambridge, Cambridge University Press, 1987, 264.
3 Lawrance, Alan, *China's Foreign Relations since 1949*, London, Boston, Routledge and Kegan Paul, 1975, 21–3.
4 *Selected Works of Mao Zedong*, vol. 4, 379.
5 *Liu Shaoqi Xuanji* (Selected Works of Liu Shaoqi), vol. 2, Beijing People's Publishing House, 1985, 261, 262.
6 *China and the Soviet Union, 1949–84*, Keesing's International Studies, Harlow, Essex, Longman Group Limited, 1985, 7.
7 Up to this event, China respected the leading role of the Soviet Party in the Eastern bloc. This had a practical diplomatic connotation. In the belief that the Soviet 'older brother' had gathered more experience and was better informed, the Chinese government and its missions abroad would consult their Soviet counterparts on any issue they considered important (Personal Notes).
8 *The Historical Experience of the Dictatorship of the Proletariat*, Beijing, Foreign Languages Press, 1964, 7.
9 *The Polemics of the International Communist Movement*, Beijing, Foreign Languages Press, 1965, 64.
10 Wang Nianyi, 'Mao Zedong Tongzhi Fadong "Wenhua Dageming" Shi Dui Xingshide Guji' (Comrade Mao Zedong's estimate of the situation at the time he launched the Great Cultural Revolution), *Dangshi Yanjiu Ziliao*, no. 4, 1989, 772.
11 See also: Barbara Barnouin, 'Dissonant voice in international communism', in Harish Kapur (ed.), *The End of an Isolation: China after Mao*, Dordrecht, Boston, Lancaster, Martinus Nijhoff Publishers, 1985, 207.
12 Barnouin and Yu, 14.
13 Ibid.

14 *Pékin Information*, no. 24, 14 June 1965, 11–21.
15 *Polemics*, 7.
16 Lawrance, 183.
17 Ibid.
18 Ibid.
19 *PR*, no. 41, 1965, 14.
20 *PR*, no. 34, 19 August 1966, 7.
21 Keesing's, 76.
22 *Pravda*, 27 November 1966.
23 *History of the CCP*, 310.
24 Ibid., 318.
25 Personal Notes.
26 Statement of the Government of the People's Republic of China, 29 October 1971, in: *Irresistible Historical Trend*, Appendix II, Document 7.
27 Ibid., 1.
28 Myers, James T., Domes, Jürgen and Von Groeling, Eric, *Chinese Politics, Documents and Analysis*, Columbia, South Carolina, University of South Carolina Press, 1989, vol. 2, 213.
29 Speech by Qiao Guanhua, Chairman of the delegation of the People's Republic of China, at the Plenary Meeting of the 26th Session of the UN General Assembly, 15 November 1971, Appendix II, Document 7.
30 Deng Xiaoping at the Special Session of the UN General Assembly, 10 April 1974, Appendix II, Document 10; see also Myers et al., vol. 2, 213–1964.
31 Ibid.
32 Ibid., 214.
33 *Unite to Win Still Greater Victories*, Beijing, Foreign Languages Press, 1972, 1, 2. See Appendix II, Document 9.
34 Ibid. 2, 3.
35 Harding, Harry (ed.), *China's Foreign Relations in the 1980s*, New Haven, London, Yale University Press, 1984, 192.
36 *PR*, 4 November 1977, 10–41.
37 Ibid.
38 Keesing's, 133.
39 *The Cambridge History of China*, vol. 14, 60; see also Barnouin and Yu, 25–6.
40 Barnouin and Yu, 27.
41 *Chinese Communist Affairs: Facts and Features*, vol. 1, no. 3, 29 November 1967, 24–5.
42 Lieberthal, Kenneth, 'The foreign policy debate in Peking as seen through allegorical articles, 1973–76', *China Quarterly*, no. 71, September 1977; Ross, Robert S., 'From Lin Biao to Deng Xiaoping: elite instability and China's US Policy', *China Quarterly*, no. 118, June 1989.
43 Lieberthal, Kenneth, 'Domestic politics and foreign policy', in Harry Harding (ed.), *China's Foreign Relations in the 1980s*, New Haven and London, Yale University Press, 1984, 52.

44 See Chapter 4 on the differences on 'revolutionary' foreign policy between Zhou Enlai and Chen Yi on the one hand and the Cultural Revolution Group on the other.

45 Kissinger, Henry, *The White House Years*, London, Weidenfeld and Nicolson and Michael Joseph, 1979, 1061.

46 Zhang Yunsheng, *Maojiawan Jishi* (A Factual Account about Maojiawan), Beijing, Spring and Autumn Press, 1988, 329 (Zhang was one of Lin Biao's secretaries who wrote about his experiences).

47 Ibid., 330.

48 Personal Notes.

49 *PR*, no. 41, 1965.

50 Personal Notes, Beijing, 1989.

51 Ibid.

52 Personal Notes.

53 An Jianshe, 207.

54 This institute was also known as the 1st Foreign Languages Institute. The 2nd Foreign Languages Institute was placed under the jurisdiction of the Ministry of Foreign Trade.

55 The group included Chen Boda, then the CCP's leading theoretician and Mao's political secretary; Xu Liqun and Yao Zhen, deputy ministers of the CC propaganda department, Wang Li, deputy minister of the CC International Liaison Department; Wu Lengxi, director of the Xinhua News Agency and editor-in-chief of the *People's Daily*; Qiao Guanhua, vice minister of foreign affairs; Guan Feng, deputy chief editor of *Red Flag*; Deng Liqun, deputy chief of the political research division of the CC general office. See: Ye Yonglie, 'Wang Li da Ke Wen' (Interview with Wang Li) *Lianhe Shibao*, Shanghai, 23 Dec. 1988.

56 Personal Notes.

57 An Jianshe, 207.

58 *History of the CCP*, 326.

59 Zhu Lin, *Dashi Furen Huiyilu* (Memories of an Ambassador's Wife), Beijing, World Affairs Press, 1991, 140.

60 *History of the CCP*, 327.

61 Personal Notes.

62 The article stated that the Cultural Revolution 'fundamentally defeated the global counter-revolutionary strategy of US imperialism', which had always aimed at promoting 'peaceful evolution' in China, and 'prevented a big reverse and retrogression of world history; it has re-opened that channel leading to communism that was blocked by modern revisionism, and advanced the international communist movement and world revolution to an entirely new stage'. The article concluded that the Cultural Revolution 'is a gigantic struggle of strategic importance between world revolutionary forces and counter-revolutionary forces' (*PR*, no. 14, 1967, 25).

63 Enlarged meetings of the Politburo (Mao and Lin Biao participated only rarely) included the entire CCRG; enlarged meetings of the Standing Committee of the Politburo had Ye Jianying (not a member

of the CCRG), Jiang Qing and Wang Li as regular participants. See:
Wang Nianyi, 'Guanyu Eryue Niliude Yixia Ziliao'.

64 Cong Jin, *Quzhe Fazhande Suiyue* (Years of Advance in Zigzags), Henan, Henan Publishing House, 1989, 501–2.
65 *History of the CCP*, 309.
66 Ibid., 309.
67 Han Nianlong (ed.), *Diplomacy of Contemporary China*, Hong Kong, New Horizon Press, 1990, 259.
68 Personal Notes.
69 Ibid.
70 See Chapter 3.
71 For more details, see Chapter 3.
72 See Appendix II, Documents 2 and 3.
73 Appendix II, Document 2; see also: Tie Zhuwei, 235.
74 Ibid., 236; see also *Ye Jianying Zhuanlue* (A Brief Biography of Ye Jianying), Beijing, Military Science Press, 1987, 271.
75 See: Qian Jiang, *Pingpong Waijiao Shimu* (The Process of Ping-Pong Diplomacy), Beijing, The East Press, 1987, 125; Kissinger, *The White House Years*, 709–10.
76 Ibid., 710.
77 Interview, Beijing, March 1989.
78 Chen Dengde, *Mao Zedong + Nixon Zai 1972* (Mao Zedong and Nixon in 1972, Beijing, Kunlun Press, 1988, 259; see also Kissinger, *The White House Years*, 784.
79 Chen Dengde, 260.
80 Ibid.

3 Revolutionary diplomacy

1 As a commentary in the *People's Daily* pointed out succinctly: 'The rapid and extensive dissemination of the great and all-conquering thought of Mao Tse-tung is the most important feature of the excellent international situation today. The world has entered upon a new era which has Mao Tse-tung's Thought as its great banner. The study and application of Mao Tse-tung's Thought has become a mass movement on a global scale, of a magnitude and with a far-reaching influence never before witnessed in the history of the development of Marxism-Leninism' (*PR*, no. 43, 1967, 26–8).
2 Van Ness, Peter, *Revolution and Chinese Foreign Policy: Peking's Support of National Liberation*, Berkeley, University of California Press, 1970. 203–4.
3 *PR*, no. 6, 1967, 23.
4 Ibid.
5 Zheng Derong, 421.
6 *PR*, no. 6, 1867, 25.
7 People's Daily, 27 January 1967.
8 Zheng Derong, 421.
9 *PR*, no. 7, 1967, 6, 10.

10 *PR*, no. 6, 1967, 30.
11 Interview with the former rebel leader in question, in Beijing, March 1989.
12 *PR*, 4 February 1967.
13 Kapur, Harish, *Distant Neighbours: China and Europe*, London, Pinter Publishers, 1990, 92; *PR*, 16 June 1967.
14 New China News Agency, Foreign Ministry Statement, 15 May 1967, in *PR*, no. 21, 1967, 14.
15 Ibid.
16 Van Ness, 217; *PR*, no. 22, 1967, 50–2.
17 Yu Chenggen, 'Zhou Enlai Yaokung "Fanying Kangbao" Neimu' (Zhou commands from a distance 'The Fight Against the Violent Repression Committed by the British'), *The Nineties*, 96/5 and 96/6.
18 Ibid.
19 According to an interview conducted in Beijing in 1993, the note was drafted by an official of the European area department. It was submitted to Zhou Enlai when he was in a state of utter fatigue. Zhou later said that this was one of the rare occasions in his life when he was so overworked and tired that he approved a memorandum of the Foreign Ministry without realizing its consequences.
20 *PD*, 22 August 1967.
21 *The Times*, 23 August 1967.
22 Personal Notes, Beijing 1989.
23 *PR*, no. 37, 8 September 1967, 37.
24 Personal Notes.
25 *PR*, no. 11, 1967, 38.
26 Van Ness, 101–10.
27 *PR*, no. 43, 1967, 6.
28 *PR*, no. 17, 1966.
29 Zheng Derong, 427.
30 Ibid.
31 *PR*, no. 19, 1967.
32 *PR*, no. 45, 1967.
33 *PR*, 13, 1967, 29–30.
34 Van Ness, 225–6.
35 *PR*, no. 31, 1965.
36 Van Ness, 225–6.
37 *PR*, 7 July 1967, 17–18.
38 *PR*, no. 30, 1967, 39.
39 *PR*, no. 31, 1967, 28.
40 *PR*, no. 34, 1967, 36–7.
41 *PR*, no. 35, 1967, 26.
42 *PR*, no. 36, 1967, 37.
43 *PR*, no. 36, 1967, 38.
44 *PR*, no. 39, 1967, 28, and no. 42, 1967, 38.
45 Ibid.
46 *PR*, no. 3, 10.
47 *PR*, 12 May 1967.
48 'Sino-Belgian Relations', *China Topics*, 1 December 1970.

49 Mehnert, Klaus, *Peking and the New Left: At Home and Abroad*, Berkeley, University of California Press, 1967, 18.
50 Kapur, *Distant Neighbours* 95.
51 Ibid., 95.
52 Wang Nianyi, *Dadongluande Niandai* (Years of Turmoil), Henan, Henan People's Publishing House, 1988, 455–9.
53 Ibid.

4 National Security Policies

1 See later part of the chapter on Sino-Soviet relations.
2 Han Nianlong (ed.) *Diplomacy of Contemporary China*, Hong Kong, New Horizon Press, 1990, 196; also see: Wang Xiangen, *Kang Mei Yuanyue Shilu* (A Factual Account of Resisting America and Assisting Vietnam), Beijing. International Cultural Development Press, 1990, 25–6.
3 Ibid., 197.
4 *People of the World, Unite and Defeat the US Aggressor and all its Lackeys*, Peking, Foreign Languages Press, 1963, 6.
5 Han Nianlong (ed.), 159. *Diplomacy of Contemporary China*.
6 Ibid., 197.
7 Chen Jian, 'China in the Vietnam War, 1964–69', *China Quarterly*, no. 142, 1995, 364.
8 PR, no. 15, 1965.
9 Han Nianlong (ed.), 161.
10 Naughton Barry, 'The Third Front: defence industrialization in the Chinese interior', *China Quarterly*, Sept. 1988, 356–7.
11 Han Nianlong (ed.), 197.
12 Ibid., 198.
13 Li Ke and Hao Shengzhang, *Wenhua Dageming Zhongde Renmin Jiefangjun* (The PLA in the Cultural Revolution), Beijing, The CCP Press for Party History Material, 1989, 341.
14 Li Ke and Hao Shengzhang, 410–42.
15 Han Nianlong (ed.), 280, 281.
16 Ibid., 281.
17 Snow, Edgar, *The Long Revolution*, New York, Vintage Books, 1973, 195, 215–16.
18 This affected not only Chinese military supplies but also 5,750 train wagons of material from other countries, including the Soviet Union. See: Wang Xiangen, 225–6.
19 Wang Nianyi, *Dadongluande Niandai*, (Years of Turmoil), Henan, Henan People's Publishing House, 1988, 300.
20 Chen Jian, 385.
21 Ibid., 282.
22 All these events have been extensively documented in Keesing's.
23 'Communiqué of the Eleventh Plenary Session of the Eighth Central Committee of the Communist Party of China, adopted on August 12, 1966', in: *PR*, no. 34, 1966, 7.

24 Keesing's, 84.
25 Brezhnev declared that communist countries in principle were in favour of national sovereignty. However, 'when internal and external forces hostile to socialism try to turn some socialist countries towards restoration of capitalism, when socialism in a country and in the socialist community as a whole is threatened, it becomes not only a problem of the country concerned but a common problem and concern of all socialist countries' (Keesing's, 85).
26 Li Ke and Hao Shengzhang, 92.
27 Ibid., 318.
28 Ibid., 319.
29 Ibid., 320–1.
30 Keesing's, 93.
31 Li and Hao, 321–3.
32 Keesing's, 94.
33 PR, no. 10, 7 March 1969, 5.
34 Ibid., 8.
35 Keesing's, 95.
36 Ibid., 95–6.
37 Wang Nianyi, *Dadongluande Niandai*, 332.
38 'Zhonggong Wenhua Dageming Zhongyao Wenjian Huibian' (A collection of important documents of the CCP on the Cultural Revolution), *Journal of CCP Studies*, Taipei, 1991, 221.
39 *History of the CCP*, 371.
40 PD, 6 January 1969.
41 Ibid., 9 March 1969.
42 PR, no. 14, 1969.
43 Ibid., no. 49, 1973.
44 Kapur, *The Awakening Giant: China's Ascension to World Politics*, Alphen aan den Rijn, The Netherlands, Rockville, Maryland, USA, Sijthoff and Noordhoff, 1991, 51.
45 *Pravda*, 11 January 1969.
46 PR, no. 28, 11 July 1969, 6; no. 33, 15 August 1969, 3.
47 Chen Dengde, 33; Kissinger, 183.
48 Wang Nianyi, *Dadongluande Niandai*, 362.
49 *History of the CCP*, 371.
50 Zhen Derong, 467.
51 Chen Dengde, 32–4.
52 Han Nianlong (ed.), 125–6.
53 PR, no. 41, 1969.
54 Chai Chengwen, *Panmunjom Tanpan* (Panmunjom Negotiations), Beijing, People's Liberation Army Press, 1992, 47.
55 Ibid.
56 Kong Jianmin, 'Zhongguo Dasanxian Jianshede Jianan Licheng' (Difficulties concerning China's third-line construction), *Pursuit*, Beijing, no. 1, 1989, 28.
57 Schram, Stuart, *Mao Tsetung Unrehearsed*, Harmondsworth, Penguin, 1974, 285.
58 Liu Suinian and Wu Qungan, *Wenhua Dageming Shiqide Guomin*

Jingji (The National Economy during the Cultural Revolution), Harbin, Heilongjiang People's Publishing House, 1986, 39; see also: Barry Naughton, 352–86.

59 Barry Naughton convincingly argues in favour of the possibility that the tremendous economic costs attributed to a decade of Cultural Revolution can be traced back primarily to the absorption of enormous quantities of resources by third-line policies (Naughton, 381).

60 Su Caiqing, 'Wenge Chuqi Jingji Zhanxian De Yanzhong Douzheng' (Serious conflicts in the economic field during the early period of the Cultural Revolution) in Tan Zongji, *Shinian Houde Pingshou* (Critical Comments Ten Years Later), Beijing, Historical Material Press, 1987, 79.

61 Li Ke and Hao Shengzhang, 125.

62 Zhang Yunsheng, 308.

63 Su Caiqing, 'Wenhua Dageming Lishi Bianwu Sanze' (Correction of three errors on the history of the Cultural Revolution), *Dangshi Yanjiu* Studies in Party History, no. 5, 1989, 79.

64 The Political Report of the 9th Party Congress reiterated this policy as one of the tasks still to be fulfilled by the Cultural Revolution. Another of its major tasks was the campaign to purify class ranks. See Myers et al., 68–9.

65 Personal Notes.

66 'Deputy Commander Lin's No. 1 Order', in Zheng Yunsheng, 317.

67 Ibid.

68 Chai Chengwen, 49.

69 Ibid.

70 Ibid.

71 Ibid., 50.

72 Ibid.

73 Ibid., 50.

74 Keesing's, 152.

75 Kissinger, *The White House Years*, 180–2.

76 See: Chen Dengde, 16.

77 Ibid., 20.

78 Kissinger, 180.

79 Nixon, Richard, *The Memoirs of Richard Nixon*, London, Melbourne, Arrow Books, 1979, 545.

80 Dulles, Foster Rhea, *American Policy towards Communist China, 1949–1969*, New York, Thomas Y. Crowell Company, 1972, 244–5.

81 Han Nianlong (ed.), 269.

82 See: Harding, Harry, *A Fragile Relationship: The United States and China since 1972*, Washington DC, The Brookings Institution, 1992, 37–9.

83 Kissinger, 188.

84 Han Nianlong (ed.), 269.

85 Chen Dengde, 49–50; see also Han Nianlong (ed.), 269; and Dulles, 247.

86 Chen Dengde, 55.

87 Kissinger, 687.
88 Chen Dengde, 74.
89 Ibid.
90 Ibid., 87.
91 Kissinger, 698.
92 Ibid., 699.
93 This is different from Kissinger's statement on p. 701; see Han Nianlong (ed.), 220.
94 Ibid.; Kissinger, 770–1.
95 Han Nianlong (ed.), 270–1.
96 Snow, 171–3; for the Chinese account of Mao's encounter with Edgar Snow, see: Appendix II, Document 5, 'If Nixon is willing . . .'.
97 Kissinger 709, see: Qian Jiang, 121, 122.
98 Ibid., 112.
99 Interview, Beijing, March 1993.
100 Qian Jiang, 121.
101 Ibid. 125; see also Kissinger, 709–10.
102 Chen Dengde, 116.
103 PR, no. 17, 1971.
104 Kissinger, 698–700.
105 Chen Dengde, 144.
106 The Foreign Minister, Chen Yi was already critically ill. Ye Jianying was nominated because of his experience of dealing with the Americans during the civil war period in the 1940s. Other members of the group were Ji Pengfei, the acting Foreign Minister and Huang Hua and Zhang Wenjin, both career diplomats. Others were Xiong Xianghui, expert of international affairs at the general chief of staff, Wang Hairong, Mao's grand-niece employed by the Foreign Ministry, Tang Wenshang and Ji Chaozhu, both interpreters at the Foreign Ministry. See: Chen Dengde, 154.
107 Ibid., 216.
108 Kissinger explains the reasons for this secrecy in The White House Years, 725.
109 The removal of Chen Boda was but the first step towards this target. For a detailed account of these events, see: Barnouin and Yu, 213–31.
110 Ibid., 226.
111 Wei Shiyan, 'Kissinger Mimi Fang Hua Neimu' (With Kissinger on his secret visit to China), in: Liu Wusheng (ed.), Zhonggong Dangshi Fengyunlu (Major Events in CCP History), Beijing, People's Publishing House, 1990.
112 Ibid., 41.
113 Ibid., 42.
114 Ibid.
115 Kissinger, 750.
116 Ibid.
117 Wei Shiyan, 42.
118 Kissinger, 752.
119 Ibid., 752–3.

120 Ibid., 759.
121 Ibid., 759.
122 *The Great Power Struggle in China*, Hong Kong, Asian Research Centre, 463.
123 Interview in Beijing, July 1991.
124 *The Great Power Struggle in China*, 480.
125 Ibid., 480.
126 Gao Gao and Yan Jiaqi, 503.
127 Zhang Yufeng, 'Wo Gei Mao Zhuxi Dang Mishu' (I served as Chairman Mao's secretary), *Yanhuang Zisun* (The Offspring of Yan and Huang), no. 8, 1994, 5.
128 Li Zhuisui, *The Private Life of Chairman Mao*, New York, Random House, 1994, 8.
129 Ibid.
130 Winston Lord, at that time, was Kissinger's adviser on Chinese affairs and later ambassador to Beijing.
131 Zhang Yufeng, 5; see also Kissinger, 1057–8.
132 Kissinger, 789.
133 *Public Papers of the President of the United States: Richard Nixon, 1972*, Washington, Government Printing Office, 1974, 376–9 and *PR*, no. 9, 1972, 4–5.
134 Ibid.
135 Barnett, A. Doak *China and the Major Powers in East Asia*, Washington DC, The Brookings Institution, 1977, 201, note 128, 382. Harding, *China Foreign Relations*, 45–6.
136 Kissinger, Henry, *Years of Upheaval*, Little, Brown, 1982, 698.
137 See Chapter 1.
138 Harding, Harry, *A Fragile Relationship: The United States and China since 1972*, Washington, DC, The Brookings Institution, 1992, 50.
139 Kissinger, *Years of Upheaval*, 51. The German chancellor, Helmut Schmidt, who visited Beijing in 1975, also reports a Mao's preoccupation with Soviet expansionism, the inevitability of a war provoked by the Soviet Union and the dangers of Western *détente* policies – subjects which took up most of the time of the meeting between Mao and himself; see: Helmut Schmidt, *Menschen und Mächte*, Berlin, Siedler Verlag, 1987, 358–66.
140 Han Nianlong (ed.), 241–2.
141 Ibid.
142 Ibid., 255.
143 *PR*, no. 5, 1965.
144 *SCMP: (Survey of China Mainland Press)*, 19 November 1965.
145 *PR*, no. 5 1968.
146 Kapur, *The Awakening Giant*, 129–30.
147 *Letters of the Central Committee of the Communist Party of Japan in Reply to the Central Committee of the CPSU*, Beijing, Foreign Languages Press, 1965; see also: 'The modern revisionists: theory of war and peace and the judgement passed by history' (Article in *Akahata*, 14 August 1965, Beijing, Foreign Languages Press, 1966).
148 *Akahata*, 10, October 1967.

149 Kapur, *The Awakening Giant*, 126–9.
150 Han Nianlong (ed.), 292–3.
151 Ibid., 292, 293; see also Hsu, Immanuel C. Y., *The Rise of Modern China*, 3rd edn, Oxford, Oxford University Press, 1983.
152 'Wenzhai Xunkan' (Ten-day Digest), ed. by *Jilin Daily*, 1988.
153 *PR*, no. 39, 1972.
154 According to a Chinese estimate, 10 million people died during the Japanese occupation of China; see: *South China Morning Post*, 25 July 1987; Hsu, in an earlier estimate speaks of 3.2 million dead; see; Hsu, 612, 622.
155 'Wenzhai Xunkan', 1988.
156 Ibid.
157 Ibid.
158 The clause states that 'neither of the two countries should seek hegemony in the Asia-Pacific region and each country is opposed to efforts by any other country or group of countries to establish such hegemony' (*PR*, no. 40, 1972, 14).
159 Ibid.

Appendix II: Documents

Document 3: "Our view of the current situation"

1 (On 26 of July, the first Soviet Vice Foreign Minister had a meeting with the Chinese Chargé d'Affaires in the USSR, handing him a statement of the Soviet Council of Ministers to the Chinese State Council suggesting a summit meeting between the two countries. This statement was not made public. Ed. note.)

Document 4: "Ultra-left ideology interferes with Chinese foreign policy"

1 *Translator's note*: by 'bad persons', Zhou Enlai meant Wang Li, Guan Feng and Qi Benyu, members of the CCRG. They were regarded as the representatives of ultra-left ideology and were arrested at the end of August of 1967, Qi Benyu at the end of that year.

Document 6: "Wang Li's talk ..."

1 This is the résumé of the foreign policy attributed to Liu Shaoqi who was accused of capitulating to the imperialists, to the Soviet revisionists and to foreign reactionaries and of eliminating support to the anti-imperialist struggle of the suppressed people.

Document 8a: Chou En-Lai's internal report...

1 'Chou En-lai tsai i-chiu-ch'i-san nien san-yüeh tui tang-nei so-tso ti kuan-yü mu-ch'ien kuo-chi chü-shih wen-t'i ti chiang-hua,' *Fei-ch'ing yüeh-pao* [Chinese Communist Affairs Monthly], XIX: 6 (December 1976), 93–6. This translation is adapted with permission from *Issues & Studies*, XIII: 1 (January 1977), 120–7, where it was translated by Ingrid Yeh.

Document 8b: Chou En-Lai's internal report...

1 'Chou En-lai tsai i-chiu-ch'i-i nien shih-erh yüeh tui tang-nei so-tso ti kuo-chi hsing-shih pao-kao,' *Fei-ch'ing yüeh-pao* [Chinese Communist Affairs Monthly], XIX: 6 (December 1976), 90–3. This translation is adapted with permission from *Issues & Studies*, XIII: 1 (January 1977), 113–20, where it was translated by Ingrid Yeh.

BIBLIOGRAPHY

Books

An Jianshe, *Zhou Enlai de Zuihou Suiyue* (The Last Years of Zhou Enlai), Beijing, Central Documentation Press, 1995.

Barnouin, Barbara and Yu Changgen, *Ten Years of Turbulence: The Chinese Cultural Revolution*, London and New York, Graduate Institute of International Studies, Kegan Paul International, 1993.

Barnett, A. Doak, *China and the Major Powers in East Asia*, Washington DC, The Brookings Institution, 1977.

The Cambridge History of China, vols. 14 and 15. Cambridge, Cambridge University Press, 1987 and 1991.

Chai Chengwen, *Panmunjom Tanpan*, (Panmunjom Negotiations), Beijing, People's Liberation Army Press, 1992.

Chen Dengde, *Mao Zedong + Nixon Zai 1972*, (Mao Zedong and Nixon in 1972), Beijing, Kunlun Press, 1988.

China and the Soviet Union, 1949–84, Keesing's International Studies, Harlow, Essex, Longman Group Limited, 1985.

Clarke, Michael and White, Brian (eds), *Understanding Foreign Policy: The Foreign Policy Systems Approach*, Aldershot, Edgar Elgar, 1989.

Cong Jin, *Quzhe Fazhande Suiyue* (Years of Advance in Zigzags), Henan, Henan Publishing House, 1989.

Dulles, Foster Rhea, *American Policy towards Communist China, 1949–1969*, New York, Thomas Y. Crowell Company, 1972.

Frankel, Joseph, *The Making of Foreign Policy: An Analysis of Decision-Making*, London, Oxford University Press, 1963.

Gao Gao and Yan Jiaqi, *Wenhua Dageming Shinian Shi* (A Ten-Year History of the Cultural Revolution), Tianjin, Tianjin People's Publishing House, 1986.

The Great Power Struggle in China, Hong Kong, Asian Research Centre.

Han Nianlong (ed.), *Diplomacy of Contemporary China*, Hong Kong, New Horizon Press, 1990.

Harding, Harry (ed.), *China's Foreign Relations in the 1980s*, New Haven, London, Yale University Press, 1984.

Harding, Harry, *A Fragile Relationship: The United States and China since 1972*, Washington DC, The Brookings Institution, 1992.

244

History of the Chinese Communist Party: A Chronology of Events, 1919–1990, Compiled by the Central Committee of the Chinese Communist Party, Beijing, Foreign Languages Press, 1991.

Hsu, Immanuel, C. Y., *The Rise of Modern China*, 3rd edn, Oxford, Oxford University Press, 1983.

Kaplan, Frederic M., Sobin, Julian M. and Andors, Stephan, *Encyclopedia of China Today*, New York, Eurasia Press, 1979.

Kapur, Harish, *The Awakening Giant: China's Ascension to World Politics*, Alphen aan den Rijn, The Netherlands, Rockville, Maryland, USA, Sijthoff and Noordhoff, 1991.

Kapur, Harish, *Distant Neighbours: China and Europe*, London, Pinter Publishers, 1990.

Kissinger, Henry, *The White House Years*, London, Weidenfeld and Nicolson and Michael Joseph, 1979.

Kissinger, Henry, *Years of Upheaval*, Little, Brown, 1982.

Lawrance, Alan, *China's Foreign Relations since 1949*, London, Boston, Routledge and Kegan Paul, 1975.

Li Ke and Hao Shengzhang, *Wenhua Dageming Zhongde Renmin Jiefangjun* (The PLA in the Cultural Revolution), Beijing, The CCP Press for Party History Material, 1989.

Liu Wusheng (ed), *Zhonggong Dangshi Fengyunlu* (Major Events in CCP History), Beijing, People's Publishing House, 1990.

Liu Shaoqi Xuanji (Selected Works of Liu Shaoqi), vol. 2, Beijing, People's Publishing House, 1985.

Li Zhuisui, *The Private Life of Chairman Mao*, New York, Random House, 1994.

Mao Zedong, *Selected Works*, vol. 4, Beijing, Foreign Languages Press, 1975.

Mehnert, Klaus, *Peking and the New Left: At Home and Abroad*, Berkeley, University of California Press, 1967.

Myers, James T., Domes, Jürgen and Von Groeling, Eric, *Chinese Politics, Documents and Analysis*, 2 vols, Columbia, South Carolina, University of South Carolina Press, 1986.

Nixon, Richard, *The Memoirs of Richard Nixon*, London, Melbourne, Arrow Books, 1979.

Peng Cheng, *Zhongguo Zhengju Beiwanglu* (A Memorandum on the Chinese Political Situation), Beijing, The PLA Publishing House, 1989.

People of the World Unite and Defeat the US Aggressor and all its Lackeys, Peking, Foreign Languages Press, 1963.

Public Papers of the President of the United States: Richard Nixon, 1972, Washington, DC, Government Printing Office, 1974.

Qian Jiang, *Pingpong Waijiao Shimu* (The Process of Ping-Pong Diplomacy), Beijing, The East Press, 1987.

Quan Yanchi, *Mao Zedong, Man Not God*, Beijing, Foreign Languages Press, 1992.

Schmidt, Helmut, *Menschen und Mächte*, Berlin, Siedler Verlag, 1987.

Snow, Edgar, *The Long Revolution*, New York, Vintage Books, 1973.

Tie Zhuwei, *Chen Yi Yuanshuai Zai Wenhua Dageming Zhong* (Marshal

Chen Yi during the Cultural Revolution), Beijing, Historical Material Press, 1986.

Van Ness, Peter, *Revolution and Chinese Foreign Policy, Peking's Support of National Liberation*, Berkeley, University of California Press, 1970.

Wang Nianyi, *Dadongluande Niandai*, (Years of Turmoil), Henan, Henan People's Publishing House, 1988.

Wang Xiangen, *Kang Mei Yuanyue Shilu* (A Factual Account of Resisting America and Assisting Vietnam), Beijing, International Cultural Development Press, 1990.

Ye Jianying Zhuanlue, (A Brief Biography of Ye Jianying), Beijing, Military Science Press, 1987.

Zhang Yunsheng, *Maojiawan Jishi* (A Factual Account about Maojiawan), Beijing, Spring and Autumn Press, 1988. *P 305*

Zheng Derong, *Xinzhongguo Jishi, 1949–84* (Records of New China), Changchun, North-East Normal University Press, 1986.

Zhou Ming, *Lishi Zai Zheli Chensi*, (Reflections about History), vol. 1, Beijing, Huaxia Press, 1986.

Zhu Lin, *Dashi Furen Huiyilu* (Memories of an Ambassador's Wife), Beijing, World Affairs Press, 1991.

Articles

Barbara Barnouin, 'Dissonant voice in international communism', in Harish Kapur (ed.), *The End of an Isolation: China after Mao*, Dordrecht, Boston, Lancaster, Martinus Nijhoff Publishers, 1985.

Chen Jian, 'China in the Vietnam War, 1964–69', *China Quarterly*, no. 142, 1995.

Chinese Communist Affairs: Facts and Features, vol. 1, no. 3, 29 November 1967.

Gurtov, Melvin, 'The Foreign Ministry and foreign affairs during the Cultural Revolution', *China Quarterly*, October–December 1969.

Gurtov, Melvin, 'Foreign affairs during the Cultural Revolution', in Thomas Robinson, (ed.), *The Cultural Revolution in China*, Berkeley, University of California Press, 1971.

Kong Jianmin, 'Zhongguo Dasanxian Jianshede Jianan Licheng' (Difficulties concerning China's Third Line construction), *Pursuit* (Beijing), no. 1, 1989.

Lieberthal, Kenneth, 'The foreign policy debate in Peking as seen through allegorical articles, 1973–76', *China Quarterly*, no. 71, September 1977.

Lieberthal, Kenneth, 'Domestic politics and foreign policy', in Harry Harding, *China's Foreign Relations in the 1980s*, New Haven and London, Yale University Press, 1984.

Lin Qingshan, 'Sirenbang Zuguo De Pomie' (The failure of the Gang of Four to seize power), in: *Mao Zedong Sixiang Yanjiu* (The Study of Mao Zedong Thought), Sichuan Academy of Social Sciences, no. 3, 1988.

Naughton, Barry, 'The Third Front: defence industrialization in the Chinese interior', *China Quarterly*, September 1988.

Ross, Robert S., 'From Lin Biao to Deng Xiaoping: elite instability and China's US Policy', *China Quarterly*, no. 118, June 1989.

'Sino-Belgian Relations', *China Topics*, 1 December 1970.

Su Caiqing, 'Wenge Chuqi Jingji Zhanxian De Yanzhong Douzheng' (Serious conflicts in the economic field during the early period of the Cultural Revolution), in Tan Zongji (ed.), *Shinian Houde Pingshou* (Critical Comments Ten Years Later), Beijing, Historical Material Press, 1987.

Su Caiqing, 'Wenhua Dageming Lishi Bianwu Sanze' (Correction of three errors on the history of the Cultural Revolution), *Dangshi Yanjiu* (Studies in Party History), no. 5, 1989.

Wang Nianyi, 'Guanyu Eryue Niliude Yixie Ziliao' (Some facts about the February Adverse Current), in: *Dangshi Yanjiu Ziliao* (Material for the Study of Party History) no. 1 1990.

Wang Nianyi, 'Mao Zedong Tongzhi Fadong "Wenhua Dageming" Shi Dui Xingshide Guji' (Comrade Mao Zedong's estimate of the situation at the time he launched the Great Cultural Revolution), *Dangshi Yanjiu Ziliao*, no. 4, 1989.

Wei Shiyan, 'Kissinger Mimi Fang Hua Neimu' (With Kissinger on his secret visit to China), in: Liu Wusheng (ed.), *Zhonggong Dangshi Fengyunlu* (Major Events in CCP History), Beijing, People's Publishing House, 1990.

'Wenzhai Xunkan' (Ten-day Digest), ed. by *Jilin Daily*, 1988.

Yu Chenggen, 'Zhou Enlai Yaokung "Fanying Kangbao Neimu' (Zhou commands from a distance 'The Fight Against the Violent Repression Committed by the British'), *The Nineties*, 96/5 and 96/6.

Zhang Yufeng, 'Mao Zedong Zhou Enlai Wannian Ersan Shi' (A few things about Mao Zedong and Zhou Enlai's last years), *Yanhuang Zisun* (The offspring of emperors Yan and Huang), no. 1, 1989.

Zhang Yufeng, 'Wo Gei Mao Zhuxi Dang Mishu' (I served as Chairman Mao's secretary), *Yanhuang Zisun* (The Offspring of Yan and Huang), no. 8, 1994.

Documents

The Historical Experience of the Dictatorship of the Proletariat, Beijing, Foreign Languages Press, 1964.

Letters of the Central Committee of the Communist Party of Japan in reply to the Central Committee of the CPSU, Beijing, Foreign Languages Press, 1965.

Myers, James T., Domes, Jürgen and Von Groeling, Eric, *Chinese Politics, Documents and Analysis*, 2 vols, Columbia, South Carolina, University of South Carolina Press, 1968.

'Report concerning the problem of Qiao Guanhua', submitted by the Party Leading Group of the Ministry of Foreign Affairs to the Party

Central Committee and the State Council, in: *Chinese Law and Government*, vol. 10, no. 1, 1977.

'The modern revisionists: theory of war and peace and the judgement passed by history', in *Akahata*, 14 August 1965.

The Polemics of the International Communist Movement, Beijing, Foreign Languages Press, 1965.

Waishi Fenglei (Events in Foreign Relations), tabloid published by red guards, Beijing, 12 August 1967.

'Zhonggong Wenhua Dageming Wenjian Huibian' (A collection of major CCP documents on the Cultural Revolution), *Studies on the CCP*, Taipei, 1973.

'Zhonggong Wenhua Dageming Zhongyao Wenjian Huibian' (A collection of important documents of the CCP on the Cultural Revolution) *Journal of CCP Studies*, Taipei, 1991.

INDEX